Focus School Gloucester Campus 3/

Issued to:

C000181341

Parents will

up

Maths Frameworking

3rd edition

Kevin Evans, Keith Gordon,
Trevor Senior, Brian Speed,
Chris Pearce

Contents

How to use this book

Learning objectives

See what you are going to cover and what you should already know at the start of each chapter.

About this chapter

Find out the history of the maths you are going to learn and how it is used in real-life contexts.

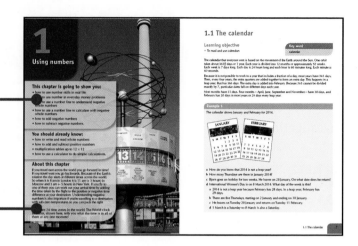

Key words

The main terms used are listed at the start of each topic and highlighted in the text the first time they come up, helping you to master the terminology you need to express yourself fluently about maths. Definitions are provided in the glossary at the back of the book.

Worked examples

Understand the topic before you start the exercises, by reading the examples in blue boxes. These take you through how to answer a question step by step.

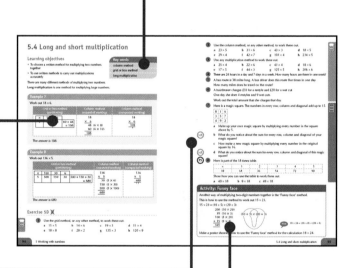

Skills focus

Practise your problem-solving, mathematical reasoning and financial skills.

Take it further

Stretch your thinking by working through the **Investigation**, **Problem solving**, **Challenge** and **Activity** sections. By tackling these you are working at a higher level.

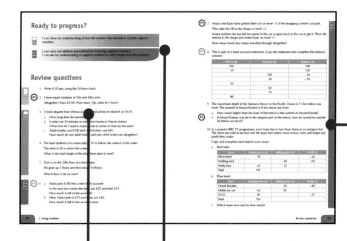

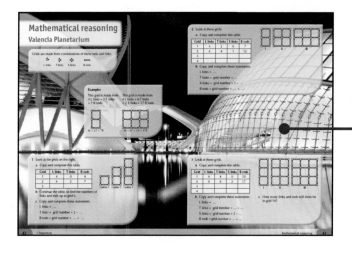

Progress indicators

Track your progress with indicators that show the difficulty level of each question.

Ready to progress?

Check whether you have achieved the expected level of progress in each chapter. The statements show you what you need to know and how you can improve.

Review questions

The review questions bring together what you've learnt in this and earlier chapters, helping you to develop your mathematical fluency.

Activity pages

Put maths into context with these colourful pages showing real-world situations involving maths. You are practising your problem-solving, reasoning and financial skills.

Interactive book, digital resources and videos

A digital version of this Pupil Book is available, with interactive classroom and homework activities, assessments, worked examples and tools that have been specially developed to help you improve your maths skills. Also included are engaging video clips that explain essential concepts, and exciting real-life videos and images that bring to life the awe and wonder of maths.

Find out more at www.collins.co.uk/connect

1
Using numbers

This chapter is going to show you:

- how to use number skills in real life
- how to use number in everyday money problems
- how to use a number line to understand negative whole numbers
- how to use a number line to calculate with negative whole numbers
- how to add negative numbers
- how to subtract negative numbers.

You should already know:

- how to write and read whole numbers
- how to add and subtract positive numbers
- multiplication tables up to 12×12
- how to use a calculator to do simple calculations.

About this chapter

If you travel east across the world you go forward in time! If you travel west you go backwards. Because of the Earth's rotation the day starts at different times across the world. So when it is 8 am in London it is 11 am (+ 3 hours) in Moscow and 3 am (– 5 hours) in New York. If you fly to one of them you can work out your arrival time by adding the time taken by the flight to the positive or negative time difference at your destination. Understanding negative numbers is also important if you're travelling to a destination with sub-zero temperatures so you can pack the right clothes.

There are 24 time zones in the world. The World Clock in Berlin, shown here, tells you what the time is in all of them at any one moment!

1.1 The calendar

Learning objective

• To read and use calendars

Key word

calendar

The **calendar** that everyone uses is based on the movement of the Earth around the Sun. One orbit takes about $365\frac{1}{4}$ days or 1 year. Each year is divided into 12 months or approximately 52 weeks. Each week is 7 days long. Each day is 24 hours long and each hour is 60 minutes long. Each minute is 60 seconds.

Because it is not possible to work to a year that includes a fraction of a day, most years have 365 days. Then, every four years, the extra quarters are added together to form an extra day. This happens in a leap year, that has 366 days. The extra day is added into February. Because 365 cannot be divided exactly by 7, particular dates fall on different days each year.

Most months have 31 days. Four months – April, June, September and November – have 30 days, and February has 28 days in most years or 29 days every leap year.

Example 1

The calendar shows January and February for 2014.

a How do you know that 2014 is not a leap year?

b How many Thursdays are there in January 2014?

c Bjorn goes on holiday for two weeks. He leaves on 28 January. On what date does he return?

d International Women's Day is on 8 March 2014. What day of the week is this?

  a 2014 is not a leap year because February has 28 days. In a leap year, February has 29 days.

  b There are five Thursdays, starting on 2 January and ending on 30 January.

  c He leaves on Tuesday 28 January and returns on Tuesday 11 February.

  d 1 March is a Saturday so 8 March is also a Saturday.

Exercise 1A

1 How many days are there in:

    a 3 weeks   **b** 12 weeks   **c** 52 weeks?

2 How many hours are there in:

    a 4 days   **b** a week   **c** July?

3 How many minutes are there in:

    a 2 hours   **b** 5 hours   **c** a day?

4 How many seconds are there in:

    a 5 minutes   **b** 24 minutes   **c** one hour?

5 How many minutes are there in:

    a 120 seconds   **b** 300 seconds?

6 How many hours and minutes are there in:

    a 200 minutes   **b** 350 minutes?

7 2016 is a leap year. When is the next leap year after that?

8 How many days are there in June, July and August altogether?

9 Judy was born on 5 August 1996. Punch was born on 6 September 1996. How many days older than Punch is Judy?

10 The calendar shows June, July and August of 2014. Saturday 12 July is circled.

    a What day of the week is 8 July?

    b What date is the third Saturday in August?

    c A family went on holiday on 4 August and returned on 18 August. How many nights were they away?

    d My last doctor's appointment was on 29 May. I was told to come back in two weeks. What date is my next appointment?

    e The first day of the school holidays is Thursday 24 July. The first day back at school is Wednesday 3 September. How many days do the school holidays last?

Problem solving: The day you were born

A Suppose the date you are looking at is 12 August 2005.

Work through this example.

Step 1: Take the last two digits of the year, multiply by 1.25 and ignore any decimals.

$05 \times 1.25 = 6.25$

Ignoring the decimal gives 6.

Step 2: Add the day.

$6 + 12 = 18$

Step 3: Add 0 for May, 1 for August, 2 for February, March or November, 3 for June, 4 for September or December, 5 for April or July, 6 for January or October.

$18 + 1 = 19$

Step 4: If the date is in the 1900s, add 1.

The date is not in the 1900s.

Step 5: If the year is a leap year and the month is January or February, subtract 1.

2005 is not a leap year.

Step 6: Divide by 7 and get the remainder.

$19 \div 7 = 2$ remainder 5

Step 7: The remainder tells you the day.

0 = Sunday, 1 = Monday, 2 = Tuesday, 3 = Wednesday, 4 = Thursday, 5 = Friday, 6 = Saturday

So 12 August 2005 was a Friday.

B Check by doing an internet search for 'Calendar 2005'.

C Now work out the day for your birthday or a friend's birthday.

1.2 The 12-hour and 24-hour clocks

Learning objectives

- To read and use 12-hour and 24-hour clocks
- To convert between the 12-hour and 24-hour systems

Key words	
12-hour clock	24-hour clock
analogue	digital

There are two types of clock.

An **analogue** clock uses the **12-hour clock** system.

A **digital** clock can use either the 12-hour or **24-hour clock** system. The time is usually represented by four digits, with a colon to separate the hours and minutes.

You can work out afternoon times as 24-hour clock times by adding 12 hours to the 12-hour clock time.

Example 2

It is half past two in the afternoon.

How many ways can you show this time, using 12-hour and 24-hour clocks?

Here are some of the ways.

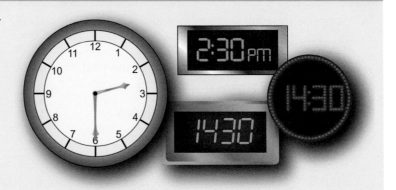

Example 3

The four clocks below show the times that Jamil gets up in the morning (clock A), has lunch (clock B), finishes work (clock C) and goes to bed (clock D).

| Clock A | Clock B | Clock C | Clock D |

a Fill in the table to show the time on each clock as 12-hour times and 24-hour times.

Clock	A	B	C	D
12-hour	6:30 am			11:00 pm
24-hour		12:45	17:15	

b How long is the time between when Jamil gets up and when he goes to bed?

c If Jamil starts work at 08:30 and takes an hour for lunch, how many hours is he at work?

   a 6:30 am is 06:30, 12:45 is 12:45 pm, 17:15 is 5:15 pm and 11:00 pm is 23:00.

Clock	A	B	C	D
12-hour	6:30 am	12:45 pm	5:15 pm	11:00 pm
24-hour	06:30	12:45	17:15	23:00

   b Jamil gets up at 06:30 and goes to bed at 23:00.

   You can use a time line to work out the difference.

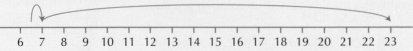

From 06:30 to 07:00 is 30 minutes. From 07:00 to 23:00 is 16 hours.

The answer is 16 hours and 30 minutes.

c 08:30 to 09:00 is 30 minutes, 09:00 to 17:00 is 8 hours and 17:00 to 17:15 is 15 minutes.

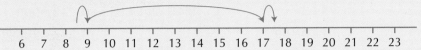

Total time is 8 hours plus 30 minutes plus 15 minutes less 1 hour for lunch.

This is 7 hours and 45 minutes.

Minutes written as fractions or decimals of an hour

The table shows some conversions between hours and minutes.

	Minutes	6	10	15	20	30	40	45
Hours	Fraction	$\frac{1}{10}$	$\frac{1}{6}$	$\frac{1}{4}$	$\frac{1}{3}$	$\frac{1}{2}$	$\frac{2}{3}$	$\frac{3}{4}$
	Decimal	0.1	0.167	0.25	0.333	0.5	0.667	0.75

Example 4

Write each time as a fraction and a decimal of an hour.

a 4 hours 30 minutes   **b** 2 hours 40 minutes   **c** 1 hour 36 minutes

   a Using the table above, 4 hours 30 minutes is $4\frac{1}{2}$ hours = 4.5 hours

   b 2 hours 40 minutes is $2\frac{2}{3}$ hours = 2.667 hours

   c 36 minutes is 6×6 minutes so 36 minutes is $\frac{6}{10}$ or $\frac{3}{5}$ hour = 0.6 hour

     1 hour 36 minutes is $1\frac{3}{5}$ hours = 1.6 hours

Note: You can use the ⊙,″ button on your calculator to input hours, minutes and seconds.

For example, pressing 4 ⊙,″ 30 ⊙,″ and then the = button will input 4 hours 30 minutes.

Now press ⊙,″ again and it will convert your time to a decimal.

Example 5

Look at this picture.

```
1 Hainault via Newbury Park    5 Mins
3 Epping                      12 Mins
              Central Line
                 20:20
```

a What time is the train to Epping due?

b Give this time according to both the 24-hour and the 12-hour clock.

   a The time on the board is 20:20. The train is due in 12 minutes, at 20:32.

   b The train is due at 20:32 or 8:32 pm.

Exercise 1B

1 Write these 12-hour clock times as 24-hour clock times.

   a   5 am   **b**   5 pm   **c**   11:20 am   **d**   12 noon

   e   5:15 pm   **f**   11:05 pm   **g**   10:45 am   **h**   12 midnight

2 Write these 24-hour clock times as 12-hour clock times, using am and pm.

   a   18:00   **b**   07:00   **c**   12:15   **d**   00:25

   e   16:20   **f**   22:30   **g**   11:07   **h**   19:25

3 How many hours and minutes are there between each pair of times?

   a   09:30 to 13:30   **b**   08:15 to 10:45   **c**   18:20 to 22:30

   d   06:22 to 09:33   **e**   06:45 to 15:30   **f**   11:12 to 23:28

4 A TV programme starts at 17:50 and finishes at 18:25. How long is the programme on for?

5 A TV programme starts at 09:55 and is 25 minutes long. At what time does it finish?

6 Copy the diagrams and fill in the missing values.

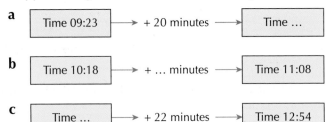

a   Time 09:23 → + 20 minutes → Time ...

b   Time 10:18 → + ... minutes → Time 11:08

c   Time ... → + 22 minutes → Time 12:54

7 Write each time as a fraction and as a decimal.

   a   2 hours 15 minutes   **b**   3 hours 45 minutes   **c**   1 hour 20 minutes

   d   3 hours 30 minutes   **e**   1 hour 40 minutes   **f**   2 hours 18 minutes

(PS) **8** This timetable shows the times of flights from Heathrow to Newcastle.

Depart Heathrow	07:20	10:05	13:20	13:45	16:30	21:00
Arrive Newcastle	08:25	11:15	14:30	14:55	17:40	22:05

   a   The 13:20 departure is delayed by 15 minutes. What is the new departure time?

   b   The 22:05 arrival is 10 minutes early. What is the new arrival time?

   c   Alan arrives at Heathrow at 09:20 to catch the next flight to Newcastle.

        What time does he arrive in Newcastle?

   d   Sarah arrives at Heathrow at 13:15. She is told she is too late for the 13:20, as check-in has closed. How long does she have to wait for the next flight that she can check in for, to depart?

(MR) **9** Jonas walks to the station each morning to catch the 07:18 train. It takes him 15 minutes to walk to the station. On the way he stops to buy a paper, which takes him 2 minutes. He likes to arrive at the station at least 5 minutes before the train is due. What is the latest time he should leave home?

10 Mobile phone calls are charged at 25p per minute for the first 3 minutes, then 10p per minute for each minute over 3 minutes.

   a How much will the following mobile phone calls cost?

   i A call lasting 2 minutes   **ii** A call lasting 8 minutes

   b After finishing a call, Jonas had a message from the phone company saying: 'Your call cost 95p.' How many minutes did the call take?

Problem solving: Times

A A school operates a two-week timetable. Year 7 have three 55-minute mathematics lessons one week and two 1-hour mathematics lessons in the second week. How much time do they spend in mathematics lessons over the two weeks?

B Jo left home at 8:05 am. It took her 8 minutes to walk to Sara's house. Sara took 5 minutes to get ready, then they both walked to school, arriving at 8:35 am. How long did it take them to walk from Sara's house to school?

C After his birthday, Adam wrote 'thank you' letters to five aunts. He took one hour to write the letters. Each letter took the same amount of time to write. How long did it take him to write each letter?

D Jonas takes 4 minutes to read each page of a comic. The comic has 16 pages. How long will it take him to read it?

E Sonia was 12 minutes late for a meeting. The meeting lasted 1 hour and 45 minutes and finished at 11:50 am. What time did Sonia arrive at the meeting?

F The first three lessons at an academy last 1 hour and 45 minutes altogether. Each lesson is the same length. How long is each lesson?

1.3 Managing money

Learning objective

• To work out everyday money problems

In England you will use these coins and notes.

The English £1 notes were replaced by £1 coins in 1984, but £1 notes are still used in the Channel Islands.

Example 6

How can you make up 12p, using exactly four coins?

The only combination, using four coins, is:

- 1p + 1p + 5p + 5p.

Example 7

Show that there are six different ways to make 7p, using coins.

You can only use 1p, 2p and 5p coins.

The combinations are:

- 1p + 1p + 1p + 1p + 1p + 1p + 1p
- 1p + 1p + 1p + 1p + 1p + 2p
- 1p + 1p + 1p + 2p + 2p
- 1p + 2p + 2p + 2p
- 1p + 1p + 5p
- 2p + 5p.

Example 8

Suppose you have been collecting 10p and 2p coins.

a Explain why it is not possible to make an odd number of pence with these coins.

b There are six ways to make 50p, using just 10p and 2p coins.

One way is 5 × 10p and 0 × 2p.

Complete a table to show all the other ways.

10p coins   2p coins

a You cannot make an odd number of pence, as both 10 and 2 are even numbers, so any combination will also be even.

b

10p coins	2p coins
5	0
4	5
3	10
2	15
1	20
0	25

Exercise 1C

FS **1** Write down all the ways of making a total of 4 pence, using just 1p and 2p coins.

FS **2** Write down all the ways of making a total of 12 pence, using just 2p and 5p coins.

FS **3** Mark buys a magazine for 25p and receives 75p change from a £1 coin. He receives exactly four coins. What coins are they?

PS **4** Zara has two 20p coins, one 2p coin and a 1p coin.

FS Ali has a 50p coin, a 10p coin and a 5p coin.

Ali owes Zara 24p. Explain how he can pay her.

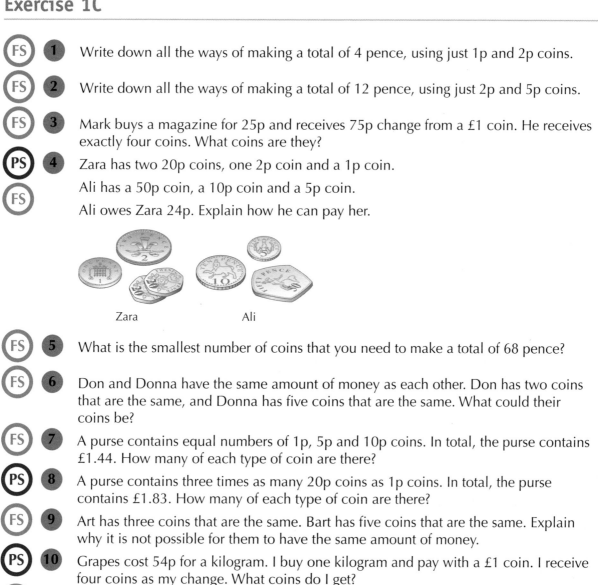

Zara   Ali

FS **5** What is the smallest number of coins that you need to make a total of 68 pence?

FS **6** Don and Donna have the same amount of money as each other. Don has two coins that are the same, and Donna has five coins that are the same. What could their coins be?

FS **7** A purse contains equal numbers of 1p, 5p and 10p coins. In total, the purse contains £1.44. How many of each type of coin are there?

PS **8** A purse contains three times as many 20p coins as 1p coins. In total, the purse contains £1.83. How many of each type of coin are there?

FS **9** Art has three coins that are the same. Bart has five coins that are the same. Explain why it is not possible for them to have the same amount of money.

PS **10** Grapes cost 54p for a kilogram. I buy one kilogram and pay with a £1 coin. I receive four coins as my change. What coins do I get?

MR **11** I buy two cans of cola for 37p each and pay with a £1 coin. I receive three coins as my change. What coins do I get?

MR **12** I buy three pencils for 21p each and pay with a £1 coin. I receive four coins as my change. What coins do I get?

Problem solving: USA money

The coins used in the USA are worth 1 cent, 5 cents, 10 cents and 25 cents. These are known as pennies, nickels, dimes and quarters.

A Mario has $1.32 in pennies, nickels and dimes. He has a total of 25 coins. There are twice as many nickels as pennies, so how many of each kind of coin does Mario have?

B Joss has 35 coins, which consist of nickels, dimes and quarters. The coins are worth $5.55. She has five more dimes than nickels.

How many nickels, dimes and quarters does she have?

1.4 Positive and negative numbers

Learning objectives

- To use a number line to order positive and negative whole numbers
- To solve problems involving negative temperatures

Key words

negative number

positive number

temperature

Look at the two pictures. What can you see?

What is the difference between the **temperatures**?

Temperature +20 °C   Temperature −5 °C

Every number has a sign. Numbers greater than 0 are called **positive numbers**. Although you do not always write it, every positive number has a positive (+) sign in front of it.

Numbers less than 0 are called **negative numbers** and must always have the negative (−) sign in front of them.

You can show the positions of positive and negative numbers on a number line.

The value of the numbers increases as you move from left to right. For example, 8 is greater than 2, 2 is greater than −5 and −5 is greater than −10.

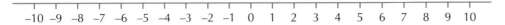

You can use the number line to compare the sizes of positive and negative numbers.

You can also use it to solve problems involving addition and subtraction.

Example 9

Which number is greater, −7 or −3?

Because −3 is further to the right on the line, it is the larger number.

Notice that −3 is closer to zero than −7 is.

Example 10

Write these temperatures in order, from lowest to highest.

8 °C, −2 °C, 10 °C, −7 °C, −3 °C, 4 °C

First, draw up a number line.

Then mark the numbers on the number line.

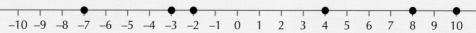

You can see that the order is:

−7 °C, −3 °C, −2 °C, 4 °C, 8 °C, 10 °C

Example 11

Work out the difference between each pair of temperatures.

a −4 °C and 6 °C   **b** −1 °C and −8 °C

Look at each of these pairs on a number line.

a

The difference is 10 degrees.

b

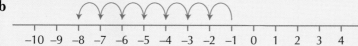

The difference is 7 degrees.

Exercise 1D

1 Write down the highest and lowest temperatures in each group.

    a 5 °C, −6 °C, 4 °C   **b** −2 °C, 6 °C, −10 °C   **c** −15 °C, −10 °C, −5 °C

2 Work out the difference between the temperatures in each pair.

    a −4 °C and 8 °C   **b** −20 °C and −10 °C   **c** 5 °C and −8 °C

3 On Monday the temperature at noon was 8 °C.

Over the next few days, these temperature changes were recorded.

Monday to Tuesday	down 5 degrees
Tuesday to Wednesday	up 2 degrees
Wednesday to Thursday	down 6 degrees
Thursday to Friday	up 1 degree

What was the temperature on Friday?

4 Put the numbers in each group in order, from smallest to largest.

   a 2, 7, 0, 9, 5   **b** −5, 7, 9, 2, 3   **c** 0, 4, −6, −8, 12

   d 1, −1, 8, −9, −15   **e** −3, −9, −12, 1, −5   **f** −9, −3, 5, −8, 4

5 State whether each of these statements is true or false.

   a 5 °C is lower than 8 °C   **b** −5 °C is lower than 8 °C

   c 5 °C is lower than −8 °C   **d** −5 °C is lower than −8 °C

   e 8 °C is lower than 5 °C   **f** −8 °C is lower than 5 °C

   g 8 °C is lower than −5 °C   **h** −8 °C is lower than −5 °C

6 Put these temperatures in order, from highest to lowest.

   16 °C, −5 °C, 10 °C, −10 °C, −6 °C

PS **7** Find the number that is halfway between the numbers on each line.

   a   −6   0   **b**   −8   −2

   c   −9   −3

Challenge: Temperatures on the Moon

Temperatures on the Moon vary depending on where light from the Sun reaches it.

When parts of the Moon are turned away from the Sun, the temperatures there can be as low as −150 °C.

When sunlight reaches the surface of the Moon, temperatures can be as high as 120 °C.

When men first landed on the Moon, on 11 July 1969, the temperature was about −20 °C.

A What is the difference between the lowest and highest temperatures on the Moon?

B Is −20 °C closer to the lowest temperature or the highest temperature?

1.5 Adding negative numbers

Learning objectives

- To carry out additions and subtractions involving negative numbers
- To use a number line to calculate with negative numbers

Key word

brackets

You can use a number line to add and subtract positive and negative numbers.

Example 12

Use a number line to work out the answers.

a $2 + (-5)$ **b** $(-7) + 4$ **c** $3 + (-2) + (-5)$

a Starting at zero and 'jumping' along the number line to 2 and then back 5 gives an answer of −3.

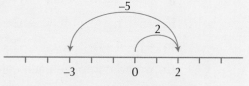

b Similarly, $(-7) + 4 = -3$.

Notice that you can use **brackets** so that you do not mistake the negative sign for a subtraction sign.

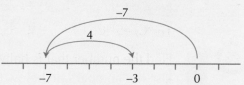

c Using two steps this time, $3 + (-2) + (-5) = -4$.

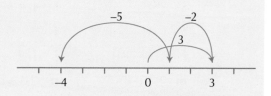

Look at these patterns.

$4 + 2 = 6$	$2 + 4 = 6$
$4 + 1 = 5$	$1 + 4 = 5$
$4 + 0 = 4$	$0 + 4 = 4$
$4 + (-1) = 3$	$(-1) + 4 = 3$
$4 + (-2) = 2$	$(-2) + 4 = 2$

Notice that $4 + (-1) = 3$ and $(-1) + 4 = 3$ have the same value as $4 - 1 = 3$

and $4 + (-2) = 2$ and $(-2) + 4 = 2$ have the same value as $4 - 2 = 2$.

Adding a negative number gives the same result as subtracting a positive number.

Example 13

Work out the answers.

a $6 + (-1)$ **b** $20 + (-5)$ **c** $(-2) + (-3)$

a $6 + -1 = 6 - 1$
$$= 5$$

b $20 + -5 = 20 - 5$
$$= 15$$

c $(-2) + (-3) = (-2) - 3$
$$= -5$$

Exercise 1E

1 Work out the answer to each of these.

    a $10 - 6$ **b** $7 - 2$ **c** $6 - 10$ **d** $4 + 8$

    e $2 - 5$ **f** $6 - 6$ **g** $-2 + 8$ **h** $-3 - 2$

    i $-5 - 1$ **j** $-2 + 9$ **k** $-5 - 5$ **l** $-10 + 8$

    m $-1 - 4 + 4$ **n** $-2 + 2 - 2$ **o** $-8 + 3 - 5$ **p** $-10 + 11 - 4$

2 Copy and complete each calculation.

    a $7 + (-1)$ **b** $9 + (-5)$ **c** $10 + (-7)$ **d** $12 + (-4)$ **e** $(-4) + (-5)$

    $= 7 - 1$ $= 9 - 5$ $= 10 -$ $=$ $=$

    $=$ $=$ $=$ $=$ $=$

3 Use the number line below to help you work out the answers.

    a $2 - 4$ **b** $6 + (-3)$ **c** $5 + (-4)$ **d** $7 + (-3)$

    e $(-3) + (-3)$ **f** $5 - 9$ **g** $(-3) + 9$ **h** $0 - 8$

    i $10 + (-4)$ **j** $(-2) + (-6)$ **k** $12 + (-9)$ **l** $5 + (-5)$

    m $7 + (-8)$ **n** $10 + (-20)$ **o** $0 + (-4)$ **p** $(-2) + (-9)$

–15 –14 –13 –12 –11 –10 –9 –8 –7 –6 –5 –4 –3 –2 –1 0 1 2 3 4 5 6 7 8 9 10 11 12 13 14 15

4 Work these out.

    a $10 + (-5)$ **b** $(-5) + (-10)$ **c** $40 - 100$ **d** $(-10) + (-10)$

    e $20 + (-10)$ **f** $(-50) + 50$ **g** $25 + (-30)$ **h** $100 - 200$

    i $12 + (-7)$ **j** $(-100) + (-90)$ **k** $15 + (-45)$ **l** $(-5) + (-15)$

5 Work these out.

    a $4 + 5 + (-8)$ **b** $10 - 1 + (-1)$ **c** $20 + (-10) + (-5)$

    d $15 + 3 + (-10)$ **e** $5 + 3 + (-2)$ **f** $8 + (-1) + (-9)$

6 Find the total of the numbers in each list.

    a $6, -4, 10$ **b** $-10, 20, 5$ **c** $-3, -8, 7$

7 In each magic square, all the rows, columns and diagonals add up to the same total.
Copy and complete the squares.

a
	1	6
	5	
4		

b
	–1	4
	3	
2		

c
1		
–4		
–3		–5

8 Alf has £20 in the bank.

He writes a cheque for £30.

How much has he got in the bank now?

Challenge: Number squares

A In this 4 by 4 magic square the numbers in all of the rows, columns and diagonals add up to −2.

−8			6
3			−3
		7	0
	2	−4	

Copy and complete the square.

B In this 4 by 4 magic square the numbers in all of the rows, columns and diagonals add up to the same number.

10		−3	7
	5		
3	1	0	
−2			−5

Copy and complete the square.

1.6 Subtracting negative numbers

Learning objective

• To carry out subtractions involving negative numbers

Look at this pattern.

$$4 - 3 = 1$$
$$4 - 2 = 2$$
$$4 - 1 = 3$$
$$4 - 0 = 4$$
$$4 - (-1) = 5$$
$$4 - (-2) = 6$$
$$4 - (-3) = 7$$

Notice that $4 - (-1) = 5$ has the same value as $4 + 1 = 5$

and $4 - (-2) = 6$ has the same value as $4 + 2 = 6$.

Subtracting a negative number is the same as adding the corresponding positive number.

Example 14

Work out the answers.

a $3 - (-4)$ **b** $10 - (-6)$ **c** $-3 - (-7)$

  a $3 - (-4) = 3 + 4 = 7$ **b** $10 - (-6) = 10 + 6 = 16$ **c** $-3 - (-7) = -3 + 7 = 4$

Exercise 1F

1 Copy and complete each calculation.

   a $8 - (-2)$ **b** $10 - (-5)$ **c** $20 - (-10)$ **d** $-15 - (-5)$ **e** $(-6) - (-6)$

     $= 8 + 2$ $= 10 + 5$ $= 20 +$ $=$

     $=$ $=$ $=$

2 Use the number line below to help work out the answers.

   a $4 - (-6)$ **b** $8 - (-1)$ **c** $(-5) - (-5)$ **d** $10 - (-2)$

   e $(-4) - (-2)$ **f** $(-1) - (-10)$ **g** $(-5) - (-10)$ **h** $(-10) - (-3)$

   i $8 - (-4)$ **j** $(-9) - (-3)$ **k** $(-7) - (-7)$ **l** $(-5) - (-5)$

   m $(-8) - (-2)$ **n** $(-10) - (-20)$ **o** $0 - (-10)$ **p** $(-2) - (-6)$

   $-15\ -14\ -13\ -12\ -11\ -10\ -9\ -8\ -7\ -6\ -5\ -4\ -3\ -2\ -1\ 0\ 1\ 2\ 3\ 4\ 5\ 6\ 7\ 8\ 9\ 10\ 11\ 12\ 13\ 14\ 15$

3 Work these out.

   a $10 - (-8)$ **b** $(-10) - (-10)$ **c** $20 - (-10)$ **d** $(-15) - (-5)$

   e $21 - (-16)$ **f** $40 - (-20)$ **g** $-25 - (-20)$ **h** $-200 - (-140)$

   i $18 - (-9)$ **j** $(-140) - (-90)$ **k** $12 - (-22)$ **l** $(-4) - (-12)$

4 Work these out.

   a $9 + 5 - (-7)$ **b** $(-4) - 2 - (-2)$ **c** $20 - (-10) + (-10)$

   d $25 + 4 - (-20)$ **e** $8 - 9 - (-3)$ **f** $(-1) - (-3) - (-4)$

5 Choose a number from each list and subtract one from the other. Repeat for at least four pairs of numbers. What are the biggest and smallest answers you can find?

A	3	−6	−4	32	9
B	−2	9	−9	−4	−2

6 Copy each statement and work out the missing numbers.

   a $9 + \ldots = 5$ **b** $10 - \ldots = 15$ **c** $\ldots + (-6) = 10$ **d** $(-4) - \ldots = 8$

7 Copy each calculation and then fill in the missing numbers.

   a $5 + +1 = 6$ **b** $-3 - 1 = -4$ **c** $4 - 1 = 3$

      $5 + 0 = 5$ $-3 - 0 = -3$ $3 - 0 = 3$

      $5 + -1 = 4$ $-3 - -1 = -2$ $2 - -1 = 3$

      $5 + -2 = \ldots$ $-3 - -2 = \ldots$ $1 - -2 = \ldots$

      $5 + \ldots = \ldots$ $-3 - \ldots = \ldots$ $0 - \ldots = \ldots$

      $5 + \ldots = \ldots$ $-3 - \ldots = \ldots$ $\ldots - \ldots = \ldots$

8 Work out the answers.

a $+5 - +2$ b $-3 - -3$ c $+8 - -5$ d $-6 + -2$ e $+9 - +2$

f $-8 - -6$ g $-5 + +5$ h $+10 - -3$ i $-2 + -2$ j $-3 + -9$

k $+4 - +5$ l $6 - -9$ m $-1 - -2 + -3$ n $-+2 + +2 - +2$ o $-1 + -6$

9 These temperatures were recorded at Glasgow Airport over one week in January.

Copy and complete the table.

Draw a number line to check your answers.

Temperature (°C)	Sun	Mon	Tue	Wed	Thu	Fri	Sat
Maximum temperature (°C)	5	0	−2		1	2	4
Minimum temperature (°C)	−4	−5		−6	−3		−1
Difference (degrees)	9		9	11		5	

10 A fish is 10 m below the surface of the water.

A fish eagle is 25 m above the surface of the water.

How many metres must the bird descend to get the fish?

Challenge: Marking a maths test

A A maths test consists of 20 questions. A correct answer earns 3 points. If an answer is wrong, the mark is −1 point.

> A computer spreadsheet is useful for this activity.

   a Work out the score for each pupil.

      i Ali gets 10 right and 10 wrong.   **ii** Bel gets 15 right and 5 wrong.

      iii Charlie gets 8 right and 12 wrong.   **iv** Dawn gets 7 right and 13 wrong.

   b What times table are all your answers in?

B Investigate what happens when a correct answer earns 3 points and a wrong answer gets −2.

Ready to progress?

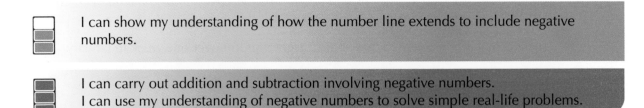

I can show my understanding of how the number line extends to include negative numbers.

I can carry out addition and subtraction involving negative numbers.
I can use my understanding of negative numbers to solve simple real-life problems.

Review questions

1   Write 8:30 pm, using the 24-hour clock.

(PS) 2   I have equal numbers of 10p and 20p coins.
    Altogether I have £3.60. How many 10p coins do I have?

3   A train departs from Vienna at 06:30 and arrives in Munich at 10:30.
    a   How long does the journey take?
    b   It takes me 30 minutes to walk from home to Vienna station.
        What time do I need to leave home to arrive in time for the train?
    c   Adult tickets cost €100 and child tickets cost €50.
        How much do two adult tickets and one child ticket cost altogether?

4   The keel (bottom) of a cruise ship is 10 m below the surface of the water.
    The deck is 20 m above the water.
    What is the total height of the ship, from deck to keel?

5   Dan is on the 20th floor of a skyscraper.
    He goes up 5 floors and then down 10 floors.
    Which floor is he on now?

(FS) 6   a   Maria puts £100 into a new bank account.
            In the next two weeks she takes out £25 and then £35.
            How much is left in her account?
        b   Next, Maria puts in £15 and takes out £50.
            How much is left in her account now?

PS 7 Anaya and Euan have parked their car on level −5 of the shopping centre's car park.

They take the lift to the shops on level +3.

Anaya realises she has left her purse in the car so goes back to the car to get it. Then she returns to the shops and meets Euan on level +1.

How many levels has Anaya travelled through altogether?

FS 8 This is part of a bank account statement. Copy the statement and complete the balance column.

Paid in (£)	Paid out (£)	Balance (£)
100		100
20		120
	100	20
	30	−10
50		
	60	
	10	
80		

9 The maximum depth of the Mariana Trench in the Pacific Ocean is 11 km below sea level. The summit of Mount Everest is 9 km above sea level.

a How much higher than the base of the trench is the summit of Mount Everest?

PS b If Mount Everest was set in the deepest part of the trench, how far would its summit be below sea level?

10 In a popular BBC TV programme, each team has to buy three items at an antiques fair. The items are sold at auction and the team that makes more money wins and keeps any profit they make.

Copy and complete each team's score sheet.

a Red team

Item	Buying price (£)	Selling price (£)	Profit (£)
Silver bowl	50		−20
Walking stick		40	+10
Teddy bear	65	55	
Total	145		

b Blue team

Item	Buying price (£)	Selling price (£)	Profit (£)
Charm bracelet		50	+40
Dinkie toy car	60	85	
Clock	80		−25
Total	150		

c Which team won and by how much?

Problem solving

Where in the UK?

A Comparing temperatures

Look at the map of the UK. It shows temperatures (°C) on one winter day.

Use it to answer these questions.

1 What is the temperature in Belfast?

2 What is the temperature in Sheffield?

3 Which is the hottest place shown?

4 Which is the coldest place shown?

5 What is the difference in temperature between Portmeirion and London?

6 How much hotter is Plymouth than Swansea?

7 Which place is at −6 °C?

8 Which place is 5 degrees colder than Norwich?

9 Which place is 6 degrees hotter than Aberdeen?

B A trip to Edinburgh

A businesswoman wants to travel from London to Edinburgh for a meeting.

She wants to return to London on the same day.

The table shows some train times.

Use these times to plan her day so that she can spend at least 4 hours in Edinburgh.

Work out all the possible trains she could use.

London (depart)	Edinburgh (arrive)	Edinburgh (depart)	London (arrive)
08:00	12:20	15:30	19:50
09:00	13:20	16:30	20:52
09:30	14:15	17:00	21:43
10:00	14:22	17:30	22:17

Aberdeen
−8

−6 Edinburgh

Belfast
−2

Sheffield
−3

3
Norwich

Portmeirion
−4

Swansea
−1

0
Bristol

London
2

Plymouth
1

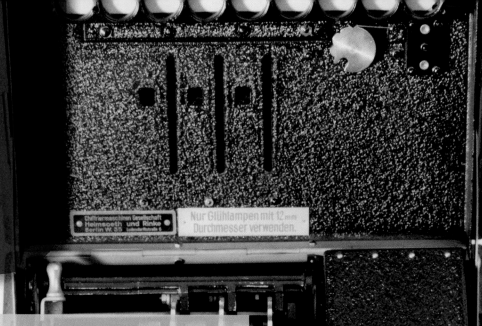

2

Sequences

This chapter is going to show you:
- how to use function machines
- how to describe some simple number patterns
- how to generate and describe some simple whole-number sequences
- how to use the special sequence called the sequence of square numbers
- how to use the special sequence called the sequence of triangular numbers.

You should already know:
- odd and even numbers
- multiplication tables up to 12×12
- how to apply the four rules of number.

About this chapter

During the Second World War, the first computer in the world was invented at Bletchley Park in the UK. At that time, Britain was at war with Germany and needed to break the coded German communications to discover what they were planning to do next. Codes are based on sequences and these were very complex ones, which were changed every day and randomly generated by a machine called Enigma. It was the job of the computer to crack each day's new code sequences from the Enigma machine – and fast. Today, coded sequences are still used in secure communications, for example, encrypting websites used for financial transactions – vital to everyday business.

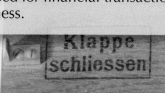

2.1 Function machines

Learning objective

- To use function machines to generate inputs and outputs

Key words

double function machine

function machine

input

inverse operation

output

A **function machine** uses a mathematical rule to change the values of numbers.

- The numbers you start with are called the **input**.
- The numbers you get after you apply the rule are the **output**.

Example 1

Complete the output box of this function machine for inputs of 1, 2, 3 and 4.

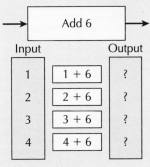

The rule is 'Add 6'.

The first input is 1.

$$1 + 6 = 7$$

The first output is 7.

$$2 + 6 = 8$$

The second output is 8.

The third input is 3.

$$3 + 6 = 9$$

The third output is 9.

The fourth input is 4.

$$4 + 6 = 10$$

The fourth output is 10.

The output box looks like this.

Output
7
8
9
10

Example 2

Complete the **double function machine** to show the outputs for inputs of 3, 5, 7 and 9.

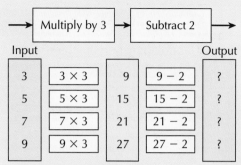

The rule is 'Multiply by 3' then 'Subtract 2'.

The first input is 3.

$3 \times 3 = 9$ and $9 - 2 = 7$

The first output is 7.

Continue in this way.

The output box looks like this.

Output

7
13
19
25

Exercise 2A

1 Work out the missing inputs or outputs for each function machine.

a
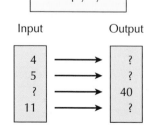

b
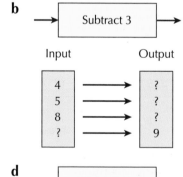

c

d
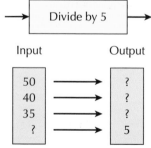

2 Complete the rule for each function machine.

a
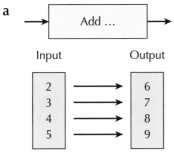

b
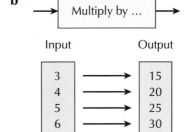

c
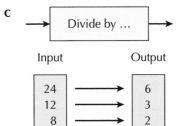

d
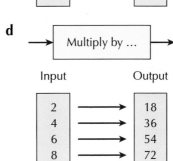

3 Work out the missing inputs or outputs for each function machine.

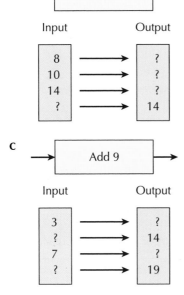

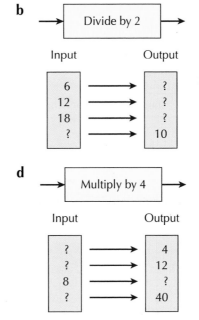

4 Make up your own function machines to show each of these functions.

Choose your four inputs for each one carefully, so that the outputs are not fractions or negative numbers.

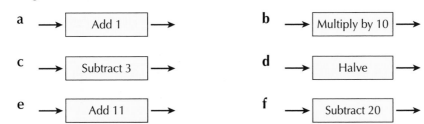

a → Add 1 →

b → Multiply by 10 →

c → Subtract 3 →

d → Halve →

e → Add 11 →

f → Subtract 20 →

5 Work out the outputs for each of these double function machines.

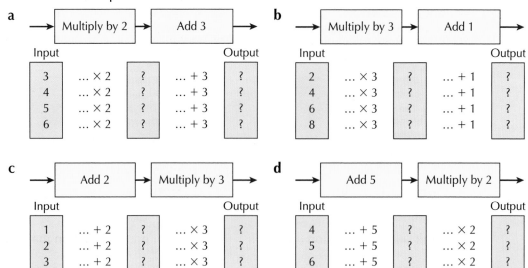

a

| Multiply by 2 | → | Add 3 | → |

Input				Output
3	... × 2	?	... + 3	?
4	... × 2	?	... + 3	?
5	... × 2	?	... + 3	?
6	... × 2	?	... + 3	?

b

| Multiply by 3 | → | Add 1 | → |

Input				Output
2	... × 3	?	... + 1	?
4	... × 3	?	... + 1	?
6	... × 3	?	... + 1	?
8	... × 3	?	... + 1	?

c

| Add 2 | → | Multiply by 3 | → |

Input				Output
1	... + 2	?	... × 3	?
2	... + 2	?	... × 3	?
3	... + 2	?	... × 3	?
4	... + 2	?	... × 3	?

d

| Add 5 | → | Multiply by 2 | → |

Input				Output
4	... + 5	?	... × 2	?
5	... + 5	?	... × 2	?
6	... + 5	?	... × 2	?
7	... + 5	?	... × 2	?

6 Draw diagrams to show each of these double function machines.
Choose your own four input numbers.

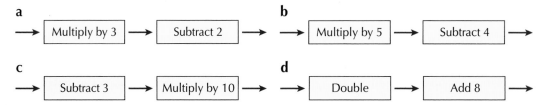

a → Multiply by 3 → Subtract 2 →

b → Multiply by 5 → Subtract 4 →

c → Subtract 3 → Multiply by 10 →

d → Double → Add 8 →

7 Copy each double function machine. Fill in the missing rules and numbers.

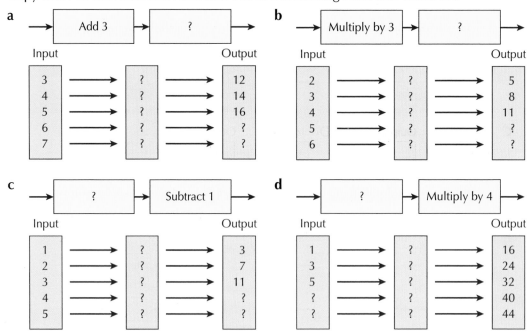

a

| Add 3 | → | ? | → |

Input				Output
3	→	?	→	12
4	→	?	→	14
5	→	?	→	16
6	→	?	→	?
7	→	?	→	?

b

| Multiply by 3 | → | ? | → |

Input				Output
2	→	?	→	5
3	→	?	→	8
4	→	?	→	11
5	→	?	→	?
6	→	?	→	?

c

| ? | → | Subtract 1 | → |

Input				Output
1	→	?	→	3
2	→	?	→	7
3	→	?	→	11
4	→	?	→	?
5	→	?	→	?

d

| ? | → | Multiply by 4 | → |

Input				Output
1	→	?	→	16
3	→	?	→	24
5	→	?	→	32
?	→	?	→	40
?	→	?	→	44

PS **8** Use **inverse operations** from each output to work out the input for each double function machine.

a

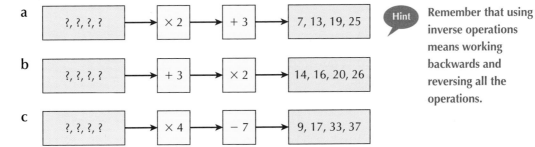

| ?, ?, ?, ? | → | × 2 | → | + 3 | → | 7, 13, 19, 25 |

Hint Remember that using inverse operations means working backwards and reversing all the operations.

b

| ?, ?, ?, ? | → | + 3 | → | × 2 | → | 14, 16, 20, 26 |

c

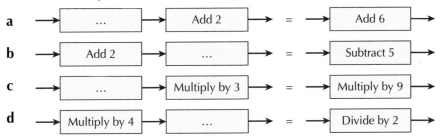

| ?, ?, ?, ? | → | × 4 | → | − 7 | → | 9, 17, 33, 37 |

9 Each of these double function machines has been replaced with a single function machine.

Work out the operation that is missing from each double function machine.

a → | ... | → | Add 2 | → = → | Add 6 | →

b → | Add 2 | → | ... | → = → | Subtract 5 | →

c → | ... | → | Multiply by 3 | → = → | Multiply by 9 | →

d → | Multiply by 4 | → | ... | → = → | Divide by 2 | →

Challenge: Double function machines

The outputs come from using two rules on the inputs, as in Question **5** above.

Draw a double function machine for each one.

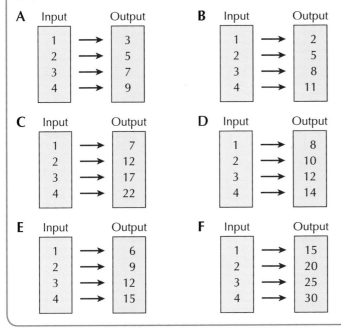

A

Input	Output
1	3
2	5
3	7
4	9

B

Input	Output
1	2
2	5
3	8
4	11

C

Input	Output
1	7
2	12
3	17
4	22

D

Input	Output
1	8
2	10
3	12
4	14

E

Input	Output
1	6
2	9
3	12
4	15

F

Input	Output
1	15
2	20
3	25
4	30

2.2 Sequences and rules

Learning objective

- To recognise, describe and write down sequences that are based on a simple rule

Key words	
first term	rule
sequence	term
term-to-term rule	

A **sequence** is a list of numbers that follow a set **rule**.

You can make up many different sequences with whole numbers, based on simple rules.

The different numbers in a sequence are called **terms**. The starting number is called the **first term**. The rule is called the **term-to-term rule**.

Example 3

Look at the rule and the starting number, then write down the first five terms of the sequence.

a Rule: Add 3   **i** Starting number 1   **ii** Starting number 2

b Rule: Double   **i** Starting number 1   **ii** Starting number 3

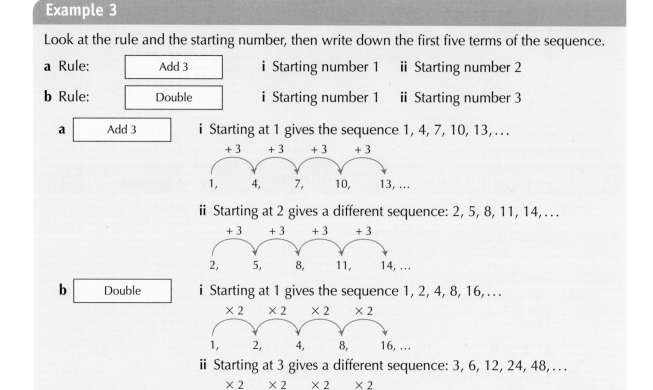

a Add 3   **i** Starting at 1 gives the sequence 1, 4, 7, 10, 13, . . .

$$+3 \quad +3 \quad +3 \quad +3$$
$$1, \quad 4, \quad 7, \quad 10, \quad 13, \ldots$$

             ii Starting at 2 gives a different sequence: 2, 5, 8, 11, 14, . . .

$$+3 \quad +3 \quad +3 \quad +3$$
$$2, \quad 5, \quad 8, \quad 11, \quad 14, \ldots$$

b Double   **i** Starting at 1 gives the sequence 1, 2, 4, 8, 16, . . .

$$\times 2 \quad \times 2 \quad \times 2 \quad \times 2$$
$$1, \quad 2, \quad 4, \quad 8, \quad 16, \ldots$$

             ii Starting at 3 gives a different sequence: 3, 6, 12, 24, 48, . . .

$$\times 2 \quad \times 2 \quad \times 2 \quad \times 2$$
$$3, \quad 6, \quad 12, \quad 24, \quad 48, \ldots$$

With different rules and different starting points, you can make many different sequences.

Exercise 2B

1 Use each term-to-term rule and the given starting point to make a sequence with four terms in it.

a Rule: | Add 3 | Start at 2.   **b** Rule: | Multiply by 3 | Start at 1.

c Rule: | Add 5 | Start at 4.   **d** Rule: | Multiply by 10 | Start at 3.

e Rule: | Add 9 | Start at 6.   **f** Rule: | Multiply by 5 | Start at 2.

g Rule: | Add 7 | Start at 3.   **h** Rule: | Multiply by 2 | Start at 5.

2 Use each term-to-term rule and the given starting point to make a sequence with four terms in it.

a Rule: | Subtract 3 | Start at 21.   **b** Rule: | Subtract 5 | Start at 31.

c Rule: | Divide by 5 | Start at 250.   **d** Rule: | Divide by 2 | Start at 32.

e Rule: | Subtract 8 | Start at 36.   **f** Rule: | Divide by 4 | Start at 64.

g Rule: | Divide by 2 | Start at 8.   **h** Rule: | Subtract 9 | Start at 45.

3 Describe the term-to-term rule of each sequence below.

Use this rule to write down the next two terms in each sequence.

a 6, 8, 10, …, …   **b** 5, 10, 15, …, …   **c** 2, 20, 200, …, …

d 1, 4, 16, …, …   **e** 2, 9, 16, …, …   **f** 30, 23, 16, …, …

g 5, 10, 20, …, …   **h** 11, 33, 55, …, …

(PS) 4 Each of these sequences uses an 'add' rule.

Write down the rule for each one.

Copy and complete each sequence.

a 2, 5, 8, …, …, 17   **b** 1, 6, …, 16, …, …

c 5, …, …, 11, …, …   **d** …, 14, …, …, 29, …

(PS) 5 Each of these sequences uses a 'multiply by' rule.

Write down the rule for each one.

Copy and complete each sequence.

a 1, 10, …, …, 10 000   **b** 3, …, …, 24, 48, …

c …, …, …, 16, 32, …   **d** 4, …, …, 108, 324

PS **6** Each of these sequences uses a 'subtract' rule.

Write down the rule for each one.

Copy and complete each sequence.

    a 52, 45, 38, …, …, 17   **b** 31, 26, …, 16, …, …

    c 45, …, …, 15, …   **d** …, 44, …, …, 26, …

PS **7** Each of these sequences uses a 'divide by' rule.

Write down the rule for each one.

Copy and complete each sequence.

    a 80, 40, …, …, 5   **b** 81, …, …, 3, 1

    c …, …, 8, …, …, 1   **d** 1250, …, …, 10, …

8 Write down the first five terms of each sequence, based on the rule.

Start each sequence with 2.

    a Add 2   **b** Multiply by 4   **c** Add 5   **d** Multiply by 10

    e Add 8   **f** Multiply by 5   **g** Add 3   **h** Multiply by 2

9 **a** The sequence below is part of a sequence with the rule 'Multiply by 2'.

    …, 20, 40, 80, …

    What are the two missing numbers?

   b The sequence below is part of a sequence with the rule 'Divide by 2'.

    …, 48, 24, 12, …, …

    What are the three missing numbers?

Challenge: Rules for sequences

A For each pair of numbers below, write down two different rules to get from the first term to the second term. Then use each rule to write down the next two terms in the sequence.

    a 1, 3, …, …   **b** 2, 8, …, …   **c** 5, 10, …, …

    d 1, 5, …, …   **e** 10, 20, …, …   **f** 3, 12, …, …

B For each sequence below, write down a rule to get from the first term to the missing second term. Then use each rule to write down the first four terms of the sequence.

    a 1, …, 7, …   **b** 1, …, 11, …   **c** 15, …, 25, …

    d 6, …, 12, …   **e** 5, …, 25, …   **f** 18, …, 22, …

2.3 Finding terms in patterns

Learning objective

• To find missing terms in a sequence

In any sequence, you will have a first term, second term, third term, fourth term and so on.

Example 4

Look at the pattern of matches, then draw the next pattern and state how many matches it will use.

Pattern 1   Pattern 2   Pattern 3   Pattern 4
3 matches   5 matches   7 matches   9 matches

You can easily draw the next pattern and count that it has 11 matches.

Pattern 5
11 matches

You can carry on doing this for as many patterns as you like.

A better way to solve the last example is to put the numbers into a table, spot the term-to-term rule and use this to work out the number of matches.

Pattern	Matches
1	3
2	5
3	7
4	9
5	11

You can carry on with this table as far as you like, but there is an easier way to work out the number of matches in, for example, the 10th pattern.

The term-to-term rule is 'Add 2'. To get from the fifth pattern to the 10th pattern, you need to add on two five more times.

$$11 + 2 \times 5 = 11 + 10 = 21$$

So there are 21 matches in the 10th pattern.

However, it is even easier to start from the first term. To get to the 10th term you need to add on two nine (10 − 1) times.

$$3 + 2 \times (10 - 1) = 3 + 2 \times 9 = 3 + 18 = 21$$

To get to the 25th term you need to add on two twenty-four times.

$$3 + 24 \times 2 = 3 + 48 = 51$$

For each series of diagrams below:

a draw the next diagram

b write down the sequence to show the numbers of matches in the first five patterns

c work out how many matches there are in:

    i the 10th

    ii the 20th pattern.

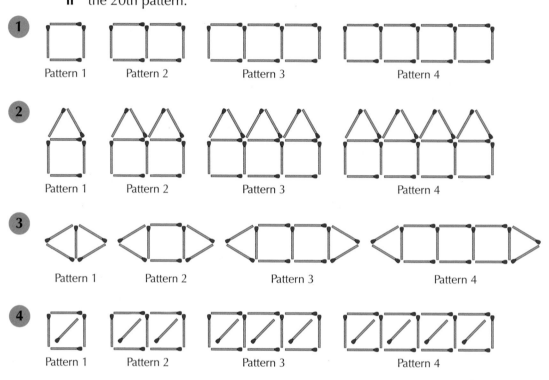

Pattern 1   Pattern 2   Pattern 3   Pattern 4

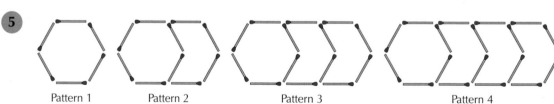

Pattern 1   Pattern 2   Pattern 3   Pattern 4

 6 For each sequence:

i write down the term-to-term rule

ii work out the 10th term.

    a 2, 4, 6, 8, ...   **b** 3, 8, 13, 18, ...   **c** 4, 10, 16, 22, ...

    d 4, 8, 12, 16, ...   **e** 7, 10, 13, 16, ...   **f** 1, 9, 17, 25, ...

Challenge: Dot patterns

A How many dots will there be in: **a** the fifth pattern **b** the 10th pattern?

Pattern 1   Pattern 2   Pattern 3   Pattern 4

B How many dots will there be in: **a** the fifth pattern **b** the 10th pattern?

Pattern 1   Pattern 2   Pattern 3   Pattern 4

C How many squares will there be in: **a** the fifth pattern **b** the 10th pattern?

Pattern 1   Pattern 2   Pattern 3   Pattern 4

2.4 The square numbers

Learning objective

To introduce the sequence of square numbers

Key words	
square numbers	squaring

When you multiply a number by itself this is called **squaring** the number. The result is a **square number**. For example:

- 4 is a square number and is the result of squaring 2 ($2 \times 2 = 4$), so 4 is the square of 2
- 9 is a square number and is the result of squaring 3 ($3 \times 3 = 9$), so 9 is the square of 3

and so on.

Instead of writing 1×1, 2×2, $3 \times 3, \ldots$, you can write 1^2, 2^2, $3^2, \ldots$.

You read this as 'one squared, two squared, three squared...'.

This table shows the first seven square numbers.

1×1	2×2	3×3	4×4	5×5	6×6	7×7
1^2	2^2	3^2	4^2	5^2	6^2	7^2
1	4	9	16	25	36	49

You can see from the bottom line of the table why they are called square numbers.

This is the start of the sequence of square numbers.

You need to learn the square numbers up to $15^2 = 225$.

Exercise 2D

1 Continue the first three rows of the table of square numbers, above, up to 10×10.

2 Use a calculator to work out the rest of the square numbers up to 15×15.

3 Use a calculator work out these squares.

    a 18^2 **b** 21^2 **c** 25^2

    d 40^2 **e** 35^2 **f** 42^2

4 Write each number below as the addition of two square numbers.
The first two have been done for you.

    a $5 = 1 + 4$ **b** $10 = 1 + 9$ **c** $13 = \ldots + \ldots$

    d $17 = \ldots + \ldots$ **e** $20 = \ldots + \ldots$ **f** $25 = \ldots + \ldots$

(PS) **5** Look at this pattern of numbers.

$1 \qquad\quad = 1 = 1^2$

$1 + 3 \quad = 4 = 2^2$

$1 + 3 + 5 = 9 = 3^2$

    a Write down the next two lines of this number pattern.

    b What is special about the numbers in the middle column, between the equals signs?

    c Without working them out, write down the answers to these calculations.

        i $1 + 3 + 5 + 7 + 9 + 11 = \ldots$

        ii $1 + 3 + 5 + 7 + 9 + 11 + 13 + 15 = \ldots$

Challenge: Triples of squares

Some pairs of square numbers are special because when you add them they give an answer that is also a square number.

For example: $3^2 + 4^2 = 9 + 16 = 25 = 5^2$

Check that each of the following additions of square numbers also gives a square number.

In each case, write out the full calculation as above.

A $6^2 + 8^2$ **B** $5^2 + 12^2$

C $7^2 + 24^2$ **D** $10^2 + 24^2$

E $8^2 + 15^2$ **F** $9^2 + 12^2$

> **Hint** Find the button on your calculator that tests if a number is a square number.
> It looks something like this.
>
>
>
> If the answer is a decimal (not a whole number), then the number you put in is not a square number.

2.5 The triangular numbers

Learning objective

• To introduce the sequence of triangular numbers

Key word

triangular number

Another well-know sequence is:

      1, 3, 6, 10, 15, 21, . . .

This is called the sequence of **triangular numbers**.

This sequence builds up like this.

First term: 1

Second term: Add 2 $2 + 1 = 3$

Third term: Add 3 to the second term $3 + 3 = 6$

Fourth term: Add 4 to the third term $4 + 6 = 10$

Fifth term: Add 5 to the fourth term $5 + 10 = 15$

This table shows you the first seven triangular numbers.

0 + 1	1 + 2	3 + 3	6 + 4	10 + 5	15 + 6	21 + 7
1	3	6	10	15	21	28
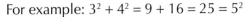						

You can see from the bottom line of the table why they are called triangular numbers.

Exercise 2E

1 Continue the first two rows of the table of triangular numbers, above, up to the 10th triangular number.

2 Continue the sequence of triangular numbers up to the 15th triangular number.

3 Write each of these numbers as the addition of two triangular numbers. The first two have been done for you.

   a $4 = 1 + 3$ **b** $7 = 1 + 6$ **c** $9 = \ldots + \ldots$

   d $11 = \ldots + \ldots$ **e** $13 = \ldots + \ldots$ **f** $16 = \ldots + \ldots$

4 Write down two numbers that are both square numbers and also triangular numbers.

(PS) **5** Look at this pattern of numbers.

$$1 \qquad\quad = 1$$
$$1 + 2 \quad\;\; = 3$$
$$1 + 2 + 3 = 6$$

   a Write down the next two lines of this number pattern.

   b What is special about the numbers on the left-hand side?

   c What is special about the numbers on the right-hand side?

   d Without working them out, write down the answers to these calculations.

      i $1 + 2 + 3 + 4 + 5 + 6 = \ldots$

     ii $1 + 2 + 3 + 4 + 5 + 6 + 7 + 8 = \ldots$

6 **a** Add up the first five pairs of consecutive triangular numbers, starting with $1 + 3, 3 + 6, 6 + 10, \ldots$.

   b What is special about the answers?

Challenge: Triangular numbers

Here is the sequence of triangular numbers.

     1, 3, 6 10, 15, 21, 28, ...

The first term is 1.   You can work this out from: $0.5 \times 1 \times 2 = 1$

The second term is 3.   You can work this out from: $0.5 \times 2 \times 3 = 3$

The third term is 6.   You can work this out from: $0.5 \times 3 \times 4 = 6$

The fourth term is 10.   You can work this out from: $0.5 \times 4 \times 5 = 10$

A Write down the next three lines in the sequence.

B Explain how you can use this pattern to work out a rule for any term in the sequence.

C Use your rule to work out:

   a the 10th triangular number   **b** the 20th triangular number

   c the 50th triangular number   **d** the 100th triangular number.

Investigation: A function machine problem

This is an investigation of a double function machine that uses a two-digit whole-number input.

Examples of two-digit whole numbers are 12, 36, 45, 71, 98.

The double function machine is:

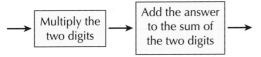

For example: start with an input of 23.

$23 \rightarrow 2 \times 3 = 6 \rightarrow 6 + 2 + 3 = 11$ So the output is 11.

Now start the investigation.

If a two-digit number input gives an output that is a single-digit number, then stop.

For example, start with an input of 14.

$14 \rightarrow 1 \times 4 = 4 \rightarrow 4 + 1 + 4 = 9$, so stop as the output is a single-digit number.

If a two-digit number gives an output that is a two-digit number, then repeat until you reach a single-digit number.

For example, start with an input of 83.

$83 \rightarrow 8 \times 3 = 24 \rightarrow 24 + 8 + 3 = 35$ Now repeat with an input of 35.

$35 \rightarrow 3 \times 5 = 15 \rightarrow 15 + 3 + 5 = 23$ Now repeat with an input of 23.

$23 \rightarrow 2 \times 3 = 6 \rightarrow 6 + 2 + 3 = 11$ Now repeat with an input of 11.

$11 \rightarrow 1 \times 1 = 1 \rightarrow 1 + 1 + 1 = 3$ Stop, as the output is a single-digit number.

A Start with an input of 31. Work out the output.

B Start with an input of 24. Work out the output.

C Start with an input of 66. Work out the output.

D Start with an input of 19. What happens?

E Start with another input that ends with 9. What happens?

F Start with an input of 91. What happens?

G Start with another input that starts with 9. What happens?

H **a** Start with an input of 56. What is the output?

   b Start with an input of 65. Explain how you know what the output is, without working it out.

Ready to progress?

I can find the output for a single function machine when I know the input value.

I can find the output for a double function machine when I know the input value.
I can write down a sequence, given the first term and a term-to-term rule.
I can give the term-to-term rule for a sequence.
I know how to work out square numbers and triangular numbers.

I can find any term in a sequence, given the first term and a term-to-term rule.

Review questions

1   Work out the missing inputs and outputs for each function machine.

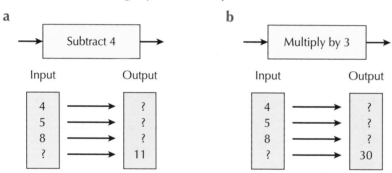

2   Here is a sequence of shapes made with grey and white tiles.

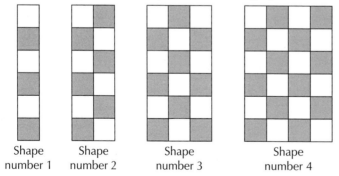

| Shape number 1 | Shape number 2 | Shape number 3 | Shape number 4 |

The number of grey tiles   = 3 × the shape number

The number of white tiles = 3 × the shape number

a   How many white tiles will there be in shape number 8?

b   Altogether, how many tiles will there be in shape number 8?

c   Altogether, how many tiles will there be in shape number 15?

d   Write down the missing number from this sentence:

The total number of tiles = … × the shape number.

3 Each of these double function machines can be replaced with a single function machine.

Work out the operation that will go in the single function machine. The first one has been done for you.

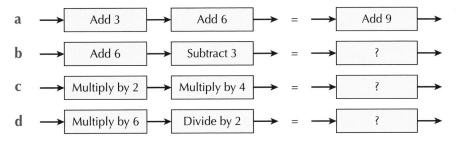

a → Add 3 → Add 6 → = → Add 9 →

b → Add 6 → Subtract 3 → = → ? →

c → Multiply by 2 → Multiply by 4 → = → ? →

d → Multiply by 6 → Divide by 2 → = → ? →

4 a Use the term-to-term rule to write the next two numbers in each sequence.

   i Rule: → Add 6 →   4   10   …   …

   ii Rule: → Multiply by 4 →   1   4   …   …

   iii Rule: → Multiply by 2 → Add 3 →   4   11   …   …

b A sequence of numbers starts like this:

      30, 22, 14

The rule is 'Subtract 8'.

Work out the first negative number in the sequence.

5 a Jeni saves £20 each week for 8 weeks. How much will she have saved after:
   i 2 weeks   **ii** 8 weeks?

b Jeni's friend Lucie already has £16 saved. She then saves £9 the first week, £11 the second week, £13 the third week and so on for 8 weeks.

Copy and complete this table for Lucie.

Week	1	2	3	4	5	6	7	8
Amount saved (£)	9	11	13	15	17			
Total amount saved (£)	25	36						

c i Who will have more money at the end of eight weeks?

   ii How much more will she have than her friend?

(MR) 6 This pattern of square numbers is made with coloured counters.

a Write down the sequence formed by the red counters.

b Write down the sequence formed by the blue counters.

c Write 49 as the sum of two triangular numbers.

d Write 100 as the sum of two triangular numbers.

Mathematical reasoning
Valencia Planetarium

Grids are made from combinations of these rods and links.

L links   T links   X links   R rods

Examples

This grid is made from 4 L links + 2 T links + 7 R rods.

This grid is made from 4 L links + 6 T links + 2 X links + 17 R rods.

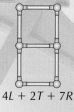

$4L + 2T + 7R$

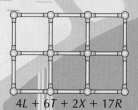

$4L + 6T + 2X + 17R$

1 Look at the grids on the right.

a Copy and complete this table.

Grid	L links	T links	R rods
1	4	0	4
2	4	2	7
3			

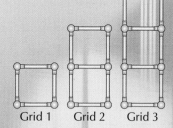

Grid 1   Grid 2   Grid 3

b Continue the table, to find the numbers of links and rods up to grid 6.

c Copy and complete these statements.

L links = ...

T links = grid number × 2 − ...

R rods = grid number × ... + ...

2 Look at these grids.

   a Copy and complete this table.

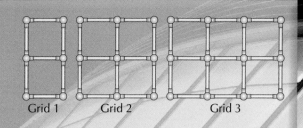

Grid 1   Grid 2   Grid 3

Grid	L links	T links	X links	R rods
1	4	2	0	7
2	4	4	1	12
3				
4				

   b Copy and complete these statements.

      L links = …

      T links = grid number × …

      X links = grid number × 1 – …

      R rods = grid number × … + …

3 Look at these grids.

   a Copy and complete this table.

Grid	L links	T links	X links	R rods
1	4	4	0	10
2	4	6	2	17
3				
4				

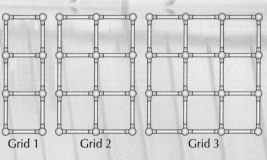

Grid 1   Grid 2   Grid 3

   b Copy and complete these statements.

      L links = …

      T links = grid number × … + …

      X links = grid number × 2 – …

      R rods = grid number × … + …

   c How many links and rods will there be in grid 10?

3

Perimeter and area

This chapter is going to show you:

- how to measure and draw lines
- how to work out the perimeter of 2D shapes
- how to work out the area of 2D shapes by counting squares
- how to work out the perimeter of a square and a rectangle by using a rule
- how to work out the area of a square and a rectangle by using a rule.

You should already know:

- the metric units of length
- how to recognise triangles, squares and rectangles
- that the perimeter of a 2D shape is the distance around its edges
- that the area of a 2D shape is the space inside it.

About this chapter

Where can you see squares and rectangles? The answer is, all around you!

People have recognised squares and rectangles for thousands of years. They discovered that these shapes can fit together easily, so they used them to build houses and plan towns and cities. For the same reasons, the blocks and bricks used to build houses are often rectangular, as are doors and windows.

This picture is a street plan of Pompeii, the ancient Roman city that was built on the slopes of Mount Vesuvius. It shows that the city was laid out in a roughly rectangular grid pattern. Sadly, the Romans did not know quite as much about volcanoes, and Pompeii was destroyed in an eruption, in 79AD.

The same idea is still used for more modern urban developments, such as Manhattan in the USA and Milton Keynes, in the UK.

3.1 Length and perimeter

Learning objectives

- To measure and draw lines
- To work out the perimeter of a shape

Key words	
centimetre	metric units
millimetre	perimeter

Length

This ruler measures length in **centimetres** and inches.

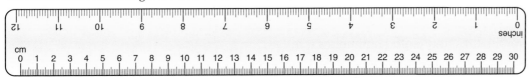

It is usually called a 30-centimetre ruler or a 12-inch ruler.

This ruler measures in centimetres and **millimetres**.

It is usually called a 30-centimetre ruler or a 300-millimetre ruler.

When measuring or drawing lines you must make sure that you use the correct **metric units.**

Make sure that you know this:

10 millimetres = 1 centimetre which is usually written as 10 mm = 1 cm

Example 1

What is the length of the blue line?
The length of the line is 6 cm.
This is the same as 60 mm.

Example 2

What is the length of the blue line?
The length of the line is 72 mm.
This is the same as 7.2 cm.

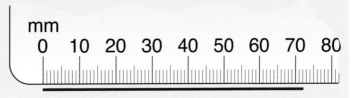

Changing units

To change centimetres into millimetres, you multiply by 10.

To change millimetres into centimetres, you divide by 10.

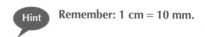

Hint Remember: 1 cm = 10 mm.

Example 3

Change 8.2 centimetres (cm) into millimetres (mm).

$8.2 \times 10 = 82$, so 8.2 cm = 82 mm

Example 4

Change 56 millimetres (mm) into centimetres (cm).

$56 \div 10 = 5.6$, so 56 mm = 5.6 cm

Perimeter

You measure the **perimeter** of a shape by adding together the lengths of all the sides.

Example 5

Work out the perimeter of this shape, which is drawn on centimetre-squared paper.

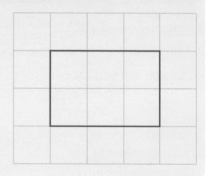

The length of the side of each square on the grid is 1 cm.

The perimeter of the shape is the distance around its edge.

So the perimeter is:

3 cm + 2 cm + 3 cm + 2 cm = 10 cm

Example 6

Work out the perimeter of this L-shape, which is drawn on centimetre-squared paper.

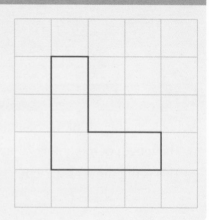

The length of the side of each square on the grid is 1 cm.

So the perimeter of the L-shape is:

1 cm + 2 cm + 2 cm + 1 cm + 3 cm + 3 cm = 12 cm

Exercise 3A

1 Copy each statement and fill in the missing numbers.

    a 4 cm = ... mm   **b** 10 cm = ... mm   **c** 7.5 cm = ... mm

    d 8.9 cm = ... mm   **e** 12.4 cm = ... mm

2 Copy each statement and fill in the missing numbers.

    a 70 mm = ... cm   **b** 140 mm = ... cm   **c** 65 mm = ... cm

    d 32 mm = ... cm   **e** 116 mm = ... cm

3 Measure the length of each line. Give your answers in centimetres.

    a _____

    b _____

    c _____

    d _____

    e _____

4 Measure the length of each line. Give your answers in millimetres.

    a _____

    b _____

    c _____

    d _____

    e _____

5 Use your ruler to draw lines of these lengths.

    a 4 cm   **b** 5.4 cm   **c** 6.8 cm   **d** 50 mm   **e** 88 mm

6 Copy these shapes onto centimetre-squared paper.

    Work out the perimeter of each shape.

a 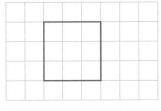   **b** 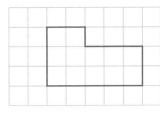   **c**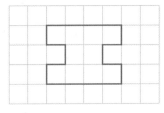

d 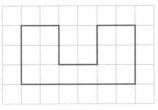   **e**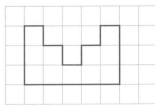

7 The shapes below are all regular shapes.

This means that the lengths of the sides on each shape are all the same.

a Use your ruler to work out the perimeter of each shape.

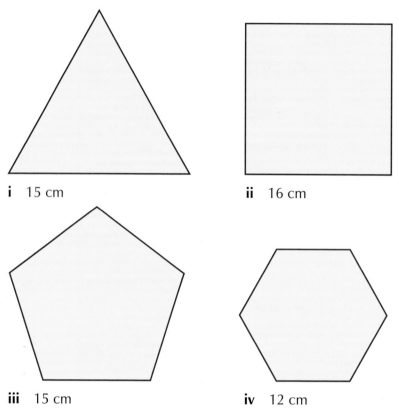

i 15 cm

ii 16 cm

iii 15 cm

iv 12 cm

b Now copy and complete this statement.

To work out the perimeter of a regular shape you multiply...by....

8 Use your ruler to measure the widths of a 1p, a 2p, a 5p, a 10p and a £1 coin. Give your answers in centimetres.

Activity: Guess the length

Work with a partner.

A Each draw five lines of different lengths, on a sheet of paper.

B Then swap papers and guess the lengths of each other's lines.

C Check by measuring each line with a ruler.

3.2 Area

Learning objective

- To work out the area of a shape by counting squares

Key words

| area | square centimetre |

The **area** of a shape is the amount of space inside it.

One way to work out the area of a shape is to count the squares inside it.

The unit of area used in this section is the **square centimetre**. This is usually written as cm².

Example 7

Work out the area of this shape, which is drawn on centimetre-squared paper.

   The area of each square on the grid is 1 cm².

   To work out the area, count the squares inside the shape.

   So, the area of this shape is 6 cm².

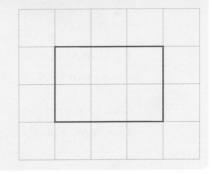

Example 8

Work out the area of this L-shape, which is drawn on centimetre-squared paper.

   The area of each square on the grid is 1 cm².

   To work out the area, count the squares inside the L-shape.

   So, the area of this L-shape is 5 cm².

Example 9

Work out the area of this shape, which is drawn on centimetre-squared paper.

The area of each square on the grid is 1 cm².

To work out the area, count the squares inside the shape.

Inside the shape there are six whole squares.

There is also one half-square and this has an area of $\frac{1}{2}$ cm².

So, the area of this shape is $6\frac{1}{2}$ cm².

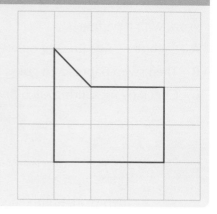

Exercise 3B

1 Copy each shape onto centimetre-squared paper.

Then work out the area of each shape.

a   **b**   **c**   **d**

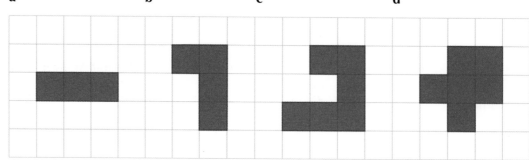

2 Copy these shapes onto centimetre-squared paper.

Then work out the area of each shape.

a   **b**   **c**

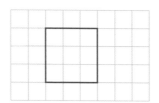
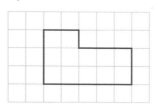
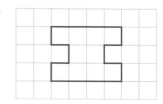

3 Copy these shapes onto centimetre-squared paper.

Then work out the area of each shape.

a   **b**

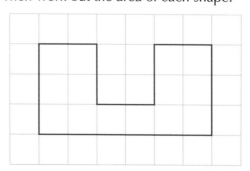
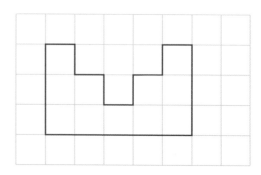

c
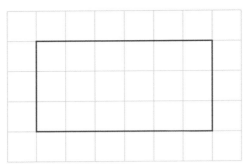

d
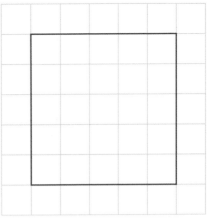

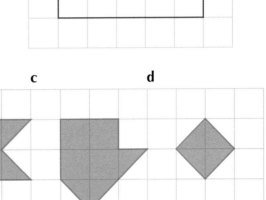

4 Copy these shapes onto centimetre-squared paper.

Then work out the area of each shape.

a   b   c   d

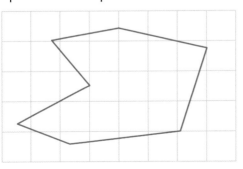

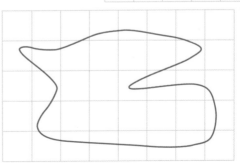

(MR) **5** On centimetre-squared paper, draw four different shapes that all have an area of 6 cm².

6 On centimetre-squared paper, draw a square that has an area of 16 cm².

Challenge: More difficult shapes

The areas of some shapes are more difficult to work out.

For these shapes, you can estimate the area, as shown in the example below.

Estimate the area of this shape.

The area of each square on the grid is 1 cm².

If at least half of a square is inside the shape, mark it with a dot.

There are 11 dotted squares.

So, an estimate for the area of the shape is 11 cm².

Now estimate the area of each of these shapes. Each square on the grid represents one square centimetre.

A

B

3.3 Perimeter and area of rectangles

Learning objectives

- To work out the perimeter of a rectangle
- To work out the area of a rectangle

Key words	
length	metre
rectangle	square
square metre	width

Perimeter of a rectangle

A **rectangle** has two measurements:

- a **length** (which is usually the longer side)
- a **width**.

The perimeter of the rectangle is the total distance around the shape.

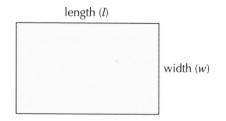

Perimeter = 2 lengths + 2 widths

Perimeter is a length. You would usually use the metric units centimetres (cm) or metres (m) to measure it.

Example 10

Work out the perimeter of the **square** and the rectangle.

a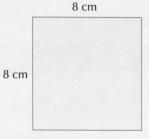

8 cm

8 cm

b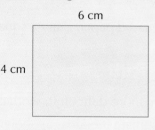

6 cm

4 cm

a Perimeter = 8 cm + 8 cm + 8 cm + 8 cm

= 4 × 8 cm

= 32 cm

b Perimeter = 6 cm + 6 cm + 4 cm + 4 cm

= 2 × 6 cm + 2 × 4 cm

= 12 cm + 8 cm

= 20 cm

Example 11

Work out the perimeter of this rectangle.

Perimeter = 6 m + 6 m + 2 m + 2 m

= 2 × 6 m + 2 × 2 m

= 12 m + 4 m

= 16 m

2 m

6 m

Area of a rectangle

The area of the rectangle is the amount of space inside the shape.

The area of each square on this grid is 1 cm².

There are 6 squares on each row and there are 3 rows.

The area can be simply worked out as $3 \times 6 = 18$ squares.

So the area of the rectangle is 18 cm².

For any rectangle:

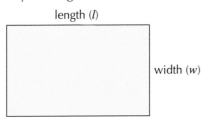

length (l)

width (w)

Area = length × width

The metric units you would usually use for area are the square centimetre (cm²) and the **square metre** (m²).

Example 12

Work out the area of the square and the rectangle.

a
8 cm

8 cm

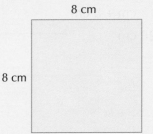

b
6 cm

4 cm

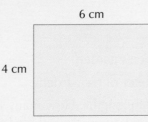

a Area = length × width
        = 8 cm × 8 cm
        = 64 cm²

b Area = length × width
        = 6 cm × 4 cm
        = 24 cm²

Example 13

Work out the area of this rectangle.

Area = length × width

= 6 m × 2 m

= 12 m²

2 m

6 m

Notice that the perimeter and area of a rectangle are usually different numbers.

Exercise 3C

1 Work out the perimeter of each square.

a 1 cm
1 cm

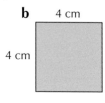
b 4 cm
4 cm

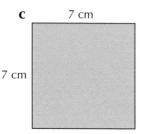
c 7 cm
7 cm

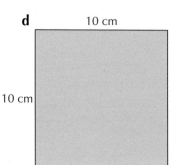
d 10 cm
10 cm

2 Work out the perimeter of each rectangle.

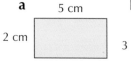
a 5 cm
2 cm

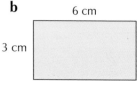
b 6 cm
3 cm

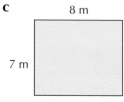
c 8 m
7 m

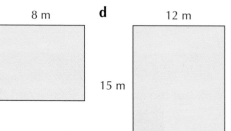
d 12 m
15 m

3 **a** This is a sketch of Ben's garden.
Work out the perimeter of his garden.

b Fencing is sold in 3 m lengths. How many lengths of fencing does Ben need, to go around the four sides of his garden?

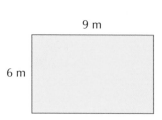
9 m
6 m

4 A square kitchen tile measures 12 cm by 12 cm. Work out the perimeter of the tile.

5 A hockey pitch measures 80 m by 60 m. Work the perimeter of the pitch.

6 Work out the area of each square.

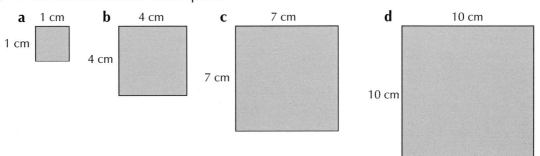

a 1 cm, 1 cm
b 4 cm, 4 cm
c 7 cm, 7 cm
d 10 cm, 10 cm

7 Work out the area of each rectangle.

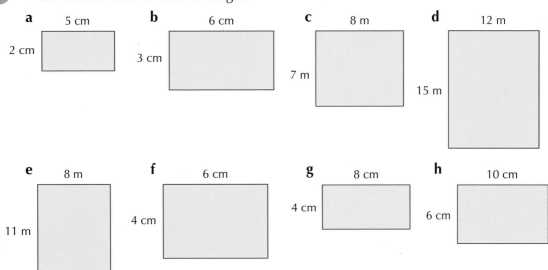

a 5 cm, 2 cm
b 6 cm, 3 cm
c 8 m, 7 m
d 12 m, 15 m

e 8 m, 11 m
f 6 cm, 4 cm
g 8 cm, 4 cm
h 10 cm, 6 cm

(MR) 8 On centimetre-squared paper, draw a square with sides of length 6 cm.

How many squares with sides of length 2 cm are needed to cover the square you have drawn?

9 Copy and complete the table for rectangles **a** to **f**.

	Length	Width	Perimeter	Area
a	4 cm	2 cm		
b	6 cm	5 cm		
c	8 cm	4 cm		
d	10 cm	9 cm		
e	8 cm	1 cm		
f	7 cm	2 cm		

Investigation: Different rectangles, same perimeter

A On centimetre-squared paper, draw as many different rectangles as you can with a perimeter of 20 cm.

B Work out the area of each one.

C Which one has the greatest area?

Ready to progress?

I can draw and measure lines.

I can find the perimeter of a shape.
I can find the area of a shape by counting squares.
I can find the perimeter of a rectangle by using perimeter = 2 lengths + 2 widths.

I can find the area of a rectangle by using area = length × width.

Review questions

1   Copy each statement and write in the missing numbers.

   a   2 cm = … mm   b   4.5 cm = … mm

   c   60 mm = … cm   d   72 mm = … cm

2   Measure the length of each line.

   Give your answers in centimetres.

   a   _____

   b   _____

   c   _____

   d   _____

3   Use your ruler to draw lines with these lengths.

   a   5 cm   b   6.5 cm   c   40 mm   d   75 mm

4   The diagram shows part of a ruler.

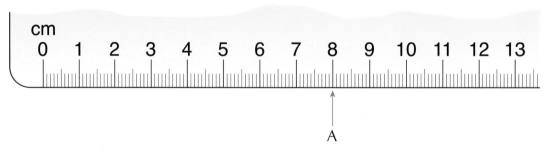

The distance between two points, A and B, is $4\frac{1}{2}$ cm.

Copy the diagram of the ruler and draw two arrows to show the points where B could be.

5   Work out the perimeter of each shape.

a

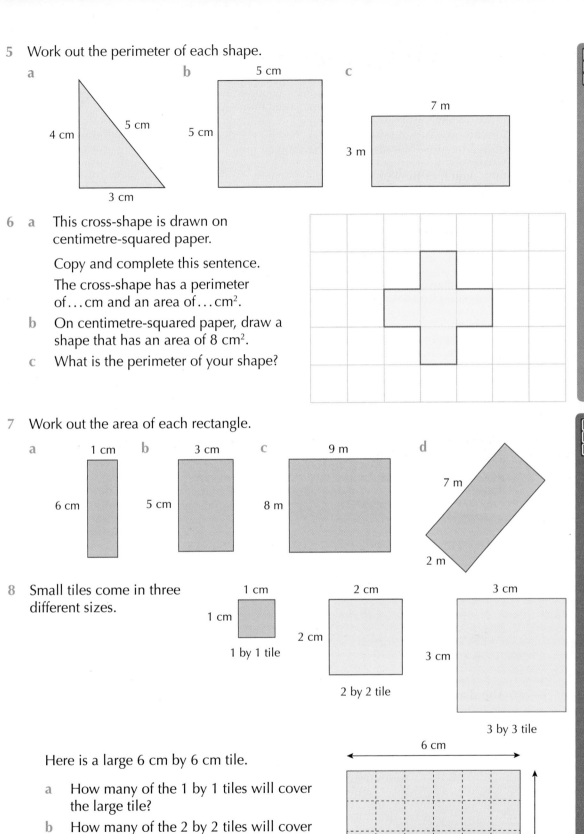

4 cm   5 cm

3 cm

b   5 cm

5 cm

c

7 m

3 m

(MR) 6 a This cross-shape is drawn on
             centimetre-squared paper.

       Copy and complete this sentence.
       The cross-shape has a perimeter
       of…cm and an area of…cm².

    b On centimetre-squared paper, draw a
       shape that has an area of 8 cm².

    c What is the perimeter of your shape?

7   Work out the area of each rectangle.

a   1 cm

6 cm

b   3 cm

5 cm

c   9 m

8 m

d

7 m

2 m

(MR) 8 Small tiles come in three
          different sizes.

1 cm

1 cm

1 by 1 tile

2 cm

2 cm

2 by 2 tile

3 cm

3 cm

3 by 3 tile

Here is a large 6 cm by 6 cm tile.

a How many of the 1 by 1 tiles will cover
   the large tile?

b How many of the 2 by 2 tiles will cover
   the large tile?

c How many of the 3 by 3 tiles will cover
   the large tile?

6 cm

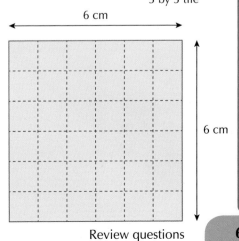

6 cm

Problem solving
Design a bedroom

1 This is a sketch of Becky's bedroom.

  a What is the perimeter of her bedroom?

  b What is the area of her bedroom?

  c Becky sees an advertisement for this carpet. How much will it cost her to carpet the bedroom?

Lille range
Regent Green

Only £6.50 per m²

1 m

1 m

Window

Window

4 m

Door

5 m

1 m

2 Becky wants posters of footballers on her bedroom walls.

They cost £8 each.

  a How many posters can she buy for £50?

  b How much money is left over?

3 These are sketches of the door and one of the windows.

The height of the bedroom is 3 m.

This is a sketch of the wall with the door.

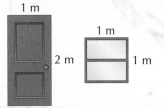

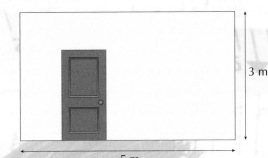

a Copy and complete these statements.

The area of the wall including the door = ____ × ____ = ____ m².

The area of the door = ____ × ____ = ____ m².

So the area of the wall without the door = _____ − _____ = ____ m².

b Now work out the area of the other three walls.

c What is the total area of all four walls?

d If a one-litre tin of paint covers 9 m², what is the smallest number of tins Becky needs, to paint the walls?

Furniture challenge

4 Becky wants to buy this furniture for her bedroom.

| Bed | Bedside table | Wardrobe | Chest of drawers | Desk |

Use the internet to find how much it would cost her to buy all this furniture.

4

Decimal numbers

This chapter is going to show you:

- how to order decimal numbers by size
- how to multiply and divide decimal numbers by 10, 100 and 1000
- how to use estimation to check your answers
- how to solve problems using decimals, with and without a calculator
- how to add and subtract decimal numbers
- how to multiply and divide decimals by whole numbers.

You should already know:

- how to write and read whole numbers and decimals
- how to write tenths and hundredths as decimals
- times tables up to 12×12
- how to use a calculator to do simple calculations.

About this chapter

The decimal number system is based on 10. Decimals have been used for so long that no one can say exactly where or when they started. They were the basis of the ancient Chinese, Hindu-Arabic and Roman number systems.

The numbers we use in Europe come from the Hindu-Arabic number system.

Often we refer to decimals when we mean decimal fractions: tenths, hundredths, thousandths and so on.

We express these as 0.1, 0.01, 0.001, etc.

4.1 Multiplying and dividing by 10, 100 and 1000

Learning objective

• To multiply and divide decimal numbers by 10, 100 and 1000

Key word

decimal

You already know how to multiply whole numbers by ten, one hundred and one thousand.

You can multiply **decimals** in the same way.

When you multiply by 10, all the digits move one place to the left.

For example: $4 \times 10 = 40$ $4.15 \times 10 = 41.5$

When you multiply by 100, all the digits move two places to the left.

For example: $4 \times 100 = 400$ $4.15 \times 100 = 415$

When you multiply by 1000, all the digits move three places to the left.

For example: $4 \times 1000 = 4000$ $4.15 \times 1000 = 4150$

Can you see that the number of places the digits move left is the same as the number of zeros in the number you are multiplying by? This is true for multiplying decimals as well as whole numbers.

Example 1

a Work out 3.5×100.   **b** Work out 4.7×10.

a
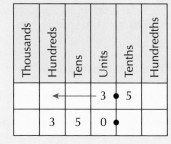

The digits move two places to the left when you multiply by 100.

$3.5 \times 100 = 350$

b
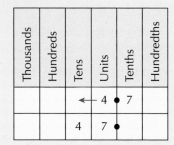

The digits move one place to the left when you multiply by 10.

$4.7 \times 10 = 47$

You can divide decimals by 10, 100 and 1000 in the same way as for whole numbers.

When you divide by 10, all the digits move one place to the right.

For example: $37 \div 10 = 3.7$ $621.8 \div 10 = 62.18$

When you divide by 100, all the digits move two places to the right.

For example: $37 \div 100 = 0.37$ $621.8 \div 100 = 6.218$

When you divide by 1000, all the digits move three places to the right.

For example: $37 \div 1000 = 0.037$ $621.8 \div 1000 = 0.6218$

This time, the number of places the digits move right is the same as the number of zeros in the number you are dividing by.

Example 2

a Work out 23 ÷ 1000.　　**b** Work out 13.6 ÷ 10.

a

Tens	Units	Tenths	Hundredths	Thousandths
2	3			
	0	0	2	3

The digits move three places to the right when you divide by 1000.

23 ÷ 1000 = 0.023

b

Tens	Units	Tenths	Hundredths	Thousandths
1	3	6		
	1	3	6	

The digits move one place to the right when you divide by 10.

13.6 ÷ 10 = 1.36

Exercise 4A

1 Eight of these numbers are divisible by 10. Write them down.

   40 55 20 26 50 35 29 110 46 10 500 625 370 690 41

2 Eight of these numbers are divisible by 100. Write them down.

   712 320 40 550 800 25 1200 600 6200 300 4000 617 1000
   670 250 000

3 Work these out, without using a calculator.

  a 14 × 10   **b** 89 × 10   **c** 7 × 100   **d** 41 × 100

  e 30 ÷ 10   **f** 8900 ÷ 10   **g** 700 ÷ 10   **h** 400 ÷ 10

  i 5800 ÷ 10   **j** 900 × 10   **k** 440 ÷ 10   **l** 64 × 10

4 Work these out, without using a calculator.

  a 4 × 10   **b** 9 × 100   **c** 7 × 100   **d** 4 × 1000

  e 3 ÷ 10   **f** 8 ÷ 100   **g** 2 ÷ 100   **h** 5 ÷ 1000

  i 8 ÷ 1000   **j** 1 × 100   **k** 4 ÷ 10   **l** 6 × 100

5 Work these out, without using a calculator.

  a 54 × 10   **b** 79 × 100   **c** 87 × 100   **d** 24 × 1000

  e 14 ÷ 10   **f** 39 ÷ 100   **g** 73 ÷ 100   **h** 65 ÷ 1000

  i 51 ÷ 1000   **j** 17 × 100   **k** 34 ÷ 10   **l** 85 × 100

6 Work these out, without using a calculator.

a	124×10	**b**	369×100	**c**	597×100	**d**	654×1000
e	$114 \div 10$	**f**	$289 \div 100$	**g**	$107 \div 100$	**h**	$235 \div 1000$
i	$143 \div 1000$	**j**	714×100	**k**	$974 \div 10$	**l**	729×100

7 Work these out, without using a calculator.

a	3.4×10	**b**	8.9×100	**c**	0.97×100	**d**	1.4×1000
e	$3.4 \div 10$	**f**	$89 \div 100$	**g**	$7 \div 100$	**h**	$7.5 \div 1000$
i	$58.3 \div 1000$	**j**	71.4×100	**k**	$0.74 \div 10$	**l**	18.9×100

8 Write down the missing number in each statement.

a $3 \times 10 = \square$ **b** $3 \times \square = 300$ **c** $3 \div 10 = \square$ **d** $3 \div \square = 0.03$

9 Work these out, without using a calculator.

a	5.6×100	**b**	0.9×100	**c**	6.7×100	**d**	0.07×100
e	3.5×100	**f**	0.8×100	**g**	$1.3 \div 100$	**h**	$0.4 \div 100$
i	$4.2 \div 100$	**j**	$0.01 \div 100$	**k**	$6.9 \div 100$	**l**	$0.03 \div 100$
m	$6.24 \div 100$	**n**	3.981×100	**o**	$17 \div 100$	**p**	7.81×100

10 Work these out, without using a calculator.

a	4.5×1000	**b**	0.87×1000	**c**	7.6×1000	**d**	0.03×1000
e	6.4×1000	**f**	0.82×1000	**g**	$4.6 \div 1000$	**h**	$0.5 \div 1000$
i	$2.4 \div 1000$	**j**	$0.03 \div 1000$	**k**	$9.7 \div 1000$	**l**	$0.02 \div 1000$
m	$3.1 \div 1000$	**n**	8.2×1000	**o**	$23 \div 1000$	**p**	8.7×1000

11 Copy and complete this shopping bill, then work out the total.

> 1000 sweets at £0.04 each   = ...
> 100 packets of mints at £0.32 each = ...
> 10 cans of lemonade at £0.75 each = ...

(MR) 12 How would you explain to someone how to multiply and divide a number by one million?

(PS) 13 Owen was looking in a shop at the price of long nails.

He saw three different ways of buying the same sort of nails.

> Buy a packet of 100 for £1.50
> Buy a box of 1000 for £14
> Count your own and buy at 1p each.

Which is the cheapest way for Owen to buy 2000 of these nails?

Explain your answer.

Activity: Billions and billions

A Find out about the difference between an American billion and a UK billion, before 1975.

B Explain how to multiply and divide by an American billion and a pre-1975 UK billion.

4.2 Ordering decimals

Learning objective

- To order decimal numbers according to size

Key words	
decimal point	order
place value	

Name	Leroy	Myrtle	Shehab	Baby Jane	Pete	Connie
Age	37 years 4 months	21	32	9 months	57	68 years 3 months
Height	170 cm	154 cm	189 cm	55 cm	150 cm	180 cm
Weight	75 kg	50.3 kg	68 kg	7.5 kg	85 kg	76.3 kg

Look at the people in the picture. How would you put them in **order**?

When you compare the sizes of numbers, you have to consider the **place value** of each digit.

It helps if you put the numbers in a table, like the one in the example below.

Remember that the **decimal point** separates the whole-number part of the number from the decimal-fraction part.

Example 3

Put the numbers 2.33, 2.03 and 2.304 in order, from smallest to largest.

    Put the numbers in a table.

    Fill up the extra decimal places with zeros.

    Now work across the table from the left.

    You can see that all of the numbers have the same units digit.

    Two of them have the same tenths digit, and two have the same hundredths digit.

Thousands	Hundreds	Tens	Units	Tenths	Hundredths	Thousandths
			2	3	3	0
			2	0	3	0
			2	3	0	4

But only one has a digit in the thousandths.

So the smallest number is 2.03 because it has no tenths. Both of the other numbers have tenths.

Next is 2.304 because it has fewer hundredths than 2.33, even though is has the same number of tenths.

Then 2.33 is the largest.

Written in order, the numbers are:

2.03, 2.304, 2.33

Example 4

Put the correct sign, > or <, between the numbers in each pair.

a 6.05 and 6.046   **b** 0.06 and 0.065

a Rewrite both numbers so that they have the same number of decimal places.

6.050...6.046

Both numbers have the same units and tenths digits, but the hundredths digit is bigger in the first number.

So 6.050 is bigger than 6.046.

6.05 > 6.046

b Rewrite both numbers so that they have the same number of decimal places.

0.060...0.065

Both numbers have the same units, tenths and hundredths digits, but the second number has the bigger thousandths digit, as the first number has a zero in the thousandths.

So 0.06 is less than 0.065.

0.06 < 0.065

Exercise 4B

1. **a** Copy the table from Example 3, without the numbers. Write these numbers in your table. Make sure that you put each digit in the correct column.

   457   45   4057   4   450   5405

   b Use your answer to part **a** to write the numbers in order from smallest to largest.

2. Put each set of numbers in *ascending* order (from smallest to largest).

   a 29   69   47   75   70   **b** 907   98   203   302   92

3. Put each set of numbers in *descending* order (from largest to smallest).

   a 45   403   54   450   400   **b** 513   315   135   2531   153

4. Edinburgh is 202 miles from Leeds. York is 24 miles from Leeds.

   Which of these two cities is the greater distance from Leeds?

5 Aberdeen is 513 miles from Bristol. Fort William is 491 miles from Bristol. Which of these two towns is the smaller distance from Bristol?

6 Manchester is 39 miles from Sheffield. Nottingham is 44 miles from Sheffield.

    a Which of these two cities is the further from Sheffield?

    b How much further is it?

7 **a** Draw a table like the one in Example 3. Write these numbers in your table. Make sure that you put each digit in the correct column.

        3.46, 34, 34.6, 3.4, 3.04

    b Use your answer to part **a** to write the numbers in order, from smallest to largest.

8 Write each set of numbers in order, from smallest to largest.

    a 6.2, 0.62, 0.6, 6.02   **b** 5.4, 0.54, 0.5, 5.12   **c** 2.31, 2.03, 2.35, 21

    d 12.3, 1.85, 1.8, 1.88   **e** 75, 7.5, 0.75, 7.55   **f** 0.18, 0.018, 0.1, 0.8

9 Put these amounts of money in order, from smallest to largest.

    a 32p, £1.32, £0.30, 130p, £0.03   **b** €0.05, €1.05, €15, €0.55, €5

10 Put these times in order.

    1 hour 20 minutes, 35 minutes, half an hour, one and a half hours

11 Put the correct sign, > or <, between the numbers or amounts in each pair.

    a 0.42…0.44   **b** 0.51…0.50   **c** 7.89…7.99

    d 3.75 km…3.7 km   **e** 5.43 kg…5.5 kg   **f** £0.08…16p

12 Write each statement in words.

    a 1.5 < 1.55   **b** £0.32 > 22p   **c** 3.7 < 4.7

    d £0.50 > 5p   **e** 3.5 < 3.55 < 3.6   **f** £0.12 < 22p < £0.32

    g 3.7 < 3.75 < 3.8   **h** £0.05 < 15p < £0.50

13 These are the names of four brothers, and their heights.

    David: 158 cm   Malcolm: 157.6 cm   Brian: 158.3 cm   Kevin: 157.7 cm

    a Who is the tallest and what is his height?

    b Who is the smallest and what is his height?

Investigation: Reciprocals

A Choose a set of five consecutive integers (whole numbers), such as 3, 4, 5, 6, 7.

B Use a calculator to work out the reciprocal of each of your five numbers.

C Put your answers in order, from smallest to largest.

D Repeat with any five consecutive two-digit whole numbers, such as 12, 13, 14, 15, 16.

E What do you notice?

 Hint The reciprocal of a number is the answer when the number is divided into 1. That is: 1 ÷ 3, 1 ÷ 4, 1 ÷ 5, 1 ÷ 6, 1 ÷ 7

4.3 Estimates

Learning objective

- To estimate calculations in order to spot possible errors

Key words

| approximation | estimate |
| inverse operation | round |

TOWN v CITY

CROWD	41 923
SCORE	1 – 2
TIME OF FIRST GOAL	42 min 13 sec
PRICE OF A PIE	£2.95
CHILDREN	33% off normal ticket prices

Suppose you were telling a friend about the game. Which of the numbers above would you **round** up or down to a sensible **approximation**? Which ones must you give exactly?

You can also use rounding to make a quick **estimate** of the answer to a calculation, to check if your accurate answer is about right.

Here are some quick ways to check an answer.

- For a multiplication, check that the final digit is correct by multiplying the last digits of the numbers in the question.

- Round the numbers and do a mental calculation to see if an answer is about the right size.

- Use the **inverse operation** – see example 7 to find out how to do this.

Example 5

Round each number to the nearest: **i** 10   **ii** 100.

a 431   **b** 578   **c** 705

  i Look at the last digit.

   If it is less than 5, round the number down.

   If it is 5 or greater, round the number up.

   a 431 ≈ 430   **b** 578 ≈ 580   **c** 705 ≈ 710

  ii Look at the tens digit then round up or down as before.

   a 431 ≈ 400   **b** 578 ≈ 600   **c** 705 ≈ 700

Example 6

Estimate answers to these calculations.

a $\dfrac{21.3 + 48.7}{6.4}$　　b 31.2×48.5　　c $359 \div 42$

   a Round the numbers on the top to $20 + 50 = 70$. Round 6.4 to 7. Then $70 \div 7 = 10$.

   b Round to 30×50, which is $3 \times 5 \times 100 = 1500$.

   c Round to $360 \div 40$, which is $36 \div 4 = 9$.

Example 7

Explain why these calculations must be wrong.

a $23 \times 45 = 1053$　　　　b $19 \times 59 = 121$

   a The last digit should be 5, because the product of the last digits (3 and 5) is 15.
   That is, $23 \times 45 = \ldots 5$

   b The answer is roughly $20 \times 60 = 1200$.

Example 8

Use the inverse operation to check if each calculation is correct.

a $450 \div 6 = 75$　　　b $310 - 59 = 249$

   a By the inverse operation, $450 = 6 \times 75$.
   Check mentally.
   $6 \times 70 = 420$, $6 \times 5 = 30$, $420 + 30 = 450$, so is true.

   b By the inverse operation, $310 = 249 + 59$.
   The sum of 249 and 59 must end in 8, as $9 + 9 = 18$, so the answer cannot be correct.

Exercise 4C

 1 The number line shows the ages of ten members of a family.

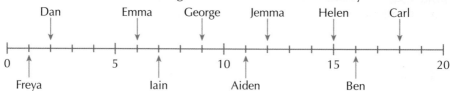

Copy and complete this table.

Name	Aiden	Ben	Carl	Dan	Emma	Freya	George	Helen	Iain	Jemma
Age										
Age (to nearest 10 years)										

2 The price of a dishwasher was £435.

Sam was offered a discount of £99.

She was told that the new price was £344.

How could she tell this was wrong?

3 The price of a bike was £282.

Chris was offered a part-exchange discount of £135 off the marked price. He was told the new price was £138.

How could he tell that this was wrong?

4 The price of a hi-fi advertised in a shop was £467.

Gianni was told that the same hi-fi was being sold for exactly half the price, in a local market, where the price was £237.

How could Gianni tell that this information was not correct?

5 These are the attendances at FA cup matches.

	Game	Attendance
a	Charlton v Walsall	18 573
b	Chelsea v West Ham	33 443
c	Everton v Leyton Orient	35 851
d	Gillingham v Bristol Rovers	17 624
e	Preston v Sheffield Wednesday	13 068
f	Rotherham v Crewe	8477
g	Tottenham v Bolton	26 820
h	Fulham v Southampton	7563

Ben says: These all add up to over 170 000.

How can you quickly check that Ben is correct?

6 Explain why these calculations must be wrong.

    a $21 \times 7 = 146$ **b** $32 \times 5 = 146$ **c** $22 \times 4 = 86$

    d $35 \times 5 = 160$ **e** $99 \times 9 = 198$ **f** $67 \times 7 = 426$

7 Explain why these calculations must be wrong.

    a $35 \times 22 = 777$ **b** $36 \times 44 = 1548$ **c** $71 \times 38 = 1689$

    d $54 \times 37 = 1999$ **e** $53 \times 47 = 2419$ **f** $38 \times 27 = 1025$

8 Use an inverse operation to check these calculations.

    a $203 - 96 = 107$ **b** $315 - 30 = 285$ **c** $401 - 61 = 350$

    d $243 - 59 = 148$ **e** $522 - 58 = 446$ **f** $719 - 37 = 682$

9 Use an inverse operation to check these calculations.

    a $450 \div 50 = 9$ **b** $144 \div 3 = 58$ **c** $210 \div 6 = 35$

    d $455 - 5 = 92$ **e** $520 \div 100 = 5$ **f** $225 \div 5 = 45$

10 Explain why these calculations must be wrong.

    a $15 \times 32 = 484$ **b** $41 \times 23 = 643$ **c** $43.6 + 62.4 = 200$

    d $240 \div 6 = 25$ **e** $243 - 50 = 107$ **f** $450 \div 8.8 = 40$

 11 A man bought 98 kg of grain at a cost of $4.15 per kg.

    What is the approximate total cost of this grain?

12 Estimate the answer to each problem.

    a $687 - 92$ **b** 107×19 **c** $98 \div 21$ **d** $796 + 95$

    e 511×103 **f** $34.7 \div 6.9$ **g** 98×8.8 **h** $58.7 \div 6.1$

 13 Eve bought five cans of lemonade at 46p per can. The shopkeeper asked her for £3.30.

    Without working out the correct answer, explain how Eve can tell that this is wrong.

 14 One cake costs 53p. I need six cakes. Will £3 be enough to pay for them?

    Explain your answer clearly.

15 Mrs Roberts took all her class of 28 children to a theme park.

    It cost £4.15 for each child to go into the theme park. Mrs Roberts got in free.

    a Approximately how much did Mrs Roberts have to pay altogether for the class to go into the theme park?

    b Mrs Roberts had £20 available to spend. She saw that ice creams were 55p each. How did Mrs Roberts estimate if she had enough money to pay for the ice creams?

    c All of the children queued at the same stall for a drink. Mrs Roberts noticed that each child took approximately 32 seconds to get served. Approximately, how long did Mrs Roberts have to wait until al the class were served with their drinks?

Challenge: Rugby

A Read this article from a newspaper.

> A crowd of 6832 saw Katy McLean kick 27 points and set up 2 tries as England eased to a 32–3 win over Canada. The tries were scored after 12 minutes 45 seconds and 23 minutes 14 seconds. Canada's Karen Paquin, aged 23 years and 14 days, was sent to the sin bin after only 9.7 minutes, to be followed by England's Rowena Burnfield after 17 minutes.
>
> It was also reported that half-time food for spectators was expensive, a burger costing £5.98 and a drink of tea costing £3.10 without sugar and £3.80 with sugar.

B Now rewrite it with all the numbers rounded as you would expect.

C Explain why some numbers have not been rounded at all.

4.4 Adding and subtracting decimals

Learning objective

• To add and subtract decimal numbers

You can add and subtract decimals in the same way as you add and subtract whole numbers. As with whole numbers it is important to get the place values in the right place. You need to take care with the decimal point.

Example 9

Work these out.   **a** $4 + 0.86 + 0.07$ **b** $6 - 1.45$

a Whole numbers have no decimal places, but it helps to write a decimal point after the units digit and show the decimal place values with zeros.

Then you can line up the decimal points and place values of all the numbers in the addition.

```
  4 . 0 0
  0 . 8 6
+ 0 . 0 7
─────────
  4 . 9 3
      ₁
```

b As in part **a**, put a decimal point and zeros after the whole number to show the place values, and line up the decimal points.

```
  ⁵6̶ . ⁹0̶ ¹0
- 1 . 4 5
─────────
  4 . 5 5
```

Example 10

Nazia has done 4.3 km of a 20 km bike ride. How far does Nazia still have to go?

You need to subtract 4.3 km from 20 km.

```
  ¹2ⁱ0̸ . ⁱ0̸
−    4 . 3
  1 5 . 7
```

Nazia still has to go 15.7 km.

Example 11

Kilroy has to reduce the weight in his suitcase by 3 kg. So far he has taken out 0.65 kg. How much more does he need to take out?

This gives:

```
  ²3̸ . ⁹0̸ ⁱ0̸
− 0 . 6 5
  2 . 3 5
```

Kilroy still has to take out 2.35 kg.

Exercise 4D

1 Use the column method to work out each addition.

    a $371 + 142$ **b** $326 + 157$ **c** $678 + 459$ **d** $962 + 70$

    e $479 + 120$ **f** $608 + 216$ **g** $12 + 341 + 456$ **h** $7657 + 3125 + 608$

2 Use the column method to work out each subtraction.

    a $371 − 142$ **b** $326 − 157$ **c** $678 − 459$ **d** $962 − 70$

    e $479 − 12$ **f** $608 − 216$ **g** $120 + 341 − 456$ **h** $7657 + 3125 − 608$

3 Work these out, without using a calculator.

    a $2.4 + 3.5$ **b** $7.2 + 3.9$ **c** $2.5 + 3.7$ **d** $5.5 + 3.6$

    e $9.8 − 7.1$ **f** $4.8 − 2.3$ **g** $7.2 − 3.7$ **h** $7.6 − 6.8$

4 Work these out, without using a calculator.

    a $5 − 3.7$ **b** $6 − 1.9$ **c** $9 − 3.4$ **d** $11 − 2.7$

    e $6 − 1.8$ **f** $12 − 2.6$ **g** $14 − 2.3$ **h** $5 − 4.9$

5 Write down the change you would get from £10 if you bought goods worth:

    a £3.50   **b** £7.99   **c** £5.14

    d £3.75   **e** £2.83   **f** 30p

6 What change would you get at the checkout If you paid with a £20 note for a pair of socks at £3.50, a T-shirt at £4.50 and two scarves at £2.50 each.

7 Work these out, without using a calculator.

a	2.34 + 3.25	**b**	7.22 + 3.19	**c**	7.44 + 1.15	**d**	2.64 + 3.25
e	3.25 + 2.17	**f**	6.35 + 4.36	**g**	8.15 + 7.27	**h**	3.45 + 6.76
i	8.68 − 6.17	**j**	7.48 − 2.33	**k**	9.42 − 3.21	**l**	8.64 − 6.53
m	5.32 − 3.17	**n**	8.56 − 5.38	**o**	8.16 − 3.24	**p**	9.15 − 6.86

8 Work these out, without using a calculator.

a	6 − 3.27	**b**	7 − 1.82	**c**	10 − 4.56	**d**	13 − 3.61
e	8 − 2.73	**f**	14 − 3.54	**g**	15 − 4.71	**h**	6 − 3.84

9 James pours 0.34 litres of water from a jug containing 2 litres. How much is left?

10 Emily cuts 1.37 metres of ribbon from a roll that holds 4 metres. How much ribbon is left?

11 The three legs of a relay are 2 km, 3.8 km and 1.7 km. How far is the race altogether?

Activity: Can you estimate well?

A Estimate the length of your little finger.

B Now measure it. Were you close?

C Draw five straight lines in your book of various lengths without measuring.
Estimate the length of each one.

D Measure the length of each one, were you closer than before?

E Repeat for five more lines, your estmates should be better this time.

4.5 Multiplying and dividing decimals

Learning objective

• To be able to multiply and divide decimal numbers by any whole number

When you add together 1.2 + 1.2 + 1.2 + 1.2, you get 4.8.

This sum can be written as 4 × 1.2 = 4.8.

It can also be written as 4.8 ÷ 4 = 1.2.

You are now going to look at how to multiply and divide decimals by whole numbers.

These two operations are just like any other type of division and multiplication but you need to be sure where to put the decimal point.

As a general rule, there will be the same number of decimal places in the answer as there were in the original problem.

Example 12

Work these out.   **a** 5×3.7 **b** 8×4.3 **c** 9×1.08 **d** 6×3.5

Each of these can be set out in columns.

a	3.7	**b**	4.3	**c**	1.08	**d**	3.5
×	5	×	8	×	9	×	6
	18.5		34.4		9.72		21.0

You see that the decimal point in the answer stays in the same place as it is in the decimal number you are multiplying. It has the same number of decimal places after it, in both the question and the answer.

Example 13

Work these out.   **a** $22.8 \div 6$ **b** $33.6 \div 7$ **c** $9.59 \div 7$ **d** $26.2 \div 5$

These can be set out as short divisions.

a $6\overline{)22.{}^{4}8}$ = 3.8   **b** $7\overline{)33.{}^{5}6}$ = 4.8   **c** $7\overline{)9.{}^{2}5{}9}$ = 1.37   **d** $5\overline{)26.{}^{1}2{}0}$ = 5.24

Once again, the decimal point stays in the same place. Notice that you need to write in an extra zero in part **d**, to complete the division. This means that the answer has one more decimal place than the number being divided.

Exercise 4E

 1 Work these out, without using a calculator.

a	35×5	**b**	43×8	**c**	16×3	**d**	27×4
e	5×43	**f**	8×62	**g**	3×83	**h**	9×52

 2 Work these out, without using a calculator.

a	$96 \div 8$	**b**	$98 \div 7$	**c**	$87 \div 3$	**d**	$95 \div 5$
e	$72 \div 4$	**f**	$57 \div 3$	**g**	$84 \div 6$	**h**	$85 \div 5$

 3 Work these out, without using a calculator.

a	3.15×5	**b**	7.32×8	**c**	4.72×3	**d**	5.32×6
e	7×4.31	**f**	2×9.86	**g**	4×6.35	**h**	9×6.15

 4 Work these out, without using a calculator.

a	$18.4 \div 8$	**b**	$38.5 \div 7$	**c**	$25.2 \div 3$	**d**	$33.5 \div 5$
e	$6.28 \div 4$	**f**	$5.91 \div 3$	**g**	$7.62 \div 3$	**h**	$33.6 \div 8$

 5 Work these out, without using a calculator.

a	1.1×5	**b**	2.1×4	**c**	1.3×2	**d**	2.1×6
e	5×4.1	**f**	3×6.2	**g**	4×8.1	**h**	5×6.1

6 Work these out, without using a calculator.

    a 4 ÷ 2   **b** 3 ÷ 2   **c** 5 ÷ 2   **d** 7 ÷ 2

    e 9 ÷ 2   **f** 11 ÷ 2   **g** 13 ÷ 2   **h** 15 ÷ 2

 7 Select the larger number from each pair, without using a calculator.

    a 17 × 3 or 7 × 13   **b** 15 × 5 or 12 × 6   **c** 18 × 4 or 14 × 5

 8 Work these out, without using a calculator.

    a 4.5 × 5   **b** 3.2 × 8   **c** 2.7 × 3   **d** 4.2 × 4

    e 5 × 3.7   **f** 8 × 5.2   **g** 3 × 7.5   **h** 9 × 6.1

 9 Work these out, without using a calculator.

    a 16.8 ÷ 8   **b** 35.7 ÷ 7   **c** 24.9 ÷ 3   **d** 30.5 ÷ 5

    e 6.8 ÷ 4   **f** 5.1 ÷ 3   **g** 7.2 ÷ 3   **h** 22.5 ÷ 5

10 Joseph cuts a piece of wood, 3.5 metres long, into five equal pieces.
How long is each piece?

11 A cake weighing 1.56 kg is cut into six equal pieces.
How much does each piece weigh?

 12 Eight cans of orange cost £6.
How much is one can?

 13 Ten pens cost £8.50.
How much would four pens cost?

14 Four bars of metal each weigh 2.8 kg.
How much do they weigh altogether?

 15 Eight buns cost £2.72.
How much would three buns cost?

 16 Eight packs of cards cost £12.80.
How much would five packs cost?

 17 Given that 53 × 47 = 2491, write down, without calculating, the value of:

    a 53 × 470   **b** 530 × 47   **c** 53 × 4.7   **d** 5.3 × 47.

18 I went into a shop with £10. I wanted to buy two packets of pasta at £1.85 each and three bottles of sauce at £1.35 each. Will I have enough to buy a box of chocolates costing £2.50 as well?

Reasoning: The same digits

A Use a calculator to work these out.

    a 46 × 34   **b** 4.6 × 34   **c** 4.6 × 3.4   **d** 0.46 × 0.34

B You will notice that the digits of all the answers are the same but that the decimal point is in different places. Can you explain a rule for placing the decimal point?

C Use your rule to write down the answers to the problems below, given that 152 × 45 = 6840.

    a 15.2 × 4.5   **b** 1.52 × 45   **c** 0.152 × 4.5   **d** 1520 × 450

Ready to progress?

I can order decimals by size.

I can add and subtract decimal numbers.
I can multiply and divide decimal numbers by 10, 100 and 1000.
I can estimate answers and check if an answer is about right.
I can multiply and divide decimals by any whole number.

Review questions

1   Here is part of the 36 times table.

   1 × 36 = 36

   2 × 36 = 72

   3 × 36 = 108

   4 × 36 = 144

   5 × 36 = 180

   6 × 36 = 216

   7 × 36 = 252

   8 × 36 = 288

   9 × 36 = 324

   10 × 36 = 360

   Use the 36 times table to help you work out the missing numbers.

   a 288 ÷ 8 = ☐   b 180 ÷ 36 = ☐   c 11 × 36 = ☐

2   Which of these numbers is closer to 1000?

       996   1006

   Explain how you can tell.

3   At a mathematics competition there are 112 pupils altogether.

   The pupils are in teams of seven and come from different schools.

   How many teams are there at the competition?

4   Chris, Josh and George made buns to sell on a charity stall.

They made 80 buns altogether.

Chris sold 13 buns.

Josh sold 24 buns.

George sold 16 buns.

a   How many buns were left?

b   Josh sold his buns for 50p each.

How much money did he get from selling his buns?

5   Write these numbers in order of size, with the smallest on the left.

5.38   53.8   8.35   8.53   5.83

6   A meal in a restaurant costs the same for each person.

The total cost for five people is £83.65.

What is the total cost for three people?

7   The table shows how much it costs to go to a theatre.

	Afternoon	Evening
Adult	£8.40	£20.50
Child (14 or under)	£6.50	£17.50
Senior citizen (60 or over)	£6.25	£18.00

Mrs Keys (aged 35), her daughter (aged 8), her son (aged 6) and her mother (aged 64) want to go to the cinema.

How much will they save if they go in the afternoon rather than the evening?

Show your working.

8   Look at the shapes below. All the lengths are in centimetres.

a   Which shape has the longest perimeter?

b   Which shape has the smallest area?

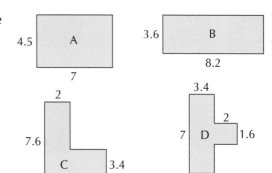

9   Write down the next three numbers in each sequence.

a   4, 5.5, 6, 7.5, ..., ..., ...

b   1, 3.7, 6.4, ..., ..., ...

c   7.4, 7.3, 7.2, 7.1, ..., ..., ...

Financial skills
Shopping for leisure

All sorts of things are advertised in magazines and newspapers.

The Bishop family, Pat Visser and Abbas Elliot all saw this advertisement in a local paper.

Lildi

Table £48.85 each

Chairs £37.45 each

Cubed planter £8.85 each

Outdoor speakers £39.15 each

Mats £4.75 each

Fuchsia £1.65 each

Cushions £6.95 each

Tapestry cube £15.35 each

Living for less

The Bishop family

They decided to buy:

- a folding table with wooden top
- four multi-position chairs
- a cubed planter.

How much will this cost them?

A gift for Pat Visser

Pat had been given a £50 gift voucher.

She thought she would like to buy:

- two tapestry cubes
- three printed cushions
- a patterned mat.

Estimate if she can buy all these with the gift voucher.

Abbas' outdoor area

Abbas wanted to create an outdoor area with wireless outdoor speakers, a table, some chairs, some mats and some plants, all for less than £200.

Select from the advertisement what Abbas can buy. Get as close to the £200 as you can.

5

Working with numbers

This chapter is going to show you:

- how to round whole numbers
- the order of operations
- how to carry out long multiplication
- how to carry out long division
- how to calculate with measurements.

You should already know:

- how to square a number
- multiplication tables up to 12×12
- place value of digits in a number such as 23.508
- how to use a calculator to do simple calculations
- how to convert units of measurement.

About this chapter

Your school is organising its summer fête, but where should it locate the star attraction: a giant chessboard with an area of 9 m²? The organisers need to work out how long its sides are in order to see where it will fit. As the board is a square, its area is the length of one of its sides squared. This means that the length is the square root of the area. So if the area is 9 m² the sides will be 3 m long. Most square roots are not whole numbers, however. If the chessboard had an area of 10 m², the organisers would need either to approximate the square root or to use a calculator to find it, and then round it up, to be sure of having enough space to fit the board.

5.1 Square numbers

Learning objective

• To recognise and use square numbers up to 225 (15×15)

Key words

integer	power
square number	squaring

When you multiply any number by itself, you are **squaring** the number. You can write it as a number to the **power** of 2, for example, $4 \times 4 = 4^2 = 16$.

When you multiply an **integer** (whole number) by itself, the result is called a **square number**.

You need to learn all of the first 15 square numbers.

1×1	2×2	3×3	4×4	5×5
1^2	2^2	3^2	4^2	5^2
1	4	9	16	25

6×6	7×7	8×8	9×9	10×10
6^2	7^2	8^2	9^2	10^2
36	49	64	81	100

11×11	12×12	13×13	14×14	15×15
11^2	12^2	13^2	14^2	15^2
121	144	169	196	225

Example 1

Work out the value of 18^2.

18^2 is 18×18.

Using a calculator, either key in 18×18 or use the squaring key $\boxed{x^2}$.

$18^2 = 324$

Exercise 5A

  1 Look at this pattern of additions.

$1 \quad 1+3 \quad 1+3+5 \quad 1+3+5+7 \quad 1+3+5+7+9$

a Work out the answers for the addition pattern.

b What is special about the answers?

c Write the number 49 as a sum of odd numbers.

2   **a**   Copy this multiplication table. Fill in the gaps.

×	1	2	3	4	5	6	7	8	9	10	11	12
1	1	2										
2	2			8								
3												
4						24						
5			15									
6							42			60		
7	7								63			
8												
9					45			72				
10												
11												132
12											132	144

b   Shade in all the square numbers. What do you notice?

3   Copy this table of numbers and their squares. Fill in the gaps.

Number	Number × number	Number²	Number squared
1	1 × 1	1²	1
2	2 × 2	2²	
	3 × 3	3²	
			16
5			
	6 × 6		
			49
			64
			81
		10²	
11			
	12 × 12		
		13²	
			196
15			

4 **a** Write down the square numbers less than 200 that:

    i have a 5 as one of the digits

    ii have a 3 as one of the digits

    iii have a 9 as one of the digits.

  b Is there any digit (0–9) that does not appear in any of the first 15 square numbers?

MR **5** Copy each table. Fill in the gaps.

The first one has been done for you.

a

3^2	4^2	5^2
9	16	25
9 + 16 = 25		

b

5^2	12^2	13^2
25		
25 + … = …		

c

7^2	24^2	25^2
… + … = …		

d

9^2	40^2	41^2
… + … = …		

MR **6** Work out which calculation has the larger answer in each pair.

  a $(3^2 + 4^2)$ or $(2^2 + 5^2)$

  b $(7^2 + 6^2)$ or $(3^2 + 8^2)$

  c $(9^2 + 1^2)$ or $(5^2 + 8^2)$

MR **7** Work out which calculation has the larger answer in each pair.

  a $(13^2 - 5^2)$ or $(12^2 - 4^2)$

  b $(15^2 - 9^2)$ or $(14^2 - 8^2)$

  c $(11^2 - 7^2)$ or $(10^2 - 6^2)$

Problem solving: Squares and products

A a Choose a number, for example, 8.

  b Square your number and write down the answer.

  c Write down the whole numbers either side of your first number, for example, 7 and 9.

  d Multiply these two numbers together and write down the answer.

  e What do you notice about your two answers?

B a Repeat, choosing a different starting number.

  b What do you notice about these two answers?

5.2 Rounding

Learning objective

- To round numbers to the nearest whole number, 10, 100 or 1000

Key words	
round	round down
round up	

To **round** numbers – to the nearest 10, 100 or 1000 – you need to use what you know about place value. You must always look at the digit to the right of the digit you are rounding. For example:

- if you are rounding to the nearest 10, look at the units digit
- if you are rounding to the nearest 100, look at the tens digit

and so on.

If the digit is 4, 3, 2, 1 or 0, **round down**. If the digit is 5, 6, 7, 8 or 9, **round up**.

When you are rounding, you can use the special symbol, ≈, which means 'is approximately equal to'. For example, if you round 38 to the nearest 10, you could write '38 ≈ 40', which means '38 is approximately equal to 40'.

Example 2

Round each number to the nearest:

i 10   **ii** 100   **iii** 1000.

a 1312   **b** 1527   **c** 4128   **d** 3554

  i Look at the units digit.

    If its value is less than 5, round the number down. If its value is 5 or more, round up.

  a 1312 ≈ 1310   **b** 1527 ≈ 1530   **c** 4128 ≈ 4130   **d** 3554 ≈ 3550

  ii Look at the tens digit. Round down or up, as before.

  a 1312 ≈ 1300   **b** 1527 ≈ 1500   **c** 4128 ≈ 4100   **d** 3554 ≈ 3600

  iii Look at the hundreds digit. Round down or up, as before.

  a 1312 ≈ 1000   **b** 1527 ≈ 2000   **c** 4128 ≈ 4000   **d** 3554 ≈ 4000

Look at this picture.

Can you see anything wrong?

It shows that the woman who weighs 60 kg balances the man who weighs 110 kg, when both measures are rounded to the nearest 100 kg!

This example shows that you need to round numbers sensibly, depending on what you are using them for.

Example 3

Round each number to the nearest whole number.

a 1.3 **b** 4.8 **c** 6.25 **d** 8.51

Look at the number after the decimal point. Round down or up, as before.

a 1.3 ≈ 1 **b** 4.8 ≈ 5 **c** 6.25 ≈ 6 **d** 8.51 ≈ 9

Exercise 5B

1 The Brighton College in Abu Dhabi has 1094 students.

  a How many students is this, to the nearest 100?

  b How many students is this, to the nearest 10?

2 The price of a laptop is £269.

  a What is the price, to the nearest £100?

  b What is the price, to the nearest £10?

3 A car is advertised for sale at £7495.

  a What is the price, to the nearest £100?

  b What is the price, to the nearest £10?

4 A fridge is advertised for sale at £327.

  a What is the price, to the nearest £100?

  b What is the price, to the nearest £10?

5 A bike is advertised for sale at £1459.

  a What is the price, to the nearest £100?

  b What is the price, to the nearest £10?

6 These are the attendances at the FA Cup semi-finals and final matches in 2013.

  a Copy and complete the table.

Match	Attendance	Attendance (to nearest 100)	Attendance (to nearest 1000)
Millwall v Wigan Athletic	62 335		
Chelsea v Manchester City	85 621		
Manchester City v Wigan Athletic	86 254		

  b Why could it be misleading to use the numbers rounded to the nearest 1000 to compare the Manchester City attendances?

7 Round each number to:

  i the nearest 10   **ii** the nearest 100   **iii** the nearest 1000.

  a 4642   **b** 981   **c** 1234   **d** 5678

  e 1263   **f** 3947   **g** 2010   **h** 5999

  i 1051   **j** 6125   **k** 4203   **l** 1198

8 **a** The table shows the diameters of the planets, in kilometres. Round each diameter to the nearest 1000 km.

Planet	Earth	Jupiter	Mars	Mercury	Neptune	Saturn	Uranus	Venus
Diameter (km)	12 800	142 800	6780	5120	49 500	120 660	51 100	12 100

b Which is the smallest planet?

c Which is the largest planet?

d Which planet is the closest in size to Earth?

9 Round each number to:

i the nearest 10   **ii** the nearest whole number.

a 17.3	**b** 24.8	**c** 51.4	**d** 71.9
e 54.2	**f** 93.6	**g** 105.5	**h** 799.9
i 84.5	**j** 71.8	**k** 101.5	**l** 142.9

10 Round each number to the nearest ten.

a 7^2 **b** 3^2 **c** 8^2 **d** 12^2 **e** 5^2 **f** 13^2

11 The number of boys attending a show is 30, to the nearest 10.

The number of girls attending the show is 40, to the nearest 10.

a What are the maximum numbers of boys and of girls that could have attended the show?

b What are the minimum numbers of boys and of girls that could have attended the show?

Problem solving: Think of a rounded number

Starla and Morgan are thinking of whole numbers.

When I round my number to the nearest 10 it is 150.

When I round my number to the nearest 100 it is 200.

How many possible answers are there, if Morgan's number is the same as Starla's number?

5.3 Order of operations

Learning objective

- To use the conventions of BIDMAS to carry out calculations

Key words

BIDMAS	operation
order of operations	

Most of the time, the order in which instructions are carried out is important.

These are instructions for sending a text message on your phone.

If you attempt them in the wrong order you probably wouldn't send the message at all! Put them into the correct order.

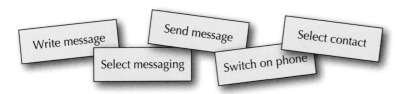

In mathematics, the order in which calculations are carried out is also important. A calculation can be made up of various different **operations**, for example, adding, subtracting, multiplying or squaring.

BIDMAS describes the **order of operations** – the order in which you should always carry out the operations.

B	Brackets
I	Indices or powers
D	Division
M	Multiplication
A	Addition
S	Subtraction

This means that you always work out calculations in brackets first, then work out the powers, then division and multiplication and, finally, addition and subtraction.

For example, in the calculation $2 + 3 \times 4$, you must do the multiplication first.

$$2 + 3 \times 4 = 2 + 12 = 14$$

Example 4

Circle the operation that you do first in each calculation. Then work out each one.

a $4 + 8 \div 2$ **b** $30 - 2 \times 4$ **c** $12 \div 3 - 1$ **d** $8 \div (4 - 2)$

a Division is done before addition, so you get $4 + (8 \div 2) = 4 + 4 = 8$.

b Multiplication is done before subtraction, so you get $30 - (2 \times 4) = 30 - 8 = 22$.

c Division is done before subtraction, so you get $(12 \div 3) - 1 = 4 - 1 = 3$.

d Brackets are done first, so you get $8 \div (4 - 2) = 8 \div 2 = 4$.

Example 5

Work out each of these, showing each step of the calculation.

a $1 + 3^2$ **b** $(1 + 3)^2$

a The order will be power, addition.

This gives:

$1 + ⟨3^2⟩ = 1 + ⟨9⟩ = 10$

b The order will be brackets, power.

This gives:

$⟨(1 + 3)^2⟩ = ⟨4^2⟩ = 16$

Example 6

Put brackets into each equation to make the calculation true.

a $7 + 1 \times 4 = 32$ **b** $2 + 1 + 3^2 = 18$ **c** $48 \div 6 - 2 = 12$

Decide which operation has been done first.

a $(7 + 1) \times 4 = 32$

b $2 + (1 + 3)^2 = 18$

c $48 \div (6 - 2) = 12$

Exercise 5C

1 Write down the answer to each calculation.

   a $(1 \times 5) + (2 \times 3)$ **b** $(4 \times 6) + (5 \times 2)$ **c** $(9 \times 3) + (4 \times 7)$ **d** $(5 \times 4) + (6 \times 7)$

   e $(8 \times 8) + (5 \times 5)$ **f** $(8 \times 2) + (7 \times 8)$ **g** $(5 \times 3) + (9 \times 8)$ **h** $(12 \times 9) + (4 \times 6)$

2 Write down the answer to each calculation.

   a $(9 \div 3) + (6 \div 3)$ **b** $(5 \times 6) + (8 \div 2)$ **c** $(7 \times 3) + (6 \div 3)$ **d** $(5 \times 9) + (8 \div 1)$

   e $(7 \times 7) + (15 \div 5)$ **f** $(9 \times 3) + (16 \div 4)$ **g** $(5 \times 7) + (21 \div 3)$ **h** $(12 \div 4) + (4 \div 2)$

3 Write down the operation that you do first in each calculation.

   Then complete the calculation.

   a $1 + 2 \times 3$ **b** $10 - 4 \div 2$ **c** $3 \times 3 + 1$ **d** $15 \div 5 - 2$

   e $(1 + 2) \times 3$ **f** $(21 - 3) \div 3$ **g** $6 \times (6 + 2)$ **h** $9 \div (3 - 2)$

4 Work these out, showing each step of the calculations.

   a $1 \times 2 + 3$ **b** $1 \times (2 + 3)$ **c** $1 + 4 \times 3$ **d** $(1 + 4) \times 3$

   e $3 \times 3 - 3$ **f** $5 + 3^2$ **g** 5×3^2 **h** $3^2 - 5$

   i $(2 + 3) \times 4$ **j** $2^2 + 3 \times 4$ **k** $4 \div 4 + 4$ **l** $3^2 \div 3 + 3$

   m $(5 + 2)^2$ **n** $5^2 + 2^2$ **o** $4 + 3^2$ **p** $24 \div (6 + 2)$

5 Put brackets into each equation to make the calculation true.

a $1 \times 5 + 4 = 9$ **b** $2 + 5 \times 3 = 21$ **c** $2 + 3 \times 2 = 10$

d $5 + 2^2 = 49$ **e** $6 + 2^2 = 64$ **f** $2 \times 5 + 3 = 16$

g $4 \times 7 + 1 = 32$ **h** $3 + 4 \times 7 = 49$ **i** $8 - 4 - 1 = 5$

j $7 - 5 \times 2 = 4$ **k** $3 + 3 \div 2 = 3$ **l** $1 + 4^2 = 25$

 6 One of the calculations $4 \times 2^2 = 64$ and $4 \times 2^2 = 16$ is wrong.

a Which is it?

b How could you add brackets to make it true?

7 Work out the value of each expression.

a $(5 + 5) \div 5$ **b** $5 \times 5 \div 5$ **c** $5 + 5 \div 5$

d $5 - 5 \div 5$ **e** $(5 - 5) \div 5$ **f** $5^2 \div 5$

g $5^2 - 5$ **h** $5^2 + 5$ **i** $5^2 \times 5$

 8 Sarah is given two $10 notes and three $20 notes.

a Write down the calculation you need to do, to work out how much she is given altogether.

b Work out the answer.

9 Beth orders six garden plants at £2.50 each.

Delivery costs £5.

a Write down the calculation you need to do to work out the total cost.

b Work out the answer.

Problem solving: All the fives

In question **7** of the last exercise, each calculation was made up of three 5s, if you think of 5^2 as 5×5.

A Work out the value of each expression.

  a $55 \div 5$ **b** $5 + 5 \times 5$ **c** $55 - 5$

B Now make up some more calculations, using three 5s, to give answers that you have not yet obtained in Question **5** or in the three calculations above.

Try to make as many different answers as you can.

C Repeat with four 5s.

For example:

$(5 + 5) \div (5 + 5)$ $5 \times (5 + 5 + 5)$.

5.4 Long and short multiplication

Learning objectives

- To choose a written method for multiplying two numbers together
- To use written methods to carry out multiplications accurately

Key words

column method

grid or box method

long multiplication

There are many different methods of multiplying two numbers.

Long multiplication is one method for multiplying large numbers.

Example 7

Work out 18×6.

Grid or box method (partitioning)				Column method (expanded working)	Column method (compacted working)

×	10	8	
6	60	48	60 + 48 = 108

Column method (expanded working):

$$\begin{array}{r} 18 \\ \times\ \ 6 \\ \hline 48 \\ 60 \\ \hline 108 \end{array}$$ (6 × 8) (6 × 10)

Column method (compacted working):

$$\begin{array}{r} 18 \\ \times\ \ 6 \\ \hline 108 \\ {\scriptstyle 4} \end{array}$$

The answer is 108.

Example 8

Work out 136×5.

Grid or box method (partitioning)					Column method (expanded working)	Column method (compacted working)

×	100	30	6	
5	500	150	30	500 + 150 + 30 = 680

Column method (expanded working):

$$\begin{array}{r} 136 \\ \times\ \ 5 \\ \hline 30 \\ 150 \\ 500 \\ \hline 680 \end{array}$$ (5 × 6) (5 × 30) (5 × 100)

Column method (compacted working):

$$\begin{array}{r} 136 \\ \times\ \ 5 \\ \hline 680 \\ {\scriptstyle 1\ 3} \end{array}$$

The answer is 680.

Exercise 5D

1. Use the grid method, or any other method, to work these out.

   a 15×5 **b** 14×6 **c** 19×3 **d** 51×4

   e 18×8 **f** 28×2 **g** 135×3 **h** 120×9

2 Use the column method, or any other method, to work these out.

   a 23 × 5   **b** 31 × 6   **c** 43 × 3   **d** 18 × 5

   e 29 × 4   **f** 42 × 7   **g** 103 × 4   **h** 234 × 5

3 Use any multiplication method to work these out.

   a 25 × 4   **b** 22 × 6   **c** 43 × 4   **d** 18 × 6

   e 17 × 5   **f** 44 × 3   **g** 125 × 5   **h** 206 × 6

4 There are 24 hours in a day and 7 days in a week. How many hours are there in one week?

5 A bus route is 38 miles long. A bus driver does this route five times in one day.

   How many miles does he travel on this route?

6 A hairdresser charges £33 for a restyle and £20 for a wet cut.

   One day she does 4 restyles and 9 wet cuts.

   Work out the total amount that she charges that day.

7 Here is a magic square. The numbers in every row, column and diagonal add up to 15.

8	1	6
3	5	7
4	9	2

   a Make up your own magic square by multiplying every number in the square above by 5.

   (MR) **b** What do you notice about the sum for every row, column and diagonal of your magic square?

   c Now make a new magic square by multiplying every number in the original square by 16.

   (MR) **d** What do you notice about the sum for every row, column and diagonal of this magic square?

(PS) 8 Here is part of the 18 times table.

×	1	2	3	4	5
18	18	36	54	72	90

   Show how you can use the table to work these out.

   a 40 × 18   **b** 9 × 18   **c** 49 × 18

Activity: Funny face

Another way of multiplying two-digit numbers together is the 'Funny face' method.

This is how to use the method to work out 15 × 23.

15 × 23 = (10 + 5) × (20 + 3)

      200 (10 × 20)

       30 (10 × 3)   (10 + 5) × (20 + 3)

     100 (5 × 20)

    + 15 (5 × 3)

     345

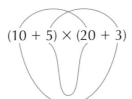

Hint: 18 × 24 = (10 + 8) × (20 + 4)

Make a poster showing how to use the 'Funny face' method for the calculation 18 × 24.

5.5 Long and short division

Learning objectives

- To choose a written method for dividing one number by another
- To use written methods to carry out divisions accurately

Key words

long division
repeated subtraction
short division

There are many different ways to work out a division calculation.

Example 9

Work out $582 \div 3$.

Long division	Short division	Repeated subtraction
$$\begin{array}{r} 194 \\ 3\overline{)582} \\ \underline{3} \\ 28 \\ \underline{27} \\ 12 \\ \underline{12} \\ 0 \end{array}$$	$$\begin{array}{r} 194 \\ 3\overline{)5^28^12} \end{array}$$	$$\begin{array}{r} 582 \\ -\ 300 \quad (100 \times 3) \\ \hline 282 \\ -\ 270 \quad (90 \times 3) \\ \hline 12 \\ -\ \ 12 \quad (4 \times 3) \\ \hline 0 \end{array}$$

The answer is 194.

Exercise 5E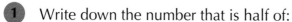

1. Write down the number that is half of:
   a 12   b 16   c 20   d 30   e 50

2. Write down the amount that is half of:
   a £10   b £24   c 14 kg   d 22 kg   e 60 m

3. Use long division, or any other method, to work these out.
   a $42 \div 3$ b $75 \div 5$ c $76 \div 4$ d $54 \div 6$
   e $124 \div 4$ f $126 \div 9$ g $496 \div 4$ h $145 \div 5$

4. Use short division, or any other method, to work these out.
   a $39 \div 3$ b $84 \div 4$ c $91 \div 7$ d $180 \div 9$
   e $144 \div 4$ f $216 \div 6$ g $424 \div 4$ h $375 \div 5$

5. Use short division, or any other method, to work these out.
   a $120 \div 3$ b $80 \div 4$ c $96 \div 6$ d $140 \div 5$
   e $180 \div 4$ f $180 \div 6$ g $360 \div 5$ h $360 \div 8$

6 Use any division method to work these out.

   a   220 ÷ 4   **b**   840 ÷ 3   **c**   189 ÷ 9   **d**   225 ÷ 5

   e   330 ÷ 6   **f**   248 ÷ 8   **g**   960 ÷ 3   **h**   777 ÷ 7

7 Which division in each pair gives the smaller answer?

   a   300 ÷ 5 or 400 ÷ 6   **b**   244 ÷ 4 or 355 ÷ 5   **c**   411 ÷ 3 or 722 ÷ 6

8 A boy saves £8 each week. He now has £96.

How many weeks has he been saving?

 9 A rope is 75 metres long. It is cut into five equal pieces.

How long is each piece?

10 Eggs are packed in boxes of 6.

How many boxes will you need, to pack 84 eggs?

Decide whether questions **11–12** involve multiplication or division. Then work out the answers.

(PS) 11 To raise money, a running club is doing a relay race of 120 kilometres. Each runner will run 8 km.

   a   How many runners are needed to cover the distance?

   b   If each runner runs 10 km, how many fewer runners are needed?

(FS) 12 A group of people go on a journey from Paris to Rome. They travel in 52-seater coaches.

Nine coaches are full. Each coach carries 52 passengers.

   a   How many passengers are there altogether?

   b   Each passenger pays £6.

      How much do the passengers pay altogether?

Activity: Cross-number puzzle

Copy and complete this puzzle.

Across	Down
1 34 × 5	2 426 ÷ 6
4 9 × 9	3 27 × 8
6 81 ÷ 9	5 3 × 90
7 64 ÷ 4	6 2733 ÷ 3
9 24 × 5	8 124 ÷ 2

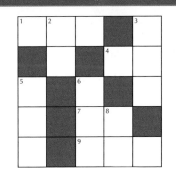

5.6 Calculations with measurements

Learning objectives

- To convert between common metric units
- To use measurements in calculations
- To recognise and use appropriate metric units

Key words	
cent-	centi-
conversion	convert
metric	mill-
milli-	

You need to know and use these **metric conversions** for length and capacity.

Length	Capacity
1 kilometre (km) = 1000 metres (m)	
1 metre (m) = 100 centimetres (cm)	1 litre (l) = 100 centilitres (cl)
1 metre (m) = 1000 millimetres (mm)	1 litre (l) = 1000 millilitres (ml)
1 centimetre (cm) = 10 millimetres (mm)	1 centilitre (cl) = 10 millilitres (ml)

Can you see the connections?

Cent- relates to hundreds and **centi-** to hundredths, for example, a century is 100 years, a centimetre is one-hundredth of a metre. There are 100 cents in a dollar.

Mill- relates to thousands and **milli-** to thousandths, for example, a millennium is 1000 years, a millilitre is one-thousandth of a litre.

You also need to know these metric conversions for mass.

Mass
1 kilogram (kg) = 1000 grams (g)
1 tonne (t) = 1000 kilograms (kg)

 Hint You will learn in science lessons that mass is the amount of 'stuff' there is in something. Its weight is the effect that gravity has on it, pulling it towards the Earth.

Example 10

Convert:

a 8 centimetres to millimetres   **b** 4000 grams to kilograms

c 2 litres to centilitres   **d** 3.5 kilograms to grams.

    a 1 cm = 10 mm   So multiply by 10.

       $8 \times 10 = 80$

       So 8 cm = 80 mm.

    b 1000 g = 1 kg   So divide by 1000.

       $4000 \div 1000 = 4$

       So 4000 g = 4 kg.

c 1 litre = 100 cl   So multiply by 100.

2 × 100 = 200

So 2 litres = 200 cl.

d 1 kg = 1000 g   So multiply by 1000.

3.5 × 1000 = 3500

So 3.5 kg = 3500 g.

Example 11

Add together 3 km 400 m and 5 km 800 m.

3 km 400 m + 5 km 800 m is the same as 3 km + 5 km + 400 m + 800 m.

3 km + 5 km + 400 m + 800 m = 8 km + 1200 m

= 8 km + 1 km 200 m   1000 m = 1 km

= 9 km 200 m

You could also change both distances:

- to kilometres, to give 3.4 km + 5.8 km = 9.2 km
- to metres, to give 3400 m + 5800 m = 9200 m.

Example 12

Choose a sensible metric unit to measure each of these.

a The width of a text book   **b** The length of a field

c The mass of a bag of sugar   **d** A large bottle of water

Choose a sensible unit. Sometimes there is more than one answer.

a Centimetre   **b** Metre   **c** Kilogram   **d** Litre

Exercise 5F

1 Round each length to the nearest 10 metres.

    a 38 m   **b** 53 m   **c** 45 m   **d** 21.5 m   **e** 37.8 m

2 Round each mass to the nearest 10 kg.

    a 47 kg   **b** 72 kg   **c** 35.3 kg   **d** 63.2 kg   **e** 41.9 kg

3 Convert each length from metres to centimetres.

    a 6 m   **b** 2 m   **c** 12 m   **d** 0.5 m   **e** 17.3 m

4 Convert each mass from kilograms to grams.

    a 7 kg   **b** 3 kg   **c** 11 kg   **d** 0.5 kg   **e** 21.4 kg

5 Convert each of the amounts in pence to pounds (£).

    a 700p   **b** 500p   **c** 150p   **d** 275p   **e** 314p

6 Convert each length from kilometres to metres.

    a 4 km   **b** 13 km   **c** 6.3 km   **d** 21.5 km   **e** 5.46 km

7 Convert each length from centimetres to millimetres.

    a 3 cm   **b** 11 cm   **c** 5.1 cm   **d** 35.6 cm   **e** 0.7 cm

8 Convert each mass from grams to kilograms.

    a 3000 g   **b** 5500 g   **c** 500 g   **d** 200 g   **e** 35 g

9 Convert each mass from kilograms to grams.

    a 4 kg   **b** 8 kg   **c** 9.5 kg   **d** 0.7 kg   **e** 0.45 kg

10 Convert each time to hours and minutes.

    a 90 minutes   **b** 130 minutes   **c** 85 minutes   **d** 200 minutes   **e** 630 minutes

(MR) **11** Pierre buys 650 grams of bananas and 2.4 kg of apples.

Is the total mass of the two items more than 3 kilograms?

Show your working.

12 Read the value from each of these scales.

a    **b** 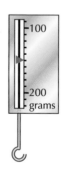   **c**

d

```
 T  T  T  T  ↑  T  T
 0        ↑ 50
```

e

```
 T  T  T  ↑  T  T  T  T
 100 ↑      200
```

f

```
 T  T  T  T  T  ↑  T  T  T  T  T
 0            ↑         20
```

Challenge: Keep the balance

The diagram shows some scales balancing.

For each part, draw the scales and divide the weights between the two pans so that the scales balance.

A

B

C

D

Ready to progress?

I can round numbers to make sensible estimates.

I know and can use squares numbers up to 15×15.

I can carry out calculations, knowing the correct order of operations.
I can use written methods to carry out calculations involving multiplications and divisions.
I can convert measurements.

Review questions

1   High Storres School has 2085 pupils.

    a   How many pupils is this, to the nearest 100?

    b   How many pupils is this, to the nearest 10?

2   This is the beginning of the sequence of square numbers.

    1, 4, 9, 16, …

    a   Write down the next two numbers in the sequence.

    b   Write down the 10th number in the sequence.

3   Work these out.

    a $5 + 6 \times 3$ b $(5 + 6) \times 3$ c $6^2 - 2^2$

 4   Which of these rectangles has the greater area?

    You must show your working.

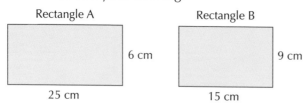

Rectangle A — 6 cm, 25 cm

Rectangle B — 9 cm, 15 cm

5   What temperature is 6 degrees higher than -2 °C?

(PS) 6 I weigh a melon.

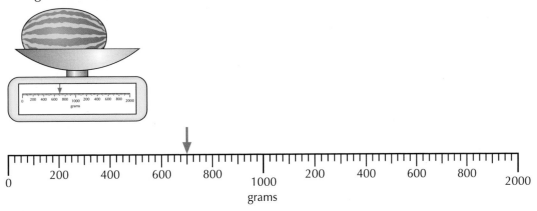

Then I weigh the melon with one banana.

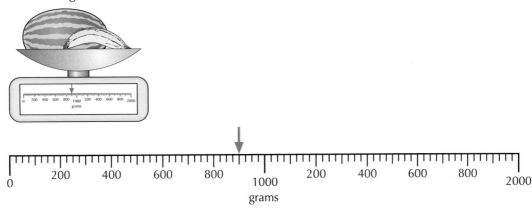

Complete the sentences below, writing in the missing numbers.

The melon weighs ... grams.

The melon and one banana weigh ... grams altogether.

One banana weighs ... grams.

 7 To work out the amount of water in a person's total body mass, divide the body mass by three and then multiply this by two.

Raza weighs 60 kg.

How much of his body is water?

 8 A builder is laying tiles on a patio.

He needs seven rows with 24 tiles in each row.

The tiles are sold in boxes of 10 tiles.

    a How many boxes does the builder need?

    b How many tiles will he have left?

Problem solving

What is your carbon footprint?

What is a carbon footprint?

It is the amount of carbon dioxide that you put into the air, because of the fuels you use.

It is measured in tonnes.

Fascinating facts

- If you turn down the heating in your house by one degree you would save about 300 kg of carbon dioxide and about £80 on your fuel bill in a year.

- If you reduce the amount of meat you eat, you will reduce your carbon footprint. 18% of all greenhouse gases are linked to meat consumption.

- The United States emits 18 tonnes of carbon dioxide per person every year.

- The United Kingdom emits 8 tonnes of carbon dioxide per person every year.

- China emits 6 tonnes of carbon dioxide per person every year.

- India emits about one-quarter of the amount that China emits, per person.

1 If 100 households turn down the heating by one Celsius degree, how much money will they save altogether in a year?

2 If 200 households turn down the heating by one Celsius degree, how many kilograms of carbon dioxide will be saved altogether in a year?

3 What percentage of greenhouse gases is linked to meat consumption?

4 The population of China is about 1 400 000 000 (1400 million). How many tonnes of carbon dioxide is emitted by the population of China?

Hint 1 tonne = 1000 kg

5 Approximately how much are the emissions of India, per person, per year?

6 Which of these statements is true?

a The United States emits more than twice as much per person as the United Kingdom does.

b China emits about one-third of the amount, per person, of the United States.

6

Statistics

This chapter is going to show you:

- how to calculate the mode, the median and the range for a set of data
- how to interpret statistical diagrams and charts
- how to collect and organise data
- how to create data-collection forms
- how to create questionnaires
- how to use frequency tables
- how to draw simple conclusions from data.

What you should already know:

- how to interpret data from tables, graphs and charts
- how to draw frequency tables and bar charts
- how to create a tally chart
- how to draw bar charts and pictograms.

About this chapter

How many people are there in the world? Or even in our country? How do they live? What do they eat and drink? How big are their families?

We find out statistics like these by carrying out censuses and surveys. Censuses are huge surveys that find out information about every single man, woman and child in a country.

In the UK a census is carried out every 10 years. When the data is analysed and interpreted it helps the government decide what it needs to do. Charts and graphs give us tools for analysing and representing statistical data – crucial for drawing the right conclusions from it.

6.1 Mode, median and range

Learning objective

* To understand the meaning of mode, median and range

Key words	
average	data
median	mode
outlier	range

Statistics is all about collecting and organising information, or **data**, then using diagrams to represent and interpret it.

When you are trying to understand or interpret data, you often need to find an **average**, for example: the average rainfall in Britain, the average weekly wage, the average mark in an examination.

But what is an average?

An average is a useful statistic because you can use it to represent a whole set of data by just a single value.

This section explains how to find two types of average: the **mode** and the **median**.

The mode is the value that occurs most often in a set of data. It is the only average that can be used for non-numerical data, such as colours or makes of car. Sometimes there may be no mode because either all the values are different, or no single value occurs more often than other values.

The median is the middle value for a set of values, when they are put in numerical order.

You also need to be able to find the **range** of a set of values. This is the difference between the largest and smallest values.

> Range = largest value – smallest value

A small range means that the values in the set of data are similar in size, whereas a large range means that the values differ a lot and therefore are more spread out.

Sometimes, one value in a set of numerical data is much larger or much smaller than the rest. This value is called an **outlier**.

Example 1

These are the ages of 11 players in a football squad.

> 23, 19, 24, 26, 27, 27, 24, 23, 20, 23, 26

Work out: **a** the mode   **b** the median   **c** the range.

First, put the ages in order.

19, 20, 23, 23, 23, 24, 24, 26, 26, 27, 27

a The mode is the number that occurs most often.

So, the mode is 23.

b The median is the number in the middle of the set.

So, the median is 24.

c The range is the largest number minus the smallest number.

27 – 19 = 8

The range is 8.

Example 2

These are the marks of ten pupils in a mental arithmetic test.

19, 18, 16, 15, 13, 14, 20, 19, 18, 12

Work out: **a** the mode   **b** the median   **c** the range.

First, put the marks in order.

12, 13, 14, 15, 16, 18, 18, 19, 19, 20

a Most of the numbers appear only once, but 18 and 19 each occur twice.

The mode is the number that appears most often.

In this case, there are two modes, 18 and 19.

b There are two numbers in the middle of the set: 16 and 18.

The median is the number that would be in the middle of these two numbers.

So, the median is 17.

c The range is the largest number minus the smallest number.

20 − 12 = 8

The range is 8.

Exercise 6A

1 Find the mode of each set of data.

   a yellow, white, blue, yellow, white, blue, yellow, blue, white, yellow

   b cloud, sun, cloud, fog, sun, sun, snow, cloud, snow, sun, rain, sun

   c I, A, E, U, I, O, E, I, A, I, A, O, E, U, I, E, I

   d ♥, ♦, ♥, ♦, ♣, ♠, ♥, ♣, ♥, ♥, ♦, ♥, ♦, ♥

2 Find the mode of each set of data.

   a 8, 7, 3, 4, 2, 10, 6, 5, 9, 5, 6, 6

   b 26, 23, 34, 17, 26, 29, 13, 16, 22, 20, 30, 23, 29, 23

   c 25, 23, 29, 17, 21, 31, 27, 19, 24, 25, 24

   d 100, 102, 108, 104, 110, 103, 106, 111, 101, 99, 102, 96, 105

3 Find the range of each set of data.

   a 12, 26, 7, 12, 17, 8, 10, 14, 25

   b 4, 2, 3, 4, 2, 1, 5, 3, 5, 1, 7, 6, 5, 6

   c 31, 34, 7, 8, 18, 25, 19, 30

   d 101, 107, 101, 98, 112, 106, 103, 107, 105

4 Find the mode and range of each set of data.

   a £1.50, £0.80, £2.65, £1.80, £3.20, £1.25, £0.80

   b 25 kg, 20 kg, 24 kg, 33 kg, 31 kg, 24 kg

   c 33 cm, 46 cm, 52 cm, 33 cm, 41 cm, 43 cm

   d 21°, 25°, 21°, 19°, 20°, 20°, 23°, 22°, 21°, 24°

5 A group of nine Year 7 pupils had their lunch in the school cafeteria. These are the amounts that they spent.

£2.40, £2.30, £2.00, £2.60, £2.30, £3.00, £3.70, £2.30, £2.90

    a Find the mode for the data.

    b Find the range for the data.

6 Find the median of each set of data.

    a 7, 6, 2, 3, 1, 9, 5, 4, 8

    b 20, 18, 29, 12, 21, 24, 8, 11, 17, 15, 25

    c 15, 13, 19, 7, 11, 21, 17, 9

    d 101, 102, 109, 105, 111, 104, 107, 112, 102, 100

7 Find the mode, range and median of each set of data.

    a £2.50, £1.80, £3.65, £3.80, £4.20, £3.25, £1.80

    b 11 kg, 6 kg, 10 kg, 19 kg, 19 kg, 14 kg, 20 kg

    c 111 cm, 124 cm, 130 cm, 111 cm, 119 cm, 121 cm, 111 cm

    d 33°, 37°, 33°, 31°, 32°, 33°, 35°, 34°, 34°, 36°, 35°

8 **a** Write down a set of three numbers that has a median of 5 and a mode of 5.

    b Write down a set of five numbers that has a median of 5 and a mode of 6.

    c Write down a list of seven numbers that has a median of 5, a mode of 4 and a range of 6.

9 These are the names of the nine people who work for a company.

Lee	Helen	Suki
Wynn	Helen	Tom
Helen	John	Tom

    a Which name is the mode?

    b One person leaves the company. A new person joins the company.

       Now the name that is the mode is Tom.

       i What is the name of the person who leaves?

       ii What is the name of the person who joins?

(MR) **10** **a** There are two children in a family.

       The range of their ages is exactly 4 years.

       What could the ages of the two children be?

       Give an example and explain why.

    b There are two children in another family.

       They are twins of the same age.

       What is the range of their ages and explain why?

Work out: **a** the mode   **b** the median   **c** the range of each set of data.

A The temperature yesterday of some UK cities

B The temperature yesterday of European cities around the world

C The number of pets each member of your class has

D The number of hours members of your class spend playing computer games in a day

6.2 Reading data from tables and charts

Learning objective

• To read data from tables and charts

Key words	
chart	frequency

You can display data in various forms. Two simple ways are tables and **charts**. In Exercise 6B you will learn some of the different ways to do this.

You will see that some charts have a column called **frequency**. This is the number of times this value occurs in the set of data.

The mode is always the value with the highest frequency.

Exercise 6B

1 The pictogram shows the amount of money collected for charity by different year groups in a school.

Year 11 | £10 | £1
Year 10 | £10 | £10 | £10
Year 9 | £10 | £10 | £10 | £10 | £1
Year 8 | £10 | £10 | £10 | £1
Year 7 | £10 | £10 | £10 | £10

Key £10 represents £10

   a   How much money did Year 7 collect?

   b   How much money did Year 8 collect?

   c   Which year group collected the most money?

   d   How much money did the groups collect altogether?

2 The pictogram shows how many CDs five friends have in their collections.

a Who has the most CDs?

b How many CDs does Harry have?

c How many CDs does Liam have?

d How many more CDs does Sophie have than Arran?

e How many CDs do the five friends have altogether?

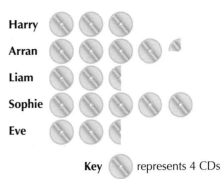

Key represents 4 CDs

3 The calendar shows the dates of the days of the month of October one year.

a What day of the week is 26 October?

b What is the date of the second Sunday in the month?

c A school's half-term holiday begins after 18 October and ends on 27 October.

How many days will Syed be in school in October?

d On what day will 5 November fall in this year?

OCTOBER

M	Tu	W	Th	F	Sa	Su
		1	2	3	4	5	6
7	8	9	10	11	12	13
14	15	16	17	18	19	20
21	22	23	24	25	26	27
28	29	30	31			

(PS) 4 The chart shows the distances, by road, between six cities in England. All of the distances are in miles.

Birmingham					
121	Leeds				
120	198	London			
89	44	204	Manchester		
68	171	57	161	Oxford	
134	24	212	71	185	York

a How many miles is it from Leeds to London?

b How many miles is it from Birmingham to Oxford?

c Which two cities are the furthest apart?

d Freya drives from Manchester to Leeds. She then drives from Leeds to York.

Then she returns home from York to Manchester.

How many miles has she driven altogether?

PS **5** This two-way table shows the results of five football teams after 28 games.

	Games won	Games lost	Games drawn
Arsenal	16	5	7
Leicester City	3	17	8
Manchester United	18	7	3
Newcastle United	17	7	4
Southampton	10	14	4

a How many games did Newcastle United win?

b Which teams drew the same number of games?

c Three points are awarded for a win, one point is awarded for a draw and no points are awarded for a lost game.

   i How many points did Southampton have after the 28 games?

   ii Which team had the most points after 28 games?

   iii Which team had the least points after 28 games?

6 The bar chart shows how the pupils in class 7BT travel to school.

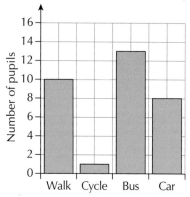

a How many pupils cycle to school?

b What is the mode for the way the pupils travel to school?

c How many pupils are there in class 7BT?

7 The graph illustrates how many pupils gained different marks, from a possible total of 10, in a spelling test.

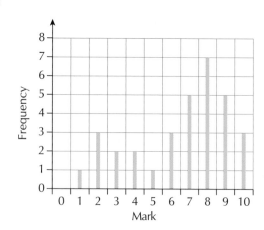

a How many pupils had a mark of 6 in the test?

b How many pupils had a mark of 8 or more in the test?

c How many pupils are there in the class altogether?

d Which mark is the mode?

8 The line graph shows the average temperature, in Celsius degrees (°C), in Bristol over a 14-hour period.

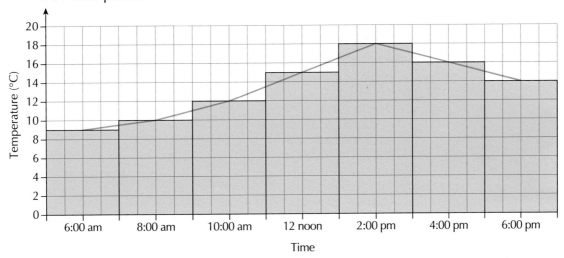

a What is the average temperature at around 8:00 am?

b What is the average temperature at midday?

c Write down the range for the temperature over the 14-hour period.

Problem solving: Places in the UK

The chart shows the names of six places in England.

Sheffield					
	London				
		Nottingham			
			Mablethorpe		
85				Solihul	
					Lincoln

A Do some research to find out the distances between the places.

Copy the chart and use what you find out to complete it.

B Which two places are the furthest apart?

C Trevor drives from Sheffield to Nottingham.

He then drives from Nottingham to Lincoln.

Then he returns home from Lincoln to Sheffield.

How many miles has he driven altogether?

6.3 Using a tally chart

Learning objective

• To create and use a tally chart

What method of transport do pupils use to travel to school – and why?

If you ask pupils this question, they will name all sorts of different methods of travelling, such as by bus, car, bike, walking, train and maybe some others.

A good way to collect this data is to fill in a **tally chart** as you ask each pupil the question. Your chart might look like this.

Type of transport	Tally	Frequency
Bus	卌 IIII	9
Car	卌	5
Bike	II	2
Walking	卌 卌 IIII	14
Other		0
	Total:	30

Notice that you use one mark to represent each pupil. When you make the fifth mark you draw it so that it slopes across the previous four. This is sometimes called a gate because it looks like a gate. Sometimes it is called a bar, because it 'bars the gate'.

It is important to use this method because, when you have collected the data, you can count it easily, in fives.

In the tally chart above, the most common type of transport is 'walking'. So 'walking' is the mode. You can also say that the **modal** form of transport is 'walking'.

When they are asked why they have chosen that particular form of transport, pupils may give answers such as those listed below.

Bus	Because it's quicker.
	Because it's too far to walk.
Car	My mum goes that way to work.
	There's no bus and it's too far.
	It's easier than the bus.
Bike	It's better than walking.
Walking	It's not too far. It's better than a crowded bus.

Look at all the reasons given by pupils. Pick out those that are common to many pupils. These reasons can be left as a table, or illustrated in different ways.

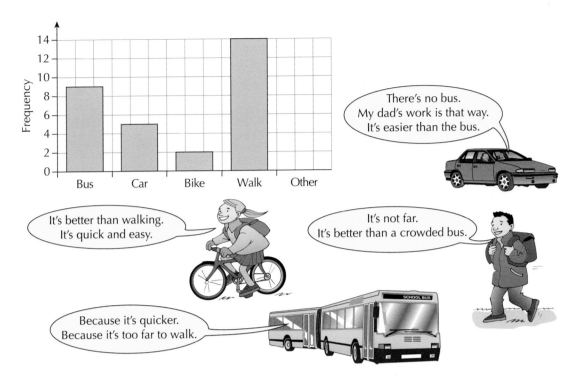

Exercise 6C

1 The pupils in a class were asked: 'Where would you like to go for your form trip?' This is how they voted.

   a Draw a bar chart to show the results of the vote.

   b Write down some suitable reasons why the pupils might have voted for each place.

   c What was the modal place chosen?

Place	Tally
Seaside	ЖН ЖН
Countryside	ЖН	
Amusement park	ЖН |||
A zoo	|||
A castle	||||

2 The pupils in a class were asked: 'What is your favourite pet?' This is how they voted.

   a Draw a chart illustrating the results.

   b Write down some suitable reasons why the students might have voted for each pet.

   c What was the modal pet chosen?

Pet	Tally
Dog	ЖН	
Cat	ЖН |||
Mice	ЖН
Guinea pig	|||
Other	||

3 The pupils in a class were asked: 'What is your favourite sport?' This is how they voted.

   a Draw a chart illustrating the results.

   b What was the modal sport chosen?

Sport	Tally
Hockey	ЖН ||
Netball	ЖН	
Football	ЖН ||||
Badminton	|||
Other	||

4 The pupils in a class were asked: 'What is your favourite school subject?' This is how they voted.

    a Draw a chart illustrating the results.

    b What was the modal subject chosen?

Subject	Tally
French	|||
Geography	ЖШ
Maths	ЖШ ЖШ ||
PE	||||
Technology	ЖШ	
Other		

5 The pupils in a class were asked: 'Find out your parents' favourite detectives on TV.' This is how they voted.

    a Draw a chart illustrating the results.

    b Which was the modal detective chosen?

Detective	Tally
Frost	ЖШ ||
Morse	||||
Scott and Bailey	ЖШ ЖШ
Poirot	ЖШ
Barnaby	|||
Other	||

(PS) **6** **a** Use your own class tally chart to draw a chart illustrating the methods of transport used by pupils to get to school.

    b Remember to ask for their reasons. Make a table of the results.

Extension Work

A Choose five different places to visit as a form trip near you.

   Create your own tally sheet, so that you can collect opinions from other pupils.

B Collect some data for this sheet, then create a bar chart with some reasons on it.

C You could try using a spreadsheet and creating graphs from your data.

6.4 Using data

Learning objective

* To understand how to use data

Key words

data-collection form   sample

Can you list six different national newspapers? There are lots of different newspapers to choose from.

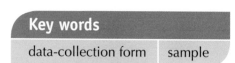

Do certain newspapers use more long words than the other newspapers?

Now think how you could answer Ted's question.

The way to find an exact answer would be to count all the words – and all their letters –in all of the newspapers, but this would take a very long time.

A better way is to take a **sample**. You could take, say, 100 words from each newspaper and find the length of each word.

Exercise 6D

Do the whole of this exercise as a class activity, so that between the whole class you will get a lot of data from different sorts of newspapers

 1 a   Select one or two pages from the newspaper given to you.

b   Create a tally chart like the one below. This is your **data-collection form.**

Number of letters	Tally	Frequency
1		
2		
3		
4		
5		

> **Hint** A data-collection form is a table that you can use to collect the results of your research. It may also be called a data-collection sheet.

c   i   Select at least two different articles.

ii   Count the letters in each word and complete the tally.

Note: numbers such as 3, 4, 5 count as 1 letter

numbers such as 15, 58 count as 2 letters

numbers such as 156, 897 count as 3 letters, and so on

ignore the hyphen in hyphenated words such as 'vice-versa'.

d   Fill in the frequency column.

e   Create a bar chart for your results.

f   What is the modal number of letters?

 2 a   Select one or two pages from the newspaper you have been given.

b   Create a data-collection form, like the one below.

Number of words	Tally	Frequency
2		
3		
4		
12		
13		

Which newspaper has the shortest sentences?

c   i   Select at least two different articles.

ii   Count the words in each sentence and complete the tally.

d   Check you have used between 50 and 100 sentences. If not choose more articles to get this number of sentences.

e   Once you have used over 50 sentences, fill in the frequency column.

f   Create a bar chart for your results.

g   What is the modal number of words?

h   Compare the different sorts of newspapers. Which has the shortest sentences?

Activity: Easy reading

Choose a book or magazine that you find easy to read and create a bar chart of the number of letters in each word for selected parts of them (either two paragraphs or two articles).

6.5 Grouped frequency

Learning objective

• To understand and use grouped frequency

Key words

class

grouped frequency

grouped frequency table

modal class

A teacher asked her class this question.

How many times have you walked to school this term?

These are the replies.

6	3	5	20	15	11	13	28	30	5	2	6
8	18	23	22	17	13	4	2	30	17	19	25
8	3	9	12	15	8						

There are too many different values to make a sensible bar chart.

You need to put the values into groups, to produce a **grouped frequency table**, like this.

Times	1–5	6–10	11–15	16–20	21–25	26–30
Frequency	7	6	6	5	3	3

The data has been put into groups, called **classes**.

Where possible, you should always make the classes the same size as each other. This means that the difference between the first and second numbers should always be the same: $5 - 1 = 4$, $10 - 6 = 4, \ldots 30 - 26 = 4$.

Now you can draw a bar chart from this data and put information on each bar, about some of the reasons.

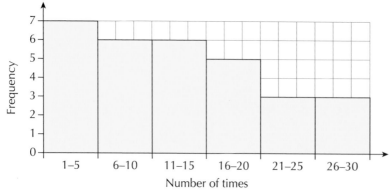

You cannot find a mode for grouped data. You have to use the **modal class**. This is the class with the most data items in it – the highest frequency – so it will be the tallest bar in a bar chart.

Exercise 6E

1 A class did a survey on how many text messages each pupil had received the day before. These are the results of the survey.

3	6	1	17	0	15	18	14	12	0	8	16
3	5	9	11	14	7	2	13	1	13	14	17
4	15	2	5	4	17	11	4	8	18	4	16
16	15	4	9	18	6	9	16	15	9	6	18
2	15	15	18	5	4	7	8	2			

a Draw a grouped frequency table with a class size of 5, like this.

Number of texts	Tally	Frequency
0–4		
5–9		
10–14		
15–19		
	Total:	

b Use the above data to complete your table.

c Draw a bar chart of the data.

d What is the modal class?

2 A teacher asked her class: 'How many times this week have you played electronic games?'

These were their replies.

4	7	10	3	24	19	7	9	30	28	3	2
1	6	20	24	14	22	8	5	24	9	8	2
1	26	25	9	14	19	16	17	4	8	12	6
28	24	7	10	30	30	7	7	1	7	23	27
26	13	5	25	12	11	6	26				

a Draw a grouped frequency table with a class size of 5, like this.

Number of times	Tally	Frequency
1–5		
6–10		
11–15		
16–20		
21–25		
26–30		
	Total:	

b Use the above data to complete your table.

c Draw a bar chart of the data.

d What is the modal class?

3 At a club, the members were asked: 'How many times have you played table football this week?'

These were their replies.

4	7	0	14	6	1	0	3	7	9	5	15
2	1	0	0	4	0	5	8	1	2	3	2
1	15	14	0	3	1	10	14	5	6	2	0
1	12	5	4	2	0	1	1	4	5	7	11
0	2	0	0	0	0	14	3	2	4	1	0
11	7	0									

a Create a grouped frequency table:

   i with a class size of 3, i.e. 0–2, 3–5, 6–8, 9–11, 12–14, 15–17

   ii with a class size of 5, i.e. 0–4, 5–9, 10–14, 15–19.

b Draw a bar chart for each frequency table.

c What is the modal class?

d Which class size seems more appropriate to use?

Challenge: Boat trips down the Ganges

In India, tourists take boat trips down the River Ganges. One week in March a boat owner recorded how many people were in his boat on the main days these trips were made.

These are the results.

Saturday:	20	24	14	18	10	30	15	11	19	23	31
	19	16	24	13	16	25	20	19	17	12	10
	11	13	24	30	22	24	15	10	26	29	27
	13	13	16	11	17	26	17	14	11	28	30
	24	18	15	19	23	28	15	11			

Sunday:	15	20	8	11	7	26	10	7	12	15	19
	25	14	9	16	10	11	14	13	11	8	7
	5	6	7	8	18	22	14	20	10	7	18
	22	23	9	7	10	8	13	8	7	5	19
	27	19	13	7	15	18	21	9	8		

Wednesday:	25	30	19	23	15	33	19	26	33	25	21
	32	18	22	32	26	24	24	23	19	15	16
	19	29	33	28	29	22	16	21	32	31	19
	19	22	16	25	31	23	20	17	33	34	29
	21	22	25	28	33	20					

A Complete a grouped frequency tally chart for each day's recorded results. (Decide on your own class size.)

B Draw a bar chart from each frequency chart.

C Comment on your results.

6.6 Data collection

Learning objective

• To gain a greater understanding of data collection

Suppose you ask a sample of the pupils in your school these questions. In other words, you will not ask not everyone, but a few from each year group.

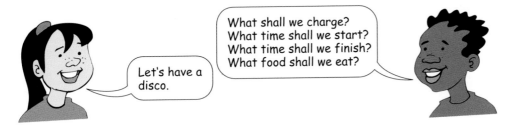

How will you record their answers, though?

You will need a suitable data-collection form. An example is shown below.

Year group	Boy or girl	How much to charge?	Time to start?	Time to finish?	What would you like to eat?
Y7	B	£1	7 pm	11 pm	snacks, burgers, chips
Y7	G	50p	7 pm	9 pm	chips, snacks, lollies
Y8	G	£2	7:30 pm	10 pm	snacks, hot dogs
Y11	B	£3	8:30 pm	11:30 pm	chocolate, pizza
↑	↑			↑	
Keep track of the age.	Try to ask equal numbers.	Once the data is collected, it can be sorted into frequency tables.			

Now, as you ask each question, you can immediately complete your data-collection form.

Collecting data

There are five stages in running this type of data collection. They are:

• deciding what questions to ask and who to ask

• creating a simple, suitable data-collection form for all the questions

• asking the questions and completing the data-collection form

• after collecting all the data, collating it in frequency tables

• analysing the data to draw conclusions from the data collected.

The size of your sample will depend on many things. It may be simply the first 50 people you come across. Or you may want a particular fraction of the available people.

In the above example, a good sample would probably be about four from each class, two boys and two girls.

Exercise 6F

A class completed the data-collection activity described above on a sample of 10 pupils from each of years 7, 8 and 9.

This is their data-collection form.

Year group	Boy or girl	How much to charge	Time to start	Time to finish	What would you like to eat?
Y7	B	50p	6:30 pm	10:00 pm	snacks, burgers, chips
Y7	G	0	7:00 pm	9:00 pm	chips, snacks, ice pops
Y8	G	£1.50	7:00 pm	10:00 pm	snacks, hot dogs
Y9	B	£2.50	8:00 pm	11:00 pm	chocolate, pizza
Y9	G	£1.50	8:00 pm	10:00 pm	pizza
Y9	B	£2	7:30 pm	9:00 pm	hot dogs, chocolate
Y8	G	£1	7:30 pm	10:30 pm	snacks
Y7	B	50p	7:00 pm	9:00 pm	snacks, burgers
Y7	B	£1	7:30 pm	10:30 pm	snacks, ice pops
Y8	B	50p	6:30 pm	9:00 pm	snacks, chips, hot dogs
Y9	G	£1.50	8:00 pm	11:00 pm	pizza, chocolate
Y9	G	£1	8:00 pm	10:30 pm	chips, pizza
Y9	G	£2	8:00 pm	11:00 pm	snacks, pizza
Y7	G	£1	7:00 pm	9:00 pm	snacks, ice pops, chocolate
Y8	B	£1.50	7:30 pm	9:30 pm	snacks, ice pops, chocolate
Y8	B	50p	8:00 pm	10:00 pm	chips, hot dogs
Y9	B	£1	8:00 pm	11:00 pm	pizza
Y7	B	0	7:00 pm	9:30 pm	snacks, hot dogs
Y8	G	50p	8:00 pm	10:00 pm	snacks, chips
Y9	B	£1.50	7:00 pm	10:30 pm	pizza
Y8	G	£1	7:30 pm	10:00 pm	chips, hot dogs, chocolate
Y8	B	£1.50	7:00 pm	9:00 pm	chips, hot dogs, ice pops
Y9	G	£2.50	6:30 pm	9:30 pm	snacks, pizza
Y9	B	£2	8:00 pm	10:30 pm	snacks, hot dogs
Y7	G	0	7:30 pm	10:00 pm	snacks, burgers, ice pops
Y7	G	0	6:30 pm	9:00 pm	snacks, pizza
Y7	G	50p	7:00 pm	9:30 pm	snacks, pizza
Y8	B	£1.50	7:30 pm	10:00 pm	snacks, chips, chocolate
Y8	G	£1	7:30 pm	9:30 pm	chips, burgers
Y7	B	50p	7:30 pm	10:00 pm	snacks, ice pops

1 **a** Copy this chart and complete the tallies for the suggested charges from each year group.

Charges	Tallies					
	Y7	Total	Y8	Total	Y9	Total
0						
25p						
50p						
75p						
£1						
£1.25						
£1.50						
£2						
£2.50						

b Comment on the differences between the year groups.

2 **a** Copy this chart and complete the tallies for the suggested starting times from each year group.

Times	Tallies					
	Y7	Total	Y8	Total	Y9	Total
6:30 pm						
7:00 pm						
7:30 pm						
8:00 pm						

b Comment on the differences between the year groups.

3 **a** Copy this chart and complete the tallies for the suggested finishing times from each year group.

Times	Tallies					
	Y7	Total	Y8	Total	Y9	Total
9:00 pm						
9:30 pm						
10:00 pm						
10:30 pm						
11:00 pm						

b Comment on the differences between the year groups.

 4 **a** Create and complete a tally chart, as before, for the food suggestions of each year.

b Comment on the differences between the year groups.

Investigation: Time for the disco

Investigate the differences between boys and girls as to the suggested length of time for the disco.

Ready to progress?

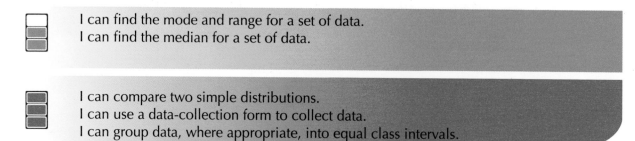

I can find the mode and range for a set of data.
I can find the median for a set of data.

I can compare two simple distributions.
I can use a data-collection form to collect data.
I can group data, where appropriate, into equal class intervals.

Review questions

1 The pupils in a class were asked: 'What is your favourite food?' This is how they voted.

Subject	Tally
Beans	|||
Burger and chips	卌
Pizza	卌 卌 ||
Sausage and mash	||||
Pasta Bake	卌	
Other		

a Draw a chart illustrating the results.

b What was the modal food chosen?

2 Sophia did a survey on the types of vehicle that arrived at her school between 10:00 am and 2:00 pm.

Vehicle	Tally
Cars	卌	
Vans	卌 |||
Lorries	|||
Taxis		

a How many vehicles arrived at Sophia's school during this survey?

b How many more vans arrived than cars?

c Sophia started drawing a bar chart to show the information.

Copy her chart and draw in the missing bars.

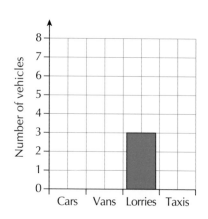

3 Twenty 11-year-old pupils were twittering about how much it cost them to travel to school on a bus. These are the amounts they paid.

40p	£1	70p	£1.20	£1	40p	70p
£1	£1	£1.20	50p	50p	£1.50	£1
50p	£1	£1.20	£1	70p	80p	

What was the modal amount spent on the bus fare?

4 These are the temperatures recorded on 12 February in 15 major towns of the UK.

| 0 °C | −5 °C | −1 °C | −2 °C | 0 °C | −3 °C | −1 °C | −2 °C |
| −5 °C | 1 °C | −4 °C | −2 °C | 0 °C | −2 °C | −3 °C | |

What was the median temperature recorded from these temperatures?

5 Kirstie was asked to make a rectangle with a piece of wire of length 12 cm.

She was told to make the length and width whole numbers of centimetres.

What is the range of areas she could make with that length of wire?

6 A sample of ten bags of flour were weighed. These are the results.

1.1 kg   1.2 kg   0.9 kg   1 kg   0.9 kg   1.1 kg   1 kg   0.9 kg   1.15 kg   1.2 kg

a   What was the modal weight?

b   What was the median weight?

c   What was the range of the weights?

7 Kim was asked to draw a rectangle with an area of 30 cm². She was told to make sure that the length of each side was a whole number of centimetres.

a   Show that there are only four different sized rectangles she can draw.

b   Calculate the median of the four different perimeters.

c   What is the range of the different perimeters.

8 Lewis asked his friends on Facebook to tell him their heights. His friends sent him the following results.

156 cm	158 cm	1.49 m	153 cm	1.62 m	143 cm
152 cm	158 cm	157 cm	1.42 m	148 cm	1.52 m
155 cm	162 cm	1.5 m	144 cm	1.47 m	144 cm
1.4 m	150 cm	142 cm	148 cm	1.55 m	1.37 m
157 cm	148 cm	141 cm	1.35 m	155 cm	1.36 m

Put the heights into a grouped frequency tally chart.

What is the modal class?

Challenge
Trains in Europe

We had a great holiday – wonderful views from the train and the freedom to go where we wanted in Europe. We were surprised how easy it was to get from one country to the next. We were able to go to some amazing places. It was unforgettable!

Train travel in Europe is getting easier each year. Look at the statistics for some of the European countries, gathered for a recent year.

Table A   The total number of passenger kilometres for some European countries

This shows how many billion kilometres all the countries' passengers have made in total.

Passenger kilometres	
Country	**Billion**
UK	62.7
France	88.1
Germany	79.2
Italy	40.6
Switzerland	18

Table B   The total number of rail journeys made in each country for this year

Railway journeys made	
Country	**Number of journeys (million)**
UK	1500
France	1100
Germany	1900
Italy	600
Switzerland	450

Table C   The average number of kilometres each person in the country travelled on the railways in that year

Kilometres travelled on train	
Country	**Average distance (kilometres)**
UK	770
France	1370
Germany	910
Italy	780
Switzerland	2422

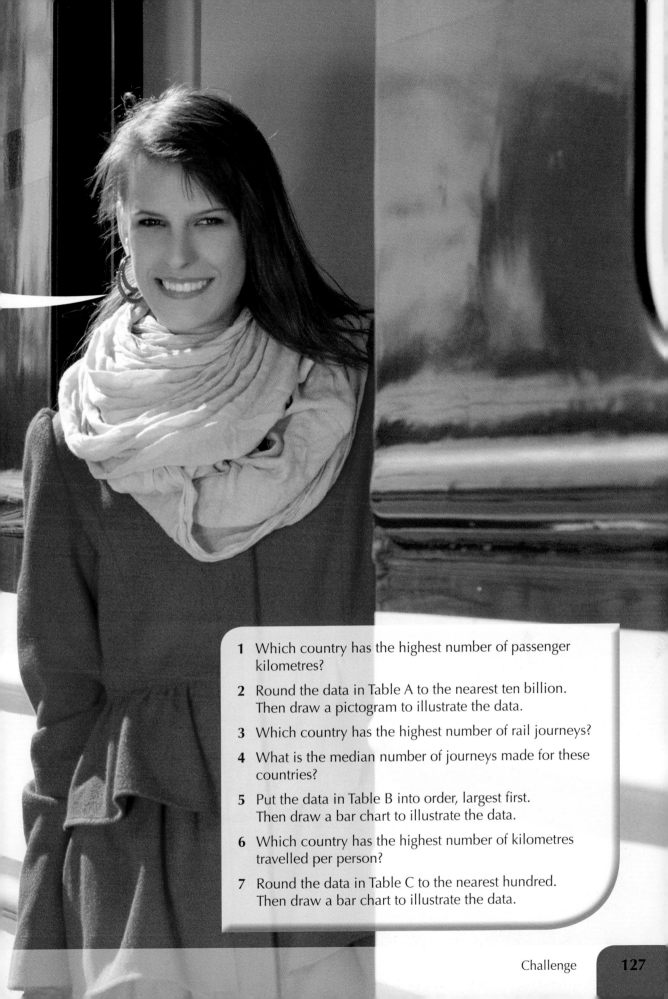

1 Which country has the highest number of passenger kilometres?

2 Round the data in Table A to the nearest ten billion. Then draw a pictogram to illustrate the data.

3 Which country has the highest number of rail journeys?

4 What is the median number of journeys made for these countries?

5 Put the data in Table B into order, largest first. Then draw a bar chart to illustrate the data.

6 Which country has the highest number of kilometres travelled per person?

7 Round the data in Table C to the nearest hundred. Then draw a bar chart to illustrate the data.

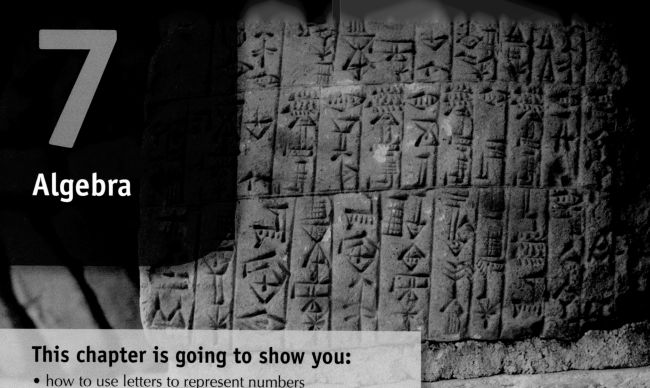

7

Algebra

This chapter is going to show you:

- how to use letters to represent numbers
- how to use the rules (conventions) of algebra
- how to simplify algebraic expressions
- how to use and write formulae.

You should already know:

- how to apply the rules of arithmetic
- the meaning of the words 'term' and 'expression'.

About this chapter

Algebra uses letters instead of numbers to describe and solve problems. It is a universal language and its rules are used all over the world.

Mathematicians have been developing the rules of algebra for over 3000 years. We know that the Babylonians (Babylon was situated in the southern part of today's Iraq) used a form of algebra because they wrote on clay tablets, some of which have survived until today.

Today, we use algebra to help us solve all sorts of problems, from the simplest to the most complex, for example, working out the area of carpet needed for a floor or designing the shape of a racing car to minimise wind resistance.

7.1 Expressions and substitution

Learning objectives

- To use algebra to write simple expressions
- To substitute numbers into expressions to work out their value

Key words

expression	substitute
term	variable

In algebra, you use letters to represent numbers. You can treat the letters in the same way as you treat numbers.

Look at this triangle.

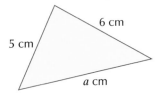

The lengths of two of the sides are given.

The length of the third side is unknown. It is represented by a letter.

An **expression** for the perimeter, in centimetres, of the triangle is $5 + 6 + a$ or $11 + a$.

You can also write the perimeter as $a + 11$.

The letter a is called a **variable**. It can take different values.

In the expression $11 + a$, the 11 and the a are called **terms**.

You can **substitute** different values for a into the formula to work out the perimeter.

- If $a = 9$, the perimeter is 20. $11 + 9 = 20$
- If $a = 7.3$, the perimeter is 18.3. $11 + 7.3 = 18.3$

You know that in a rectangle, opposite sides are the same length.

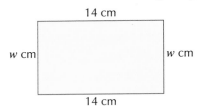

This rectangle is 14 cm long and w cm wide.

The perimeter, in centimetres, is $w + 14 + w + 14$.

You can simplify that to $2w + 28$. $14 + 14 = 28$

You write $w + w$ as $2w$.

- If $w = 9$, then the perimeter is $2 \times 9 + 28 = 18 + 28 = 46$.
- If $w = 10.5$, then the perimeter is $2 \times 10.5 + 28 = 21 + 28 = 49$.

Example 1

This rectangle is l cm long and 10 cm wide.

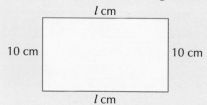

l cm

10 cm   10 cm

l cm

a Work out an expression for the perimeter of the rectangle.

b Find the value of the perimeter if:

   i $l = 8$ **ii** $l = 15.5$.

   a The perimeter, in centimetres, is $10 + l + 10 + l$.

      Write $l + l$ as $2l$. $10 + 10 = 20$

      Now you can simplify the expression to $2l + 20$.

   b i If $l = 8$, then the perimeter is $2 \times 8 + 20 = 16 + 20 = 36$ cm.

     ii If $l = 15.5$, then the perimeter is $2 \times 15.5 + 20 = 31 + 20 = 51$ cm.

Example 2

Dave is d years old.

Sophie is three years older than Dave.

Mark is nine years younger than Dave.

Gail's age is four times Dave's age.

Work out an expression, in terms of d, for:

a Sophie's age   **b** Mark's age   **c** Gail's age.

   a Sophie's age is $d + 3$.   Add 3 onto d You can also write this as $3 + d$.

   b Mark's age is $d - 9$.   Subtract 9 from d.

   c Gail's age is $4d$.   Write $4 \times d$ as $4d$.   Do not put in the $\times$ sign.

Exercise 7A

1 Find the value of each unknown.

   a $a + 4 = 5$ **b** $b - 3 = 2$ **c** $8 - c = 2$ **d** $10 - d = 2$

2 Find the value of each unknown.

   a $2 \times a = 12$ **b** $b \times 3 = 9$ **c** $20 \div c = 5$ **d** $c \div 10 = 7$

3 Each side of this square is t cm long.

   Show that an expression for the perimeter
   of the square is $4t$.

   t cm

4 Write an expression for the perimeter, in centimetres, of each triangle.

a

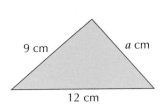

9 cm   *a* cm

12 cm

b

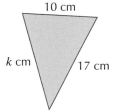

10 cm

k cm   17 cm

c

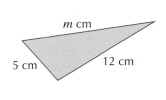

m cm

5 cm   12 cm

5 Write an expression for the perimeter, in centimetres, of each rectangle.

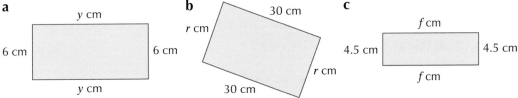

a

y cm

6 cm   6 cm

y cm

b

30 cm

r cm

r cm

30 cm

c

f cm

4.5 cm   4.5 cm

f cm

6 Each side of this hexagon is *h* cm long.

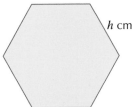

h cm

Write down an expression for the perimeter of the hexagon.

7 All the sides of this pentagon are *s* cm long.

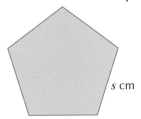

s cm

Write down an expression for the perimeter of the pentagon.

8 Alan is *h* cm tall.

   a Jenny is 4 cm taller than Alan. Explain why an expression for Jenny's height is *h* + 4.

   b Karl is 9 cm shorter than Alan. Write down an expression for Karl's height.

   c The height of a tree is six times Alan's height. Write an expression for the height of the tree.

9 Lauren runs a race in *m* minutes.

   a Mike takes 4.5 minutes longer than Lauren. Explain why an expression for Mike's time is *m* + 4.5.

   b Jordan takes twice as long as Lauren. Write down an expression for Jordan's time.

10 Look at this triangle.

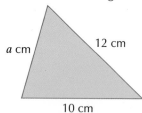

a cm

12 cm

10 cm

(MR)

a Show that the perimeter of the triangle, in centimetres, is $a + 22$.
b Work out the value of $a + 22$ if $a = 9$.
c Work out the value of $a + 22$ if $a = 10.5$.
d Work out the value of $a + 22$ if $a = 8.7$.

11 You are given the expression $x - 5$.
Work out the value of the expression if:
  a $x = 12$ **b** $x = 9.5$ **c** $x = 100$ **d** $x = 5$.

12 You are give the expression $5t + 3$.
Work out the value of the expression if:
  a $t = 2$ **b** $t = 4$ **c** $t = 6$ **d** $t = 1.5$.

13 You are given the expression $3u - 5$.
Work out the value of the expression if:
  a $u = 4$ **b** $u = 8$ **c** $u = 2$ **d** $u = 10$.

14 The area of the square is A cm². The area of the triangle is B cm².

A cm²   *B* cm²

Work out an expression for the area of each of these shapes.

a    **b**    **c**   **d**

(PS) **15** Here are the shapes from question **14** again.

A cm²   *B* cm²

Draw shapes that have areas of:

  a $4A$ cm²   **b** $2A + B$ cm²   **c** $A + 4B$ cm²   **d** $2A + 2B$ cm²

16 Write an expression for the perimeter of each shape.
The first one has been done for you.

a
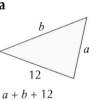
$a + b + 12$

b

c
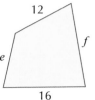

d

e
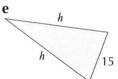

f
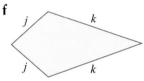

g

Investigation: Making shapes

The areas of these two shapes are C cm² and D cm².

C cm²

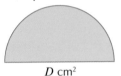
D cm²

Draw shapes that have these areas.

a $2C$ cm²   **b** $2D$ cm²   **c** $C + D$ cm²   **d** $C + 2D$ cm²

e $4C$ cm²   **f** $4C + 4D$ cm²

7.2 Simplifying expressions

Learning objective

- To learn the rules for simplifying expressions

Key words

| like terms | simplify |

The lengths of the sides of this triangle are 13 cm, a cm and $2a$ cm.

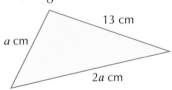

The perimeter is the sum of these three lengths.

The perimeter is $13 + a + 2a = 13 + 3a$.

You can add a and $2a$ to make $3a$. This is called adding **like terms**.

You cannot **simplify** the expression any more than this.

You could also write it as $3a + 13$.

Example 3

Write the perimeter of each shape as simply as possible.

a

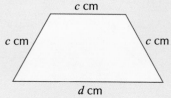

b

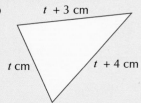

a The perimeter is:

$c + c + c + d = 3c + d$ Add the three c terms together.

b The perimeter is:

$t + t + 3 + t + 4 = 3t + 7$ $t + t + t = 3t$ and $3 + 4 = 7$

Example 4

Simplify each expression.

a $2a + 3a - a$ **b** $2f + 8 + 4f - 5$ **c** $6w + 2v - w$

a $2a + 3a - a = 4a$ The total number of as is $2 + 3 - 1 = 4$.

b $2f + 8 + 4f - 5 = 6f + 3$ $2f + 4f = 6f$ and $8 - 5 = 3$

You cannot simplify any further.

c $6w + 2v - w = 5w + 2v$ $6w - w = 5w$

You cannot simplify any further.

Example 5

Look at these two number walls. The number in each brick is the sum of the numbers in the two bricks below it.

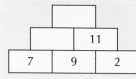
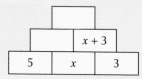

a Work out the two missing numbers in the first number wall.

b Work out the two missing expressions in the second number wall.

  a The numbers below the empty brick in the second row are 7 and 9.

    The number in the empty brick is $7 + 9 = 16$.

    Then the number in the top row is $16 + 11 = 27$.

  b The missing expression in the second row is $x + 5$.

    You could also write this as $5 + x$.

    The missing expression in the top brick is:

    $x + 5 + x + 3 = 2x + 8$ Because $x + x = 2x$ and $5 + 3 = 8$.

Exercise 7B

1 Simplify each expression.

    a $a + a$ **b** $b + 2b$ **c** $6c + c$ **d** $d + d + d$

    e $x + 2x + x$ **f** $z + z + 2z$ **g** $8k + k + k$ **h** $p + 7p + p$

    i $4q + 2q + q$ **j** $2x + 3x + 10x$ **k** $4y + y + 5y$ **l** $5z - z - z$

2 Simplify each expression.

    a $3c + 2c$ **b** $7d + 4d$ **c** $7p + 3p$ **d** $2x + 6x + 4x$

    e $4t + 3t + t$ **f** $9m - 3m$ **g** $5q - 3q$ **h** $7a - 3a$

    i $4p - 2p$ **j** $8w + 3w - w$ **k** $7t + 3t - 5t$ **l** $6g - g - 3g$

3 Write an expression for the perimeter of each shape.

Write your answers as simply as possible.

    a 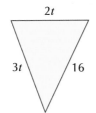   **b** 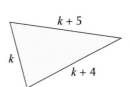   **c**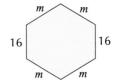

    d 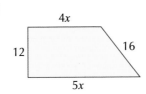   **e** 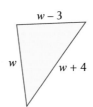   **f**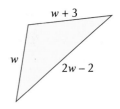

4 The areas of the different parts in these shapes are given.

Write an expression for the total area of each shape, as simply as possible.

    a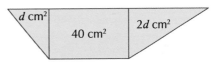

    b 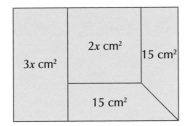   **d**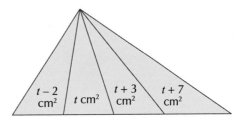

5 Simplify each expression as much as possible.

    a $2x + 5x + 2x$ **b** $y + 2y + 3y$ **c** $5e + 2e - 3e$

    d $2w + 2w - w$ **e** $8n - 2n - 2n$ **f** $3k - k + 4k$

6 Simplify each expression as much as possible.

  a $3 + 2a + 4 + 6a$ **b** $2m + 3 + 2m - m$ **c** $6 + 4t + 3 + 5t$

  d $4p - 2 - 3p - 4$ **e** $2 + 5x + 6 + 3x$ **f** $2a + 4 + 9 + 3a$

7 Simplify each expression as much as possible.

  a $a + 2b + 3a + 4b$ **b** $6x + 4y - 2x - 3y$ **c** $4e + 2f + 5f - f$

  d $6x + 2y - y - 5x$ **e** $2 + 5x + 6 + 3x$ **f** $2a + 4 + 9 + 3a$

8 Work out the missing number or expression at the top of each number wall.

a 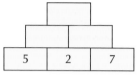   **b** 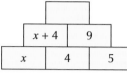   **c**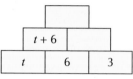

d 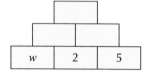   **e** 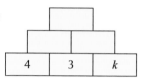   **f**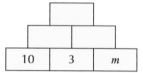

9 Work out the missing expression at the top of each number wall.

a 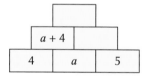   **b** 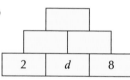   **c**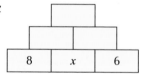

10 Work out the missing expression at the top of each number wall.

a 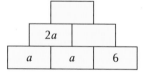   **b** 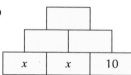   **c**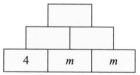

11 Work out the missing expression at the top of each number wall.

a 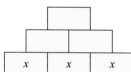   **b**    **c**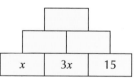

PS **12** There are some missing terms in these number sentences. Work out what they are.

  a $2x + 3x + \blacklozenge = 8x$

  b $\blacklozenge + x - 3 - \blacklozenge = 4x - 5$

  c $2a + \blacklozenge - b + \blacklozenge = 4a + 4b$

Challenge: Making addition sentences

Here are 10 expression cards.

$x + 1$ $x - 1$ $2x + 1$ $2x + 3$ $2x$

$x + 2$ $x - 2$ $3x + 4$ $3x - 1$ $2x - 1$

Use the right expression cards to make these additions correct.

a $x + 2$ + ⬚ = $2x$

b ⬚ + ⬚ = $2x + 3$

c $x + 1$ + ⬚ = $3x + 4$

d $x - 2$ + ⬚ = $3x - 1$

e ⬚ + ⬚ = $2x - 1$

f ⬚ + ⬚ + ⬚ = $3x - 1$

7.3 Using formulae

Learning objective

• To use formulae

Key words

| formula | formulae |

You have already used simple **formulae** in Chapter 3.

Remember that you can write a **formula** in words or you can use letters.

length (*l*)

width (*w*)

The perimeter of the rectangle is equal to 2 lengths + 2 widths.

$P = 2l + 2w$ or $2(l + w)$

Example 6

A formula for changing pounds into New Zealand dollars is $z = 2p$, where p is the number of pounds (£) and z is the number of New Zealand dollars ($).

Change each amount into New Zealand dollars.

a £20   **b** £86   **c** £7.40

  a $p = 20$ so $z = 2 \times 20 = 40$

    £20 is $40.

  b $p = 86$ so $z = 2 \times 86 = 172$

    £86 is $172.

  c $p = 7.40$ so $z = 2 \times 7.40 = 14.80$

    £7.40 is $14.80.

Example 7

The formula for the area (A), in cm², of this rectangle is $A = 5t + 15$.

Work out the value of A if: **a** $t = 4$ **b** $t = 8$.

  a If $t = 4$ then $A = 5 \times 4 + 15$

                $= 20 + 15$ Work out the multiplication first.

                $= 35$

  b If $t = 8$ then $A = 5 \times 8 + 15$

                $= 40 + 15$

                $= 55$

Exercise 7C

1   A cleaner uses this formula to work out the cost for each job:

       $c = 8h$

where c is the cost (in £) and h is the number of hours worked.

Calculate what the cleaner charges to work for:

a   2 hours   **b**   5 hours   **c**   10 hours.

2 A mechanic uses this formula to work out the cost for repairing a car:

$$c = 35t$$

where c is the cost (in £) and t is the time (in hours) to do the repair.

Calculate what the mechanic charges to complete the work in:

a 2 hours   **b** 4 hours   **c** 8 hours

3 Journeys can be measured in kilometres or in miles.
You can use this formula to convert miles into kilometres:

$$k = 1.6m$$

where m is the number of miles and k is the number of kilometres.

Use the formula to convert these distances from miles to kilometres.

a 30 miles   **b** 10 miles   **c** 20 miles

4 An old unit of measurement of length was the foot.
You can use this formula to convert centimetres into feet:

$$f = \frac{c}{30}$$

where c is the number of centimetres and f is the number of feet.
Convert these distances into feet.

a 60 cm   **b** 150 cm   **c** 3 metres

 5 If the perimeter of a square is p, the length of each side, s, is given by the formula $s = \dfrac{p}{4}$.

Find the value of s if p is:

a 12   **b** 20   **c** 68.

6 The formula for the perimeter, p cm, of a rectangle that is 4 cm wide is:

$$p = 2l + 8$$

where l is the length (in centimetres).

a Work out the value of p if $l = 5$.

b Work out the value of p if $l = 20$.

 c Another formula for the perimeter of a rectangle is $p = 2(l + w)$, where w is the width (in centimetres).

Show that this gives the same answers for parts **a** and **b**.

 7 The formula to convert from pounds (£) to Hong Kong dollars (HK$) is:

$$d = 12.6p$$

where d is the number of Hong Kong dollars and p is the number of pounds.

Convert into Hong Kong dollars:

a £20   **b** £50   **c** £238.

(FS) **8** A formula to convert from euros (€) to pounds (£) is:

$$p = \frac{e}{1.2}$$

where e is the number of euros and p is the number of pounds.

Convert into pounds:

a €12   b €60   c €300.

(FS) **9** A plumber uses this formula to work out the cost when he visits a house to do a job:

$$c = 40 + 25h$$

where £c is the cost and the job takes h hours.

Work out the cost, if the job takes:

a 1 hour   b 2 hours   c 3 hours.

10 a A formula for the area, A, of this rectangle is $A = 5(x + 10)$.

Work out the value of A if:

i $x = 4$ **ii** $x = 10$.

b A formula for the perimeter, P, of the rectangle is $P = 2(x + 15)$.

Work out the value of P if:

i $x = 4$ **ii** $x = 8$.

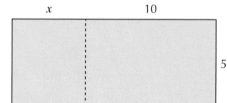

Challenge: Lines and dots

A pattern is made from lines and dots.

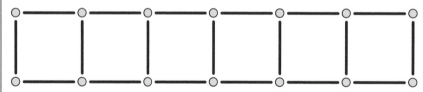

This particular pattern has six squares.

The pattern continues by adding squares on the end.

If the pattern has N squares:

- a formula for the number of lines, L, is $L = 3N + 1$
- a formula for the number of dots, D, is $D = 2N + 2$.

A Show that these formulae give the correct numbers of lines and dots if $N = 6$.

B Work out the numbers of lines and dots if the pattern is continued to make 10 squares.

C Work out the numbers of lines and dots if the pattern is continued to make 20 squares.

D Work out the numbers of lines and dots if the pattern is continued to make 100 squares.

7.4 Writing formulae

Learning objective

• To write formulae

Sometimes you will need to create your own formula to represent a statement or to solve a problem.

Example 8

Katie is k years old. Jon is j years old.

Jon is 5 years younger that Katie.

Write a formula for j in terms of k.

    A formula for j will start with $j = \ldots$

    Subtract 5 years from Katie's age to find Jon's age.

    The formula is $j = k - 5$.

Example 9

£1 is worth 4 Brazilian reals.

Write a formula to convert pounds into reals.

Use R for the number of reals and P for the number of pounds.

    To change pounds into reals you multiply by 4.

    The formula is $R = 4P$.

Example 10

a Work out a formula for the area, A, of this rectangle, in terms of t.

b Work out a formula for the perimeter, P, in terms of t.

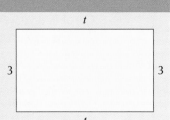

    a The area is the length × the width.

        $A = 3t$ The length is t, the width is 3.

    b The perimeter is $t + 3 + t + 3$.

        A formula for this is $P = 2t + 6$.   You could also write $P = 2(t + 3)$.

1 £1 is worth 102 Indian rupees.

Write a formula to convert pounds into rupees.

Use R for the number of rupees and P for the number of pounds.

Write your answer in the form $R = \ldots$

(FS) **2** £1 is worth 1.7 Australian dollars.

Write a formula to convert pounds into Australian dollars.

Use A for the number of Australian dollars and P for the number of pounds.

(FS) **3** 1 euro is worth 8.3 Swedish krona.

Write a formula to convert euros into Swedish krona.

Use K for the number of krona and E for the number of euros.

4 Petrol costs £1.36 per litre.

  a Work out the cost of 20 litres of petrol.

  b Write down a formula for the cost, c pounds, of l litres of petrol.

5 **a** Write a formula for the area, A, in cm², of this rectangle.

  b Write a formula for the perimeter, P cm, of the rectangle.

6 **a** Write an expression for the length of this rectangle.

  b Write a formula for the area, A, in cm², of the rectangle.

  c Write a formula for the perimeter, P cm, of the rectangle.

7 Carol is c years old. Tom is t years old. Amir is a years old.

  a Carol is 7 years older than Tom. Write a formula for Carol's age in terms of Tom's age.

    Your formula should start with $c = \ldots$

  b Amir is twice as old as Carol. Write a formula for Amir's age in terms of Tom's age.

8 Apples cost 20 pence each and oranges cost 30 pence each.

  a Write down an expression for the cost, in pence, of x apples.

  b Write down an expression for the cost, in pence, of y oranges.

  c Write down an expression for the total cost, t, in pence, of x apples and y oranges.

9 A football team gets 3 points for a win and 1 point for a draw.

    a A team had 7 wins and 4 draws. Work out the number of points they earned.

    b A team had 4 wins and 7 draws. Work out the number of points they earned.

    c Work out a formula for the number of points, p, for a team that wins w matches and draws in d matches.

10 Look at this number wall.

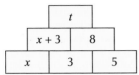

Work out a formula for the top number, t, in terms of x.

11 Here are some more number walls.

a   **b**   **c**

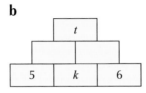 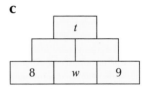

Write a formula for the top number, t, for each wall.

Investigation: Dots and squares

You will need centimetre-square dotted paper for this investigation.

Here are four shapes.

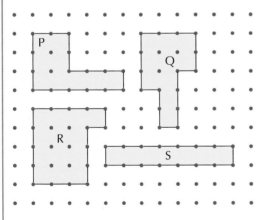

A Check that each shape has 16 dots on the perimeter.

B For each shape, work out the area, a, and the number of dots, i, inside the shape. For example, in shape P $a = 9$ and $i = 2$.

C Look at your answers to part **A** and work out a formula for a in terms of i.

D Draw some shapes of your own, with 16 dots on the outside. Check whether your formula is correct for your shapes.

Ready to progress?

 I can write simple algebraic expressions.

 I can substitute numbers into algebraic expressions, such as $2n + 3$.
I can simplify algebraic expressions such as $2a + 5a$.
I can substitute values into simple formulae.
I can construct simple formulae to show connections between variables.

Review questions

1 Write an expression for the perimeter, in cm, of each triangle. Write your answers as simply as possible.

   a   **b**   **c**

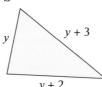

2 You are told that $a = 4$.

Work out the value of each expression.

   a $3a$ **b** $3 + a$ **c** $2a + 5$ **d** $2(a + 5)$

   e $5a - 3$ **f** $5(a - 3)$ **g** $20 - a$ **h** $\dfrac{a}{2}$

 3 You are told that $t = 7$ and $w = 16$.

Show that $3(t + w)$ and $3t + 3w$ have the same value.

4 Simplify each expression as much as possible.

   a $t + t + 6 - 2$ **b** $2x + 3x$ **c** $2a + 3b + 4b - a$

   e $d + 5 + 4d - 3$ **f** $6 + 5A - 2 - 3A$ **g** $2w - 10 + 8w - 15$

5 All the lengths in this shape are given in centimetres.

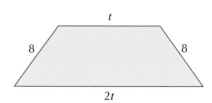

   a   Show that a formula for the perimeter, p, of this shape, in cm, is $p = 16 + 3t$.

   b   Work out the value of p if:

      i $t = 6$ **ii** $t = 11$ **iii** $t = 9.5$.

(FS) 6 The formula for changing US dollars ($) into pounds is:

$$P = 0.8D$$

where P is the number of pounds and D is the number of dollars.

Change each amount into pounds.

   a $20   **b** $500   **c** $16.50

7 For each number wall, write a formula for t in terms of c.

a 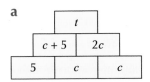   **b** 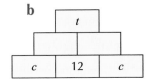   **c**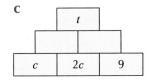

 8   Graham has £G.

Lily has £20 more than Graham.

Kazuo has twice as much as Graham.

   a   Write an expression, in terms of G, for the amount Lily has.

   b   Write an expression, in terms of G, for the amount Kazuo has.

   c   The total amount all three have is £T. Write a formula for T in terms of G.

   d   Work out the value of T if $G = 55$.

9 **a**   Work out the value of $3n - 1$ if:

      i $n = 1$ **ii** $n = 2$ **iii** $n = 3$ **iv** $n = 4$ **v** $n = 5$.

   b   The five answers to part **a** are the first five numbers of a sequence.

      i Work out the sixth number in the sequence, without using the formula.

      ii Check that the formula gives the correct answer.

   c   Use the formula to find:

      i the 10th number in the sequence

      ii the 20th number in the sequence.

Problem solving

Winter sports

You can hire equipment for snowboarding.

The cost depends on the number of days for which you want to hire the equipment.

A hire company uses these formulae to work out the cost.

	Snowboarding
Adults	$C = 8 + 16D$
Children	$C = 4 + 12D$

C is the cost in pounds.
D is the number of days of hire.

1 Work out the cost of snowboarding for one adult, for five days.

2 Work out the cost of snowboarding for one child, for four days.

3 Work out the difference in the cost of three days snowboarding for an adult or a child.

4 Work out the difference in the cost of 12 days snowboarding for an adult or a child.

5 Work out the total cost for a family of two adults and two children to hire equipment for eight days.

6 **a** Copy and complete this table.

Number of days	6	7	8	9	10
Snowboard hire for one adult (£)					

   b What is the extra cost for one extra day's hire?

7 a Draw axes like this on graph paper.

b Plot crosses to show the cost of equipment hire for one adult for from one to ten days. One cross has been plotted for you. You will find some of the costs you need in your table from Q6.

c Draw a dashed line through your ten points. It should be a straight line.

d On the same graph, plot and join crosses to show the cost of equipment hire for one child.

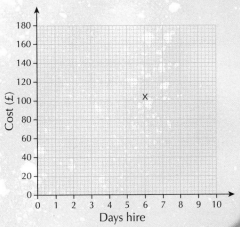

8

Fractions

This chapter is going to show you:

- how to find equivalent fractions
- how to write a fraction in its simplest form
- how to add and subtract fractions with the same and different denominators
- how to convert a simple improper fraction to a mixed number
- how to convert a mixed number into an improper fraction
- how to add and subtract mixed numbers.

You should already know:

- how to recognise and use simple fractions
- how to compare and order fractions with the same denominator.

About this chapter

For thousands of years the fraction system used in Europe was similar to the ancient Egyptian one. Egyptian fractions were all unitary fractions, that means they only had 1 as a numerator, for example, $\frac{1}{2}, \frac{1}{4}, \frac{1}{6}$. Big fractions were written as unitary fractions added together, for example, $\frac{3}{4}$ would be $\frac{1}{2} + \frac{1}{4}$.

The fractions $\frac{1}{2}, \frac{1}{4}, \frac{1}{8}, \frac{1}{16}$ and $\frac{1}{64}$ were sacred. They were linked to the Eye of the Horus, an Egyptian god, and were all used as measures for grain. You will have a chance to try Egyptian fractions in this chapter!

8.1 Equivalent fractions

Learning objectives

- To find simple equivalent fractions
- To write fractions in their simplest form

Key words	
denominator	equivalent
equivalent fraction	numerator
simplest form	simplify

Here are three rectangles.

The same fraction of each rectangle is yellow.

Look at the first rectangle. The yellow area is $\frac{3}{4}$ of the whole.

    That is 3 parts out of 4.

In the second rectangle, the yellow area is $\frac{6}{8}$ of the whole.

    That is 6 parts out of 8.

In the third rectangle, the yellow area is $\frac{9}{12}$ of the whole.

    That is 9 parts out of 12.

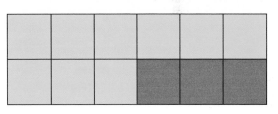

All three fractions are the same size. They are **equivalent**.

$$\frac{3}{4} = \frac{6}{8} = \frac{9}{12}$$

In the fraction $\frac{3}{4}$, 3 is the **numerator** and 4 is the **denominator**.

You can find **equivalent fractions** by multiplying both the numerator and the denominator of a fraction by the same number.

For example, if you multiply by 6: $3 \times 6 = 18$ and $4 \times 6 = 24$.

So $\frac{3}{4} = \frac{18}{24}$ and these are equivalent fractions.

Example 1

Complete these equivalent fractions.   **a** $\frac{1}{3} = \frac{\Box}{15}$ **b** $\frac{5}{8} = \frac{20}{\Box}$

  a $15 \div 3 = 5$ The denominator has been multiplied by 5.

     $1 \times 5 = 5$ Multiply the numerator by 5.

     $\frac{1}{3} = \frac{5}{15}$ The missing number is 5.

  b $20 \div 5 = 4$ The numerator has been multiplied by 4.

     $8 \times 4 = 32$ Multiply the denominator by 4.

     $\frac{5}{8} = \frac{20}{32}$ The missing number is 32.

A fraction is in its **simplest form** if you cannot divide both numerator and denominator by any whole number, other than 1. To **simplify** a fraction, write it in its simplest form.

Example 2

Write each fraction in its simplest form.

a $\frac{12}{16}$ **b** $\frac{12}{18}$

a You can divide both 12 and 16 by 4.

$\frac{12}{16} = \frac{3}{4}$ $12 \div 4 = 3$ and $16 \div 4 = 4$

b You can divide both 12 and 18 by 2.

$\frac{12}{18} = \frac{6}{9}$ $12 \div 2 = 6$ and $18 \div 2 = 9$

You can simplify it again because you can divide both 6 and 9 by 3.

$\frac{6}{9} = \frac{2}{3}$ $6 \div 3 = 2$ and $9 \div 3 = 3$

This is now its simplest form.

In the last part of Example 2, you could get the answer in one step by dividing both 12 and 18 by 6. Always check that you have simplified the fraction as much as possible.

Exercise 8A

1 What equivalent fractions do these diagrams show?
The first one has been done for you.

a 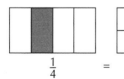 **b**

$\frac{1}{4}$ $=$ $\frac{2}{8}$

c 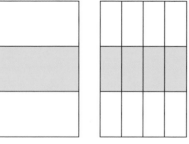 **d**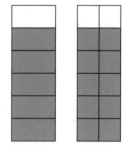

2 Draw two diagrams to show that $\frac{2}{5}$ is equivalent to $\frac{4}{10}$.

3 Complete these equivalent fractions.

a $\frac{3}{4} = \frac{9}{\square}$ **b** $\frac{1}{5} = \frac{\square}{20}$ **c** $\frac{2}{3} = \frac{8}{\square}$ **d** $\frac{5}{8} = \frac{15}{\square}$

4 Are these pairs of fractions equivalent? Say yes or no.

a $\frac{1}{3}$ and $\frac{8}{24}$ **b** $\frac{3}{4}$ and $\frac{15}{24}$ **c** $\frac{5}{8}$ and $\frac{10}{16}$ **d** $\frac{2}{5}$ and $\frac{10}{30}$

5

Multiples of 3	3	6	9	12	15
Multiples of 4	4	8	12	16	20
Multiples of 5	5	10	15	20	25

Use the multiples of 3, 4 and 5 in the table to write four fractions that are equivalent to:

a $\frac{3}{4}$ **b** $\frac{3}{5}$ **c** $\frac{4}{5}$

6 **a** Which fractions are equivalent to $\frac{1}{3}$?

b Which one is equivalent to $\frac{1}{4}$?

$\frac{5}{10}$ $\frac{5}{15}$ $\frac{8}{24}$ $\frac{12}{48}$ $\frac{9}{28}$

7 Write these fractions as simply as possible.

a $\frac{15}{20}$ **b** $\frac{15}{25}$ **c** $\frac{15}{30}$ **d** $\frac{15}{40}$

8 Write these fractions as simply as possible.

a $\frac{8}{12}$ **b** $\frac{8}{16}$ **c** $\frac{8}{18}$ **d** $\frac{8}{40}$

9 Write these fractions as simply as possible

a $\frac{9}{12}$ **b** $\frac{10}{16}$ **c** $\frac{12}{30}$ **d** $\frac{18}{24}$

(PS) **10** This compass rose has eight divisions around its face.
What fraction of a turn takes you from:

a N to E clockwise **b** E to S clockwise
c NE to SW clockwise **d** S to W anticlockwise
e NW to SW clockwise **f** N to SE clockwise?

Write your fractions in their simplest form.

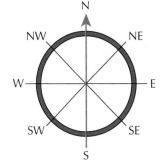

11 Write each of these fractions as simply as you can.
Some cannot be simplified.

a $\frac{12}{20}$ **b** $\frac{3}{20}$ **c** $\frac{14}{20}$ **d** $\frac{15}{20}$

e $\frac{16}{20}$ **f** $\frac{17}{20}$ **g** $\frac{18}{20}$

Problem solving: Fractions of shapes

A What fraction of this shape is blue? Give your answer in its simplest form.

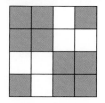

B What fraction of this shape is blue? Give your answer in its simplest form.

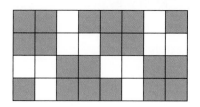

8.2 Comparing fractions

Learning objective

• To compare and order two fractions

Key word

fraction wall

You can compare fractions to each other, in terms of size. For example, $\frac{6}{8}$ is equivalent to $\frac{3}{4}$ but $\frac{1}{2}$ is bigger than $\frac{1}{4}$.

You can use a **fraction wall** to compare and order fractions.

$\frac{1}{8}$	$\frac{1}{8}$	$\frac{1}{8}$	$\frac{1}{8}$	$\frac{1}{8}$	$\frac{1}{8}$	$\frac{1}{8}$	$\frac{1}{8}$
$\frac{1}{7}$	$\frac{1}{7}$	$\frac{1}{7}$	$\frac{1}{7}$	$\frac{1}{7}$	$\frac{1}{7}$	$\frac{1}{7}$	
$\frac{1}{6}$		$\frac{1}{6}$	$\frac{1}{6}$	$\frac{1}{6}$	$\frac{1}{6}$	$\frac{1}{6}$	
$\frac{1}{5}$		$\frac{1}{5}$	$\frac{1}{5}$	$\frac{1}{5}$		$\frac{1}{5}$	
$\frac{1}{4}$		$\frac{1}{4}$		$\frac{1}{4}$		$\frac{1}{4}$	
$\frac{1}{3}$			$\frac{1}{3}$		$\frac{1}{3}$		
$\frac{1}{2}$				$\frac{1}{2}$			
1							

For example, look at the row for sixths.

The fraction $\frac{4}{6}$ is represented by four bricks, counting from left to right.

Now you compare the rows for sixths and thirds.

$\frac{1}{6}$	$\frac{1}{6}$	$\frac{1}{6}$	$\frac{1}{6}$	$\frac{1}{6}$	$\frac{1}{6}$

$\frac{1}{3}$		$\frac{1}{3}$		$\frac{1}{3}$	

You can see that $\frac{2}{3} = \frac{4}{6}$. They are equivalent fractions.

Example 3

a Use the fraction wall to decide which is smaller, $\frac{2}{3}$ or $\frac{3}{4}$.

b Check, by writing each fraction in twelfths.

    a Compare the rows for thirds and quarters.

$\frac{1}{4}$	$\frac{1}{4}$	$\frac{1}{4}$	$\frac{1}{4}$

$\frac{1}{3}$	$\frac{1}{3}$	$\frac{1}{3}$

You can see that $\frac{2}{3}$ is smaller than $\frac{3}{4}$.

b You need to find the missing number, in the sentence:

$$\frac{2}{3} = \frac{\square}{12} \qquad 3 \times 4 = 12 \text{ so multiply by } 4.$$

$$\frac{2}{3} = \frac{8}{12} \qquad 2 \times 4 = 8$$

Now you need to find the missing number, in the sentence:

$$\frac{3}{4} = \frac{\square}{12} \qquad 4 \times 3 = 12 \text{ so multiply by } 3.$$

$$\frac{3}{4} = \frac{9}{12} \qquad 3 \times 3 = 9$$

Again, this shows that $\frac{2}{3}$ is smaller than $\frac{3}{4}$.

Exercise 8B

1 Use the fraction wall to write down three fractions that are equivalent to $\frac{1}{2}$.

2 Use the fraction wall to write down fractions that are equivalent to:

    a $\frac{1}{3}$ **b** $\frac{2}{3}$ **c** $\frac{1}{4}$ **d** $\frac{3}{4}$

3 Use the fraction wall to decide which fraction is larger in each pair.

    a $\frac{1}{3}$ and $\frac{1}{5}$ **b** $\frac{2}{5}$ and $\frac{1}{3}$ **c** $\frac{4}{5}$ and $\frac{5}{6}$ **d** $\frac{4}{7}$ and $\frac{3}{8}$

    e $\frac{3}{4}$ and $\frac{4}{5}$ **f** $\frac{2}{7}$ and $\frac{1}{4}$ **g** $\frac{3}{5}$ and $\frac{4}{7}$ **h** $\frac{3}{5}$ and $\frac{5}{8}$

4 Copy and complete each number sentence.
Choose from these three phrases.

     larger than   smaller than   equal to

  a $\dfrac{6}{8}$ is ... $\dfrac{3}{4}$ **b** $\dfrac{2}{3}$ is ... $\dfrac{3}{5}$ **c** $\dfrac{4}{7}$ is ... $\dfrac{3}{4}$

  d $\dfrac{4}{6}$ is ... $\dfrac{2}{3}$ **e** $\dfrac{2}{3}$ is ... $\dfrac{5}{8}$ **f** $\dfrac{4}{7}$ is ... $\dfrac{5}{6}$

5   **a** Write each fraction in tenths

   i $\dfrac{1}{5}$ **ii** $\dfrac{2}{5}$ **iii** $\dfrac{3}{5}$ **iv** $\dfrac{4}{5}$

  b Write down which fraction is smaller.

   i $\dfrac{1}{10}$ or $\dfrac{1}{5}$ **ii** $\dfrac{7}{10}$ or $\dfrac{3}{5}$ **iii** $\dfrac{3}{10}$ or $\dfrac{2}{5}$ **iv** $\dfrac{7}{10}$ or $\dfrac{4}{5}$

6 In each part of the question:
  i write both fractions as twelfths
  ii say which fraction of the pair is larger.

  a $\dfrac{1}{2}$ and $\dfrac{1}{3}$ **b** $\dfrac{1}{3}$ and $\dfrac{1}{4}$ **c** $\dfrac{3}{4}$ and $\dfrac{5}{6}$ **d** $\dfrac{5}{6}$ and $\dfrac{2}{3}$

7 In each part of the question:
  i write the first fraction in sixteenths
  ii say which fraction of the pair is smaller.

  a $\dfrac{1}{2}$ and $\dfrac{9}{16}$ **b** $\dfrac{3}{4}$ and $\dfrac{7}{16}$ **c** $\dfrac{3}{8}$ and $\dfrac{5}{16}$ **d** $\dfrac{7}{8}$ and $\dfrac{15}{16}$

(MR) **8** Find the larger fraction in each pair.
Give a reason for each answer.

  a $\dfrac{1}{6}$ and $\dfrac{1}{4}$ **b** $\dfrac{3}{4}$ and $\dfrac{5}{8}$ **c** $\dfrac{2}{3}$ and $\dfrac{5}{9}$ **d** $\dfrac{1}{3}$ and $\dfrac{5}{12}$

Problem solving: Fraction wall

A What fractions are shown on this fraction wall?

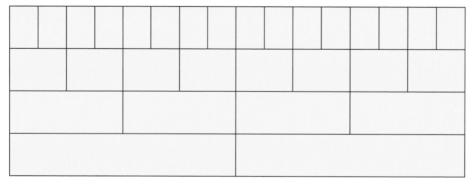

B Use the wall to put these fractions in order from smallest to largest

$\dfrac{1}{2}$ $\dfrac{1}{4}$ $\dfrac{1}{8}$ $\dfrac{1}{16}$ $\dfrac{3}{4}$ $\dfrac{3}{8}$ $\dfrac{3}{16}$ $\dfrac{5}{8}$ $\dfrac{5}{16}$ $\dfrac{7}{8}$ $\dfrac{7}{16}$ $\dfrac{9}{8}$

8.3 Adding and subtracting fractions

Learning objectives

- To add and subtract fractions with the same denominator
- To add and subtract fractions with different denominators

Key words

addition

subtraction

Fractions with the same denominator

Look at this fraction **addition**.

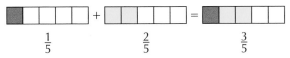

$$\frac{1}{5} \qquad \frac{2}{5} \qquad \frac{3}{5}$$

This addition is simple because both shapes are cut into pieces that are the same size, so the fractions have the same denominator.

You just add together the numerators.

Example 4

Work these out. a $\frac{3}{8} + \frac{1}{8}$ b $\frac{2}{5} + \frac{3}{5}$

In each addition, the denominators are the same, so add the numerators.

a $\frac{3}{8} + \frac{1}{8} = \frac{4}{8}$ $3 + 1 = 4$ The denominator (8) does not change.

   $= \frac{1}{2}$ 4 and 8 are both divisible by 4 so you can simplify the answer.

b $\frac{2}{5} + \frac{3}{5} = \frac{5}{5}$ $2 + 3 = 5$ The denominator does not change.

   $= 1$ 5 fifths is equal to one whole.

Subtraction of fractions with the same denominator works the same way.

Example 5

Work this out.

$\frac{3}{8} - \frac{1}{8}$

Subtract the numerators.

$\frac{3}{8} - \frac{1}{8} = \frac{2}{8}$ $3 - 1 = 2$ The denominator (8) does not change.

$\frac{2}{8} = \frac{1}{4}$ 2 and 8 are both divisible by 2 so you can simplify the answer.

---

1 Add each pair of fractions.

a $\frac{1}{5} + \frac{1}{5} = \frac{\square}{5}$ b $\frac{1}{5} + \frac{2}{5} = \frac{\square}{5}$ c $\frac{2}{5} + \frac{2}{5} = \frac{\square}{5}$ d $\frac{1}{5} + \frac{3}{5} = \frac{\square}{5}$

2 Add each pair of fractions. Write each answer as simply as possible.

a $\frac{1}{8} + \frac{1}{8} = \frac{\square}{8} = \frac{\square}{4}$ b $\frac{1}{8} + \frac{5}{8} = \frac{\square}{8} = \frac{\square}{4}$

c $\frac{3}{8} + \frac{3}{8} = \frac{\square}{8} = \frac{\square}{4}$ d $\frac{7}{8} + \frac{1}{8} = \frac{\square}{8} = \ldots$

3 Add each pair of fractions. Write each answer as simply as possible.

a $\frac{1}{10} + \frac{3}{10} = \frac{\square}{10} = \frac{\square}{5}$ b $\frac{7}{10} + \frac{1}{10} = \frac{\square}{10} = \frac{\square}{5}$

c $\frac{3}{10} + \frac{3}{10} = \frac{\square}{\square} = \frac{\square}{\square}$ d $\frac{1}{10} + \frac{9}{10} = \frac{\square}{\square} = \ldots$

4 Subtract.

a $\frac{2}{5} - \frac{1}{5} = \frac{\square}{5}$ b $\frac{4}{5} - \frac{2}{5} = \frac{\square}{5}$ c $\frac{3}{5} - \frac{1}{5} =$ d $\frac{4}{5} - \frac{3}{5} =$

5 Subtract. Write each answer as simply as possible.

a $\frac{3}{8} - \frac{1}{8} = \frac{\square}{8} = \frac{\square}{\square}$ b $\frac{5}{8} - \frac{3}{8} = \frac{\square}{8} = \frac{\square}{\square}$

c $\frac{7}{8} - \frac{1}{8} = \frac{\square}{\square} = \frac{\square}{\square}$ d $\frac{7}{8} - \frac{3}{8} = \frac{\square}{\square} = \frac{\square}{\square}$

6 Subtract. Write each answer as simply as possible.

a $\frac{3}{10} - \frac{1}{10} = \frac{\square}{10} = \frac{\square}{\square}$ b $\frac{7}{10} - \frac{3}{10} = \frac{\square}{10} = \frac{\square}{\square}$

c $\frac{9}{10} - \frac{1}{10} = \frac{\square}{\square} = \frac{\square}{\square}$ d $\frac{9}{10} - \frac{7}{10} = \frac{\square}{\square} = \frac{\square}{\square}$

7 Add the fractions in each pair. Write each answer as simply as possible.

a $\frac{1}{6} + \frac{5}{6}$ b $\frac{2}{9} + \frac{5}{9}$ c $\frac{3}{7} + \frac{2}{7}$ d $\frac{1}{12} + \frac{5}{12}$

e $\frac{7}{12} + \frac{1}{12}$ f $\frac{3}{16} + \frac{3}{16}$ g $\frac{7}{16} + \frac{3}{16}$ h $\frac{9}{16} + \frac{7}{16}$

8 Subtract. Write each answer as simply as possible.

a $\frac{5}{6} - \frac{1}{6}$ b $\frac{5}{9} - \frac{2}{9}$ c $\frac{6}{7} - \frac{2}{7}$ d $\frac{5}{12} - \frac{1}{12}$

e $\frac{7}{12} - \frac{1}{12}$ f $\frac{3}{16} - \frac{1}{16}$ g $\frac{7}{16} - \frac{3}{16}$ h $\frac{9}{16} - \frac{3}{16}$

(PS) **9** Richard cuts a cake into eighths. Mark eats one piece, Sally eats three pieces.

a What fraction does Sally eat?   b What fraction of the cake is left?

10 Amber lives $\frac{3}{8}$ of a kilometre from her friend's house. She walks there and back. What fraction of a kilometre does she walk all together?

Fractions with different denominators

Look at this fraction addition.

$$\frac{1}{4} + \frac{3}{8}$$

These fractions have different denominators.

This is part of the fraction wall from section 8.2, with $\frac{1}{4}$ and $\frac{3}{8}$ coloured.

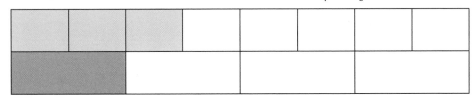

You can put them together to see that the sum is $\frac{5}{8}$.

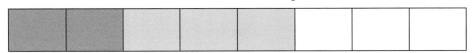

You can get this answer by changing $\frac{1}{4}$ to $\frac{2}{8}$. These are equivalent fractions.

Then:

$$\frac{1}{4} + \frac{3}{8} = \frac{2}{8} + \frac{3}{8} = \frac{5}{8}$$

Example 6

Work these out.

a $\frac{3}{10} + \frac{1}{2}$ **b** $\frac{1}{2} - \frac{1}{3}$

a To work out $\frac{3}{10} + \frac{1}{2}$ change $\frac{1}{2}$ into tenths.

$\frac{1}{2} = \frac{\square}{10}$ $10 \div 2 = 5$ so multiply the numerator by 5.

$\frac{1}{2} = \frac{5}{10}$ $1 \times 5 = 5$

So $\frac{3}{10} + \frac{1}{2} = \frac{3}{10} + \frac{5}{10} = \frac{8}{10}$ $3 + 5 = 8$ and the denominator does not change.

$\qquad\qquad = \frac{4}{5}$ You can divide 8 and 10 by 2 to simplify $\frac{8}{10}$.

b To work out $\frac{1}{2} - \frac{1}{3}$ you must change both fractions.

6 can be divided by 2 and 3 so you can change them to sixths.

$\frac{1}{2} - \frac{1}{3} = \frac{3}{6} - \frac{2}{6}$ $\frac{1}{2} = \frac{3}{6}$ and $\frac{1}{3} = \frac{2}{6}$

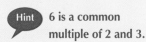

Hint 6 is a common multiple of 2 and 3.

$\qquad = \frac{1}{6}$ $3 - 2 = 1$ and the denominator does not change.

1 Complete this list of fractions equivalent to $\frac{1}{2}$.

$$\frac{1}{2} = \frac{\square}{4} = \frac{\square}{6} = \frac{\square}{8}$$

Use your answers to question **1** to help you to complete questions **2** and **3**.

Simplify your answers if you can.

2 Add these fractions.

    a $\frac{1}{4} + \frac{1}{2}$ **b** $\frac{1}{6} + \frac{1}{2}$ **c** $\frac{1}{8} + \frac{1}{2}$ **d** $\frac{1}{2} + \frac{3}{8}$

3 Do these subtractions.

    a $\frac{1}{2} - \frac{1}{4}$ **b** $\frac{1}{2} - \frac{1}{8}$ **c** $\frac{1}{2} - \frac{3}{8}$ **d** $\frac{1}{2} - \frac{1}{6}$

4 Complete this list of fractions equivalent to $\frac{1}{3}$.

$$\frac{1}{3} = \frac{\square}{6} = \frac{\square}{9} = \frac{\square}{12}$$

Use your answers to question **4** to help you to complete questions **5** and **6**.

Simplify your answers if you can.

5 Add these fractions. Simplify your answers if you can.

    a $\frac{1}{3} + \frac{1}{6}$ **b** $\frac{1}{3} + \frac{1}{9}$ **c** $\frac{1}{3} + \frac{2}{9}$ **d** $\frac{1}{3} + \frac{1}{12}$

    e $\frac{1}{3} + \frac{5}{12}$ **f** $\frac{1}{3} + \frac{7}{12}$ **g** $\frac{2}{3} + \frac{1}{6}$ **h** $\frac{2}{3} + \frac{1}{12}$

6 Do these subtractions.

    a $\frac{1}{3} - \frac{1}{6}$ **b** $\frac{1}{3} - \frac{1}{9}$ **c** $\frac{1}{3} - \frac{2}{9}$ **d** $\frac{1}{3} - \frac{1}{12}$

    e $\frac{5}{12} - \frac{1}{3}$ **f** $\frac{7}{12} - \frac{1}{3}$ **g** $\frac{2}{3} - \frac{1}{6}$ **h** $\frac{2}{3} - \frac{1}{12}$

7 Work out these additions.

Write the answers as simply as possible.

    a $\frac{1}{8} + \frac{1}{4}$ **b** $\frac{5}{8} + \frac{1}{4}$ **c** $\frac{1}{8} + \frac{3}{4}$ **d** $\frac{1}{4} + \frac{3}{8}$

    e $\frac{1}{2} + \frac{1}{10}$ **f** $\frac{1}{2} + \frac{3}{10}$ **g** $\frac{1}{4} + \frac{1}{12}$ **h** $\frac{1}{4} + \frac{7}{12}$

8 Work out these subtractions.

Write the answers as simply as possible.

a $\frac{1}{4} - \frac{1}{8}$ **b** $\frac{5}{8} - \frac{1}{4}$ **c** $\frac{1}{2} - \frac{1}{10}$ **d** $\frac{1}{2} - \frac{3}{10}$

e $\frac{3}{4} - \frac{1}{8}$ **f** $\frac{1}{4} - \frac{1}{12}$ **g** $\frac{7}{12} - \frac{1}{2}$ **h** $\frac{11}{12} - \frac{3}{4}$

9   **a** Change $\frac{1}{2}$ and $\frac{1}{3}$ to sixths.

    b Work out $\frac{1}{2} - \frac{1}{3}$.

10   **a** Change $\frac{1}{3}$, $\frac{2}{3}$ and $\frac{1}{4}$ to twelfths.

    b Work these out.

      i $\frac{1}{3} + \frac{1}{4}$ **ii** $\frac{1}{3} - \frac{1}{4}$ **iii** $\frac{2}{3} - \frac{1}{4}$ **iv** $\frac{2}{3} + \frac{1}{4}$

(PS) **11** Jonas has two cartons of milk. One contains $\frac{1}{4}$ of a litre. The other contains $\frac{3}{8}$ of a litre.
Work out the total amount of milk.

(PS) **12** Maria has some apples. She gives $\frac{1}{3}$ of them to Peter and $\frac{1}{6}$ of them to Paul.
What fraction of the original number does she have left?

Investigation: Ancient Egyptian fractions

The ancient Egyptians only used unit fractions.

These are fractions with a numerator of 1.

These are unit fractions.

$$\frac{1}{2}, \frac{1}{3}, \frac{1}{4}, \dots$$

A   **a** Work out these additions of unit fractions.

      i $\frac{1}{2} + \frac{1}{4}$ **ii** $\frac{1}{2} + \frac{1}{8}$ **iii** $\frac{1}{2} + \frac{1}{12}$

      iv $\frac{1}{2} + \frac{1}{16}$ **v** $\frac{1}{2} + \frac{1}{20}$

   b Describe any pattern you can see in your
answers to part **a**.

B   **a** Work out these additions of unit fractions. Write your answers as simply as possible.

      i $\frac{1}{2} + \frac{1}{6}$ **ii** $\frac{1}{2} + \frac{1}{10}$ **iii** $\frac{1}{2} + \frac{1}{14}$ **iv** $\frac{1}{2} + \frac{1}{18}$

   b Describe any pattern you can see in your answers to part **a**.

8.4 Mixed numbers and improper fractions

Learning objectives

• To convert mixed numbers to improper fractions

• To convert improper fractions to mixed numbers

Key words

convert

improper fraction

mixed number

This diagram shows one whole and another three quarters.

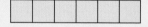

You can write this in two ways: either as $1\frac{3}{4}$ or as $\frac{7}{4}$.

$1\frac{3}{4}$ is called a **mixed number** because it has a whole number part and a fraction part.

$\frac{7}{4}$ is called an **improper fraction** because the numerator is greater than the denominator.

You can **convert** (change) improper fractions to mixed numbers and mixed numbers to improper fractions.

Example 7

Write these improper fractions as mixed numbers.

a $\dfrac{13}{6}$ **b** $\dfrac{13}{8}$

   a Here is a diagram to show 13 sixths.

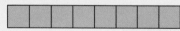 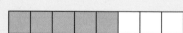

     The rectangles are divided into sixths and 13 of the sixths are shaded.

     $\frac{13}{6} = 2\frac{1}{6}$ You can get that answer by saying $13 \div 6 = 2$ remainder 1.

   b This diagram shows 13 eighths.

     $\frac{13}{8} = 1\frac{5}{8}$ You can get that answer by saying $13 \div 8 = 1$ remainder 5.

Example 8

   a How many fifths are there in 4 whole ones?

   b Work out the number of eighths in $2\frac{3}{8}$.

     a There are 5 fifths in one whole one.

     So there are 20 fifths in 4 whole ones. $4 \times 5 = 20$

b This diagram shows $2\frac{3}{8}$.

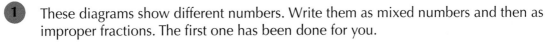

The number of eighths is $2 \times 8 + 3$.   8 for each whole one plus three more.

$$= 19$$

So $2\frac{3}{8} = \frac{19}{8}$ You read this as '19 eighths'.

Exercise 8E

1 These diagrams show different numbers. Write them as mixed numbers and then as improper fractions. The first one has been done for you.

a 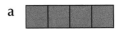 $1\frac{3}{4} = \frac{7}{4}$

b

c

d     

e 

f

2 Draw diagrams to illustrate these mixed numbers. Then write them as improper fractions.

    a $3\frac{1}{2}$ **b** $2\frac{3}{4}$ **c** $1\frac{5}{8}$ **d** $4\frac{2}{5}$

3 Work out the number of thirds in:

    a   2   **b**   4   **c**   5   **d** $2\frac{2}{3}$ **e** $4\frac{1}{3}$

4 Work out the number of eighths in each number.

    a   2   **b**   3   **c**   4   **d** $2\frac{7}{8}$ **e** $3\frac{5}{8}$

5 Write each mixed number as an improper fraction.

a $2\frac{1}{2}$ b $2\frac{1}{4}$ c $2\frac{1}{8}$ d $2\frac{5}{8}$

6 Write each mixed number as an improper fraction.

a $3\frac{1}{4}$ b $4\frac{4}{5}$ c $1\frac{9}{20}$ d $4\frac{5}{6}$

e $6\frac{3}{4}$ f $5\frac{2}{3}$ g $4\frac{7}{8}$ h $9\frac{1}{5}$

7 Write each improper fraction as a mixed number.

a $\frac{9}{4}$ b $\frac{9}{5}$ c $\frac{9}{2}$ d $\frac{13}{8}$

e $\frac{13}{6}$ f $\frac{13}{3}$ g $\frac{13}{2}$ h $\frac{25}{12}$

8 These improper fractions are not in their simplest form. Work out the simplest form for each one.

a $\frac{12}{8}$ b $\frac{14}{6}$ c $\frac{15}{6}$ d $\frac{10}{4}$

9 These improper fractions are not in their simplest form. Work out the simplest form for each one and then write it as a mixed number.

a $\frac{10}{4}$ b $\frac{18}{8}$ c $\frac{21}{6}$ d $\frac{20}{8}$

e $\frac{25}{10}$ f $\frac{16}{8}$ g $\frac{15}{10}$ h $\frac{30}{12}$

(PS) 10 Match each improper fraction to the correct mixed number.

$1\frac{5}{8}$ $1\frac{1}{2}$ $2\frac{1}{4}$ $2\frac{3}{4}$ $2\frac{1}{2}$

$\frac{10}{4}$ $\frac{9}{4}$ $\frac{12}{8}$ $\frac{22}{8}$ $\frac{13}{8}$

Challenge: Fractions in sequences

A Here is a sequence of six numbers. They increase by $\frac{3}{4}$ each time.

$\frac{3}{4}$ $\frac{6}{4}$ $\frac{9}{4}$ $\frac{12}{4}$ $\frac{15}{4}$ $\frac{18}{4}$

  a Copy the sequence but write each number as a mixed number as simply as possible.

  b Work out the next two numbers in the sequence.

B Repeat part **A** with this sequence, where the numbers increase by $\frac{3}{8}$ each time.

$\frac{3}{8}$ $\frac{6}{8}$ $\frac{9}{8}$ $\frac{12}{8}$ $\frac{15}{8}$ $\frac{18}{8}$

8.5 Calculations with mixed numbers

Learning objectives

- To add and subtract simple mixed numbers with the same denominator
- To add and subtract simple mixed numbers with different denominators

Sometimes, when you add two fractions, the answer is an improper fraction. Write it as a mixed number, as simple as possible.

Example 9

Work this out. $\frac{5}{8} + \frac{7}{8}$

$\frac{5}{8} + \frac{7}{8} = \frac{12}{8}$ The denominators are the same. Add the numerators.

$= \frac{3}{2}$ 4 is a factor of 12 and 8 so divide numerator and denominator by 4.

$= 1\frac{1}{2}$ $3 \div 2 = 1$ remainder 1

You will get the same answer if you write $\frac{12}{8}$ as a mixed number and then simplify.

$\frac{12}{8} = 1\frac{4}{8}$ $12 \div 8 = 1$ remainder 4

$= 1\frac{1}{2}$ $\frac{4}{8}$ is equivalent to $\frac{1}{2}$.

To add or subtract mixed numbers

1. Write them as improper fractions.
2. Add or subtract.
3. Write the answer as a mixed number, as simply as possible.

Example 10

Work these out.   **a** $2\frac{2}{3} + \frac{5}{6}$ **b** $4\frac{1}{2} - 1\frac{3}{4}$

a $2\frac{2}{3} + \frac{5}{6} = \frac{8}{3} + \frac{5}{6}$ $2 \times 3 + 2 = 8$ so $2\frac{2}{3} = \frac{8}{3}$

$= \frac{16}{6} + \frac{5}{6}$ Change $\frac{8}{3}$ to sixths by doubling the numerator and denominator.

$= \frac{21}{6}$ $16 + 5 = 21$

$= \frac{7}{2}$ 3 is a factor of 21 and 6. $21 \div 3 = 7$ and $6 \div 3 = 2$

$= 3\frac{1}{2}$ $7 \div 2 = 3$ remainder 1

b $4\frac{1}{2} - 1\frac{3}{4} = \frac{9}{2} - \frac{7}{4}$ Write them both as improper fractions.

$= \frac{18}{4} - \frac{7}{4}$ Change $\frac{9}{2}$ to quarters. Double the numerator and denominator.

$= \frac{11}{4}$ This cannot be simplified.

$= 2\frac{3}{4}$ $11 \div 4 = 2$ remainder 3

Exercise 8F

1 Work out these additions.
Give each answer as a mixed number, as simply as possible.

a $\frac{3}{4} + \frac{3}{4}$ **b** $\frac{7}{8} + \frac{3}{8}$ **c** $\frac{4}{5} + \frac{3}{5}$ **d** $\frac{7}{8} + \frac{9}{8}$

e $\frac{7}{12} + \frac{5}{12}$ **f** $\frac{7}{12} + \frac{11}{12}$ **g** $\frac{5}{6} + \frac{5}{6}$ **h** $\frac{9}{16} + \frac{13}{16}$

2 Work out these additions.
Give each answer as a mixed number, as simply as possible.

a $1\frac{3}{4} + \frac{3}{4}$ **b** $2\frac{1}{2} + 1\frac{1}{2}$ **c** $1\frac{3}{8} + \frac{7}{8}$ **d** $1\frac{2}{5} + \frac{4}{5}$

e $\frac{5}{6} + 1\frac{5}{6}$ **f** $1\frac{7}{12} + \frac{5}{12}$ **g** $\frac{2}{3} + 2\frac{2}{3}$ **h** $3\frac{9}{10} + \frac{3}{10}$

3 Work out these subtractions.
Give each answer as a mixed number, as simply as possible.

a $1\frac{3}{4} - \frac{1}{4}$ **b** $4\frac{1}{2} - \frac{1}{2}$ **c** $1\frac{5}{8} - \frac{3}{8}$ **d** $2\frac{1}{5} - \frac{3}{5}$

e $3\frac{1}{6} - \frac{5}{6}$ **f** $2\frac{3}{10} - \frac{7}{10}$ **g** $4\frac{1}{3} - \frac{2}{3}$ **h** $1\frac{3}{8} - \frac{7}{8}$

4 Work out these subtractions.
Give each answer as a mixed number, as simply as possible.

a $3\frac{1}{4} - 1\frac{3}{4}$ **b** $4\frac{1}{5} - 1\frac{3}{5}$ **c** $3\frac{1}{8} - 1\frac{3}{8}$ **d** $3\frac{1}{12} - 1\frac{7}{12}$

5 Work out these additions.

Give each answer as a mixed number, as simply as possible.

a $1\frac{1}{2} + \frac{3}{4}$
b $2\frac{3}{4} + \frac{1}{2}$
c $1\frac{3}{8} + 1\frac{1}{4}$
d $1\frac{2}{5} + 1\frac{3}{10}$

e $1\frac{1}{6} + \frac{7}{12}$
f $1\frac{5}{8} + \frac{3}{4}$
g $2\frac{1}{2} + 2\frac{1}{8}$
h $2\frac{2}{3} + 3\frac{1}{6}$

6 Work out these subtractions.

Give each answer as a mixed number, as simply as possible.

a $1\frac{1}{2} - \frac{3}{4}$
b $2\frac{3}{4} - \frac{1}{2}$
c $2\frac{3}{8} - 1\frac{1}{4}$
d $3\frac{2}{5} - 1\frac{3}{10}$

e $3\frac{1}{3} - 1\frac{5}{6}$
f $1\frac{5}{8} - \frac{3}{4}$
g $4\frac{1}{2} - 2\frac{5}{8}$
h $5\frac{2}{3} - 2\frac{1}{6}$

7 Work out these calculations.

Give each answer as simply as possible.

a $1\frac{1}{2} + \frac{1}{3}$
b $1\frac{2}{3} + \frac{1}{2}$
c $2\frac{1}{2} + \frac{2}{3}$
d $2\frac{1}{3} + 2\frac{1}{2}$

 Hint Change the fractions to sixths each time.

e $1\frac{1}{2} - \frac{1}{3}$
f $1\frac{2}{3} - \frac{1}{2}$
g $2\frac{1}{2} - \frac{2}{3}$
h $2\frac{1}{3} - \frac{1}{2}$

(PS) **8** The answer to each question is either $1\frac{3}{4}$ or $2\frac{1}{4}$.

Decide which it is, in each case.

a $1\frac{1}{2} + \frac{3}{4}$
b $2\frac{1}{2} - \frac{3}{4}$
c $1\frac{1}{8} + \frac{5}{8}$

d $1\frac{3}{8} + \frac{7}{8}$
e $3\frac{1}{4} - 1\frac{1}{2}$
f $4\frac{1}{2} - 2\frac{1}{4}$

Challenge: Fraction square

Here is an addition table for mixed numbers.

Copy it and fill in the gaps.

Write your answers as simply as possible.

+	$1\frac{1}{8}$	$1\frac{3}{8}$	$1\frac{1}{2}$
$1\frac{1}{4}$	$2\frac{3}{8}$		
$1\frac{5}{8}$		$3\frac{1}{8}$	
$1\frac{7}{8}$			

Ready to progress?

 I can find simple equivalent fractions.

I can write fractions in their simplest form.
I can add and subtract fractions with the same denominator.

I can add and subtract fractions with different denominators.
I can convert between mixed numbers and improper fractions.
I can add and subtract mixed numbers.

Review questions

1   Copy and complete these equivalent fractions.

   a $\dfrac{1}{4} = \dfrac{5}{\square}$ b $\dfrac{2}{3} = \dfrac{\square}{12}$ c $\dfrac{3}{8} = \dfrac{9}{\square}$ d $\dfrac{1}{5} = \dfrac{\square}{25}$

2   Work out the fraction of this rectangle that is coloured:

   a   red   b   green   c   yellow.

   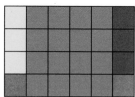

   Write your answers as simply as possible.

3   Write each improper fraction as a mixed number, as simply as possible.

   a $\dfrac{18}{12}$ b $\dfrac{20}{15}$ c $\dfrac{17}{4}$ d $\dfrac{30}{8}$

4   Here is a sequence of numbers.

   $1\frac{3}{4}$ 2 $2\frac{1}{4}$ $2\frac{1}{2}$ ...   ... $3\frac{1}{4}$ 4

   Work out the missing numbers.

5   Work out these additions and subtractions.

   Write the answers as simply as possible.

   a $\dfrac{3}{8} + \dfrac{1}{8}$ b $\dfrac{4}{5} - \dfrac{1}{5}$ c $\dfrac{5}{6} + \dfrac{5}{6}$ d $\dfrac{7}{8} - \dfrac{3}{8}$

6   Work out these additions and subtractions.

Write the answers as simply as possible.

a $1\frac{3}{8} + 2\frac{5}{8}$ b $3\frac{1}{5} - 2\frac{3}{5}$ c $1\frac{3}{4} + 3\frac{3}{4}$ d $5\frac{1}{3} - 1\frac{2}{3}$

7   Work out these additions and subtractions.

Write the answers as simply as possible.

a $2\frac{1}{8} + 2\frac{1}{2}$ b $6\frac{1}{4} - 1\frac{1}{2}$ c $4\frac{1}{3} + 1\frac{5}{6}$ d $3\frac{1}{4} - 1\frac{5}{8}$

8   Work out the perimeter of this triangle.

Give your answer as a mixed number.

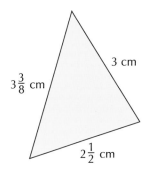

3 cm

$3\frac{3}{8}$ cm

$2\frac{1}{2}$ cm

9   Work out the missing numbers in these additions.

a $2\frac{1}{4} + \ldots = 3\frac{3}{4}$ b $4\frac{3}{5} + \ldots = 7$ c $1\frac{3}{4} + \ldots = 3\frac{1}{2}$

10 Here are seven masses.

$2\frac{1}{2}$ kg $1\frac{3}{4}$ kg $4\frac{1}{4}$ kg   2 kg $2\frac{1}{2}$ kg $4\frac{1}{2}$ kg $3\frac{1}{2}$ kg

Work out the median mass. Show your method.

PS 11 Perry is $1\frac{3}{4}$ m tall and Sherrie is $1\frac{5}{8}$ m tall.

Who is the taller, and by what fraction of a metre?

Challenge

Fractional dissections

Task 1

This rectangle has 12 squares.
It is divided into three parts.

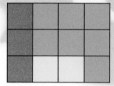

a Check that the red part is $\frac{1}{4}$, the yellow part is $\frac{1}{6}$ and the green part is $\frac{7}{12}$.

This shows that $\frac{1}{4} + \frac{1}{6} + \frac{7}{12} = 1$.

This is one way to write the whole rectangle as the sum of three fractions with different denominators (in this case 4, 6 and 12). We can call this a triple dissection of the rectangle.

b Draw a diagram to show that a different triple dissection of this rectangle is $\frac{3}{4} + \frac{1}{6} + \frac{1}{12}$.

c Draw a diagram to show that $\frac{1}{4} + \frac{1}{3} + \frac{5}{12}$. is another triple dissection of this triangle.

Task 2

a Draw a triple dissection for this rectangle.
Write down the three fractions.

b There are two different triple dissections
for this rectangle. Draw each one and write
down the three fractions each time.

Task 3

Here is a rectangle with 18 squares.

There are nine different triple dissections for this rectangle.

a One triple dissection is $\frac{1}{2} + \frac{1}{18} + \frac{4}{9}$. Illustrate this with a diagram.

b A second triple dissection is $\frac{1}{6} + \frac{1}{9} + \frac{13}{18}$. Illustrate this with a diagram.

c Work out a third triple dissection for this rectangle and illustrate it with a diagram.

Task 4

A unit fraction is a fraction with a numerator of 1.

Examples are $\frac{1}{2}$, $\frac{1}{5}$ and $\frac{1}{12}$.

a This rectangle has been divided into three unit fractions.

What are they?

b This is the same rectangle. It has been divided into four unit fractions.

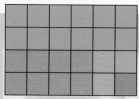

What are they?

c Now the same rectangle has been divided into six unit fractions.

What are they?

9

Angles

This chapter is going to show you:

- how to use a compass to give directions
- how to measure angles
- how to draw angles
- how to calculate angles at a point, angles on a straight line and opposite angles
- how to recognise parallel, intersecting and perpendicular lines
- how to explain the geometrical properties of triangles and quadrilaterals.

You should already know:

- the names of the different types of angle
- the names of different triangles and quadrilaterals.

About this chapter

In the past, sailors used to stay close to shore so that they could find their way by looking at the coast. Then some discovered that the height or angle of the Sun at midday, or the North Star at night, helped them work out how far north or south they were. They had observed that all of the other stars move across the sky as the Earth rotates, but the North Star is always in the same place in the night sky.

The picture shows how to find the North Star, by drawing an imaginary line from the last two stars of the constellation called the Plough, and extending it.

9.1 Using the compass to give directions

Learning objective

• To use a compass to give directions

Key words

anticlockwise	clockwise
compass	

Have you ever used a **compass**? It shows the four main directions: north, east, south and west.

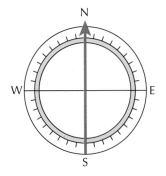

Example 1

Describe how to move from A to B on the grid.

Move 4 squares north.

Then move 3 squares west.

You can use a compass to find the amount of turn you need to get from one direction to another.

You need to know two things when you describe a turn.

• The direction of the turn, which may be **clockwise** or **anticlockwise**:

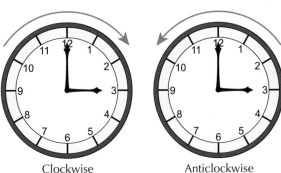

Clockwise　　　　　Anticlockwise

• The amount of turn:

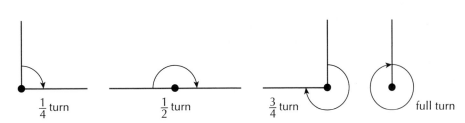

$\frac{1}{4}$ turn　　　$\frac{1}{2}$ turn　　　$\frac{3}{4}$ turn　　　full turn

Example 2

Imagine you are standing facing south.

What direction will you be facing, after you make a quarter-turn clockwise?

A quarter-turn clockwise will leave you facing west.

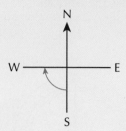

Example 3

Imagine you are standing facing east.

What direction will you be facing, after you make a three-quarter turn anticlockwise?

A three-quarter turn anticlockwise will leave you facing south.

Exercise 9A

1 Describe how to move from A to B on each grid.

a
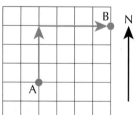

b
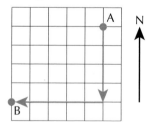

c
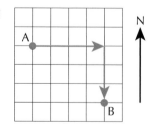

d
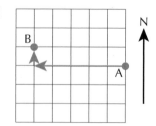

2 Copy this grid.

a Show the position of the point X after it moves 3 squares east and then 2 squares south.

b Show the position of the point X after it moves 2 squares north and then 4 squares east.

c Show the position of the point X after it moves 3 squares west and then 1 square north.

d Show the position of the point X after it moves 3 squares south and then 3 squares west.

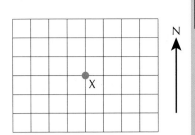

 3 Write down two different ways to move from A to B, using three compass directions.

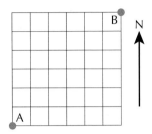

4 Describe each turn, in words.

a

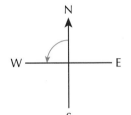

b

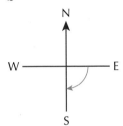

c

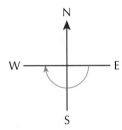

d

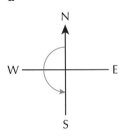

e

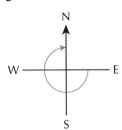

f

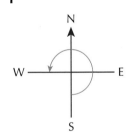

5 Copy and complete the table.

	Starting direction	Amount of turn	Finishing direction
a	North	Quarter turn clockwise	
b	West	Quarter turn anticlockwise	
c	South	Half turn clockwise	
d	East	Half turn anticlockwise	
e	North	Three-quarter turn clockwise	
f	West	Three-quarter turn anticlockwise	

6 Write down the point that is:

   a west of E   **b** north of H

   c east of F   **d** south of B.

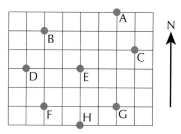

7 Look at the map of England.

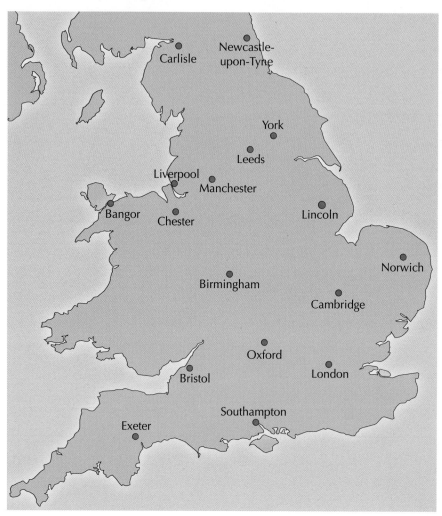

   a Which city is south of Newcastle-upon-Tyne?

   b Which city is east of Bangor?

   c Which city is west of Manchester?

   d Which city is north of Southampton?

Challenge: More directions

This compass rose shows four more compass directions.

NE stands for north-east.

SE stands for south-east.

SW stands for south-west.

NW stands for north-west.

Look at this map of Europe.

A   Name a city that is north of Rome.

B   Name a city that is south of Warsaw.

C   Name a city that is south-west of London.

D   Name a city that is north-west of Munich.

E   Name a city that is south-east of Paris.

F   Name a city that is north-east of Madrid.

9.2 Measuring angles

Learning objectives

- To know the different types of angle
- To use a protractor to measure an angle

Key words	
acute angle	angle
degrees	obtuse angle
protractor	right angle
triangle	

When two lines meet at a point they make an **angle**. Angles are measured in **degrees** (°).

Types of angle

This angle is 90° and is called a **right angle**.

This angle is 180° and is called a half turn.

This angle is 360° and is called a full turn.

This angle is less than 90° and is called an **acute angle**.

This angle is greater than 90° but is less than 180° and is called an **obtuse angle.**

Here are some acute angles.

Here are some obtuse angles.

You will need to use a protractor to measure angles.

Notice that there are two scales on the protractor.

The outer scale goes from 0° to 180° and the inner one goes from 180° to 0°.

It is important to remember to use the correct scale.

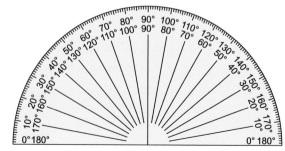

When measuring or drawing an angle, always decide first whether it is an acute angle (less than 90°) or an obtuse angle (more than 90°).

Example 4

Measure this angle.

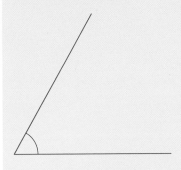

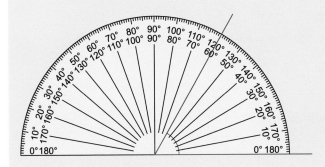

First, decide whether the angle to be measured is acute or obtuse.

This is an acute angle (less than 90°).

Place the centre of the protractor at the corner of the angle, as in the diagram.

The two angles shown on the protractor scales are 60° and 120°.

Since you are measuring an acute angle, the angle is 60°.

Example 5

Measure this obtuse angle.

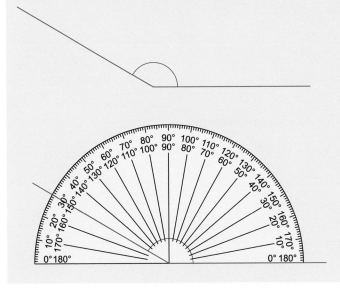

Place the centre of the protractor at the corner of the angle, as in the diagram.

The two angles shown on the protractor scales are 30° and 150°.

Since you are measuring an obtuse angle, the angle is 150°.

1 Write down whether each angle is acute or obtuse.

a   b   c   d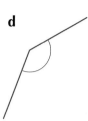

2 This shape has seven angles.

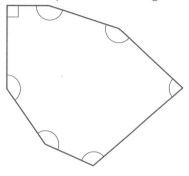

    a How many of the angles are right angles?

    b How many are acute angles?

    c How many are obtuse angles?

3 Which of these angles are acute angles?

a   b   c  d

4 Which of these angles are obtuse angles?

a   b   c   d

5 List these acute angles in order, from smallest to largest.

a  b  c 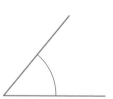 d

6 List these obtuse angles in order, from smallest to largest.

a
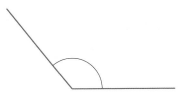

b

c
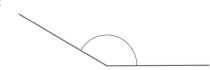

d

7 Measure each angle.

a
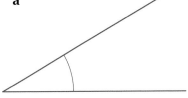

b
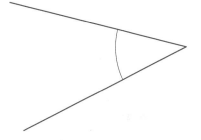

c
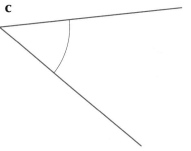

d
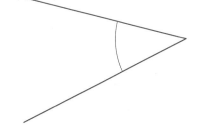

e
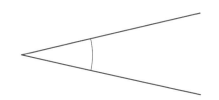

f
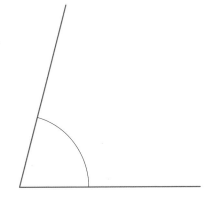

g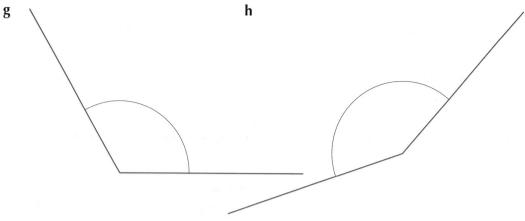 h

i j

8 **a** Measure the three angles in this **triangle**.

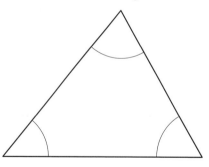

b Add the three angles together. What is the sum of the angles?

 9 **a** Measure the three angles in this triangle.

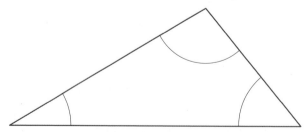

b Add the three angles together. What is the sum of the angles?

c You should now be able to complete this statement.

In any triangle, the sum of the three angles is always ….

Challenge: Estimating angles

A Copy the table below.

Angle	Estimate	Actual	Difference
1			
2			
3			
4			

B Estimate the size of each of the four angles below.

Write your estimate in the 'Estimate' column of your table.

1

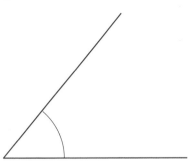

2

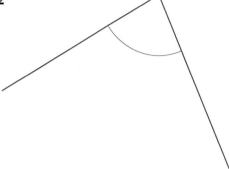

3

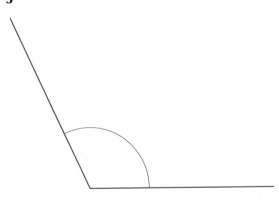

4

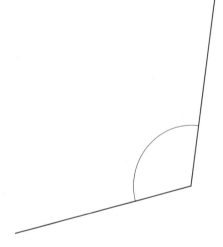

C Now measure each angle, to the nearest degree, and write the size in the 'Actual' column.

D Work out the difference between your estimate and the actual measurement for each angle and complete the 'Difference' column.

9.3 Drawing angles

Learning objective

* To use a protractor to draw an angle

Carefully follow the two examples below.

Example 6

Draw and label an angle of 70°.

First draw a line about 5 cm long.

Then place the middle of the protractor at one end of the line.

Put a mark on 70° as it is an acute angle.

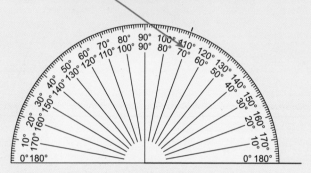

Label the angle.

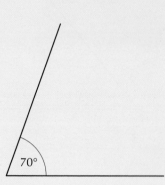

Now draw a line from the end of your first line, to the mark you have made.

Example 7

Draw and label an angle of 125°.

First draw a line about 5 cm long.

Then place the middle of the protractor at one end of the line.

Put a mark on 125° as it is an obtuse angle.

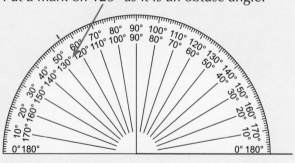

Label the angle.

125°

Now draw a line from the end of your first line, to the mark you have made.

Exercise 9C

1 Draw and label these acute angles.

    a 20°   **b** 40°   **c** 60°   **d** 80°

2 Draw and label these obtuse angles.

    a 110°   **b** 130°   **c** 150°   **d** 170°

3 Draw and label each acute angle.

    a 25°   **b** 45°   **c** 65°   **d** 85°

4 Draw and label each obtuse angle.

    a 95°   **b** 125°   **c** 135°   **d** 175°

5 Draw these angles accurately.

a

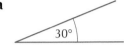

b

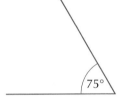

c

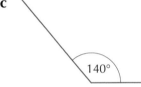

d

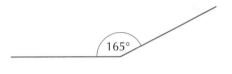

6 Draw these diagrams accurately.

a

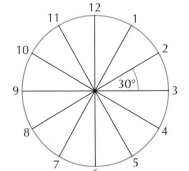

b

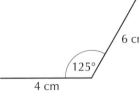

c

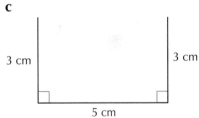

PS **7** Use these diagrams to draw an accurate clock face.

Set the clock at your favourite time of day.

Challenge: Drawing triangles

A Follow the instructions to draw this triangle accurately.

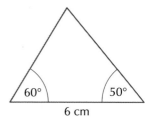

1 First draw a line 6 cm long.

2 Then draw the angle of 60°.

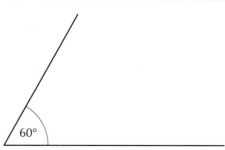

3 Then draw the angle of 50°.

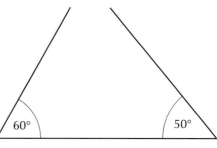

4 Then complete the triangle.

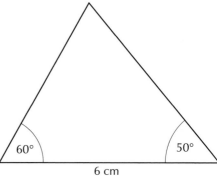

B Draw these triangles accurately.

a

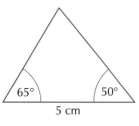

b

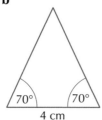

c

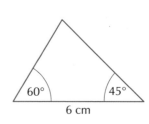

d

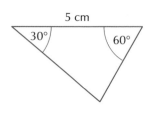

9.4 Calculating angles

Learning objectives

- To calculate angles at a point
- To calculate angles on a line
- To calculate opposite angles

Key words

angles on a straight line

angles at a point

calculate

opposite angles

You can often **calculate** (work out) the unknown angles in a diagram, from the information that you are given.

Unknown angles are usually denoted by letters, such as a, b, c, x, y,...

Remember that diagrams are not usually drawn accurately, or to scale.

Right angles

In the diagram, the square symbol means that the angle is 90°.

Example 8

Calculate the size of the angle labelled x.

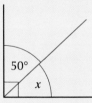

$x = 90° - 50°$

$x = 40°$

Angles on a straight line

Angles on a straight line add up to 180°.

Example 9

Calculate the size of the angle labelled b.

The two angles on a straight line add up to 180° so:

$b = 180° - 155°$

$b = 25°$

Angles at a point

Angles at a point add up to 360°.

Example 10

Calculate the size of the angle labelled *a*.

The three angles add up to 360° so:

$a = 360° - 150° - 130°$

$a = 80°$

Opposite angles

When two lines intersect, the **opposite angles** are equal.

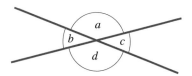

$a = d$ and $b = c$

Example 11

Calculate the sizes of the angles labelled *d* and *e*.

Give a reason for your answers.

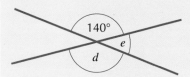

Opposite angles are equal so:

$d = 140°$

Angles on a straight line add up to 180° so:

$e = 180° - 140°$

$e = 40°$

1 Calculate the size of each unknown angle.

a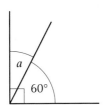

b

c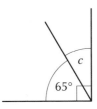

d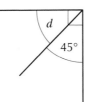

2 Calculate the size of each unknown angle.

a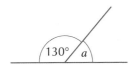

b

c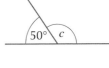

d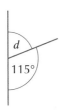

e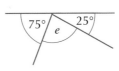

f

MR **3** Three of these angles will fit together to make a straight line.

a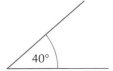

b

c

d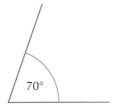

e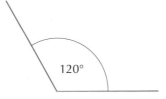

Which three are they?

4 Calculate the size of each unknown angle.

a

b
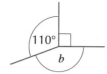

c

d
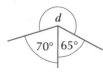

e

f
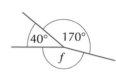

5 Calculate the size of each unknown angle.

a
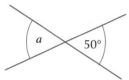

b

c
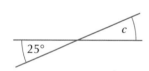

d

6 Calculate the size of each unknown angle.

a
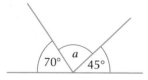

b

c
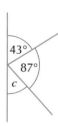

d
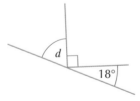

e
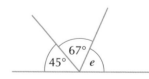

f
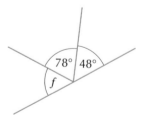

7 Calculate the size of each unknown angle.

a

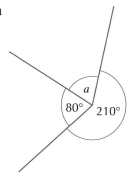

b

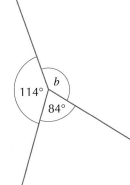

c

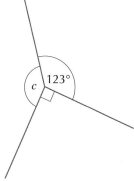

d

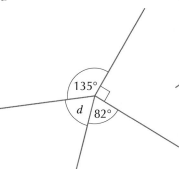

e

f

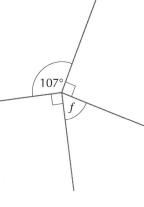

8 Calculate the size of each unknown angle.

a

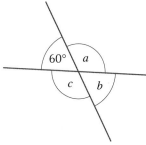

b

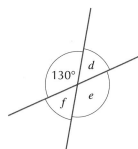

c

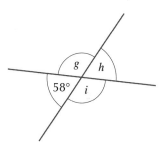

Reasoning: Calculating angles

Calculate the size of each unknown angle.

A

B

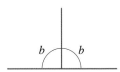

C

D

E

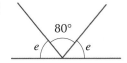

F

9.5 Properties of triangles and quadrilaterals

Learning objectives

- To understand the properties of parallel, intersecting and perpendicular lines
- To understand and use the properties of triangles
- To understand and use the properties of quadrilaterals

Key words

diagonal	geometrical properties
intersect	parallel
perpendicular	vertex, vertices

Describing lines

This line has point A at one end and point B at the other, so you can describe it as the line AB.

A ————————————————— B

Two lines will always either be **parallel** or **intersect**.

Parallel lines never meet. You show that lines are parallel by putting arrows on them.

These two lines **intersect** at a point X.

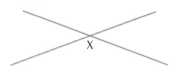

These two lines intersect at right angles.

The lines are said to be **perpendicular**.

A **diagonal** is a line that joins two corners of a shape.

This rectangle has two diagonals.

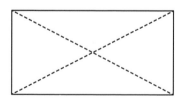

Describing angles

The angle at B can be written as:

∠B or ∠ABC or angle ABC.

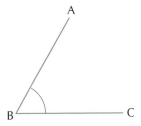

Describing triangles and quadrilaterals

The triangle can be described as triangle ABC.

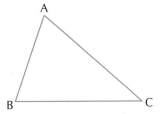

Each corner is called a **vertex**.

So it has:

- three **vertices**, A, B and C
- three angles, ∠A, ∠B and ∠C
- three sides, AB, AC and BC.

The quadrilateral can be described as quadrilateral ABCD.

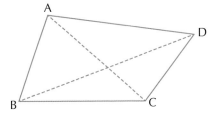

It has:

- four vertices, A, B, C and D
- four angles, ∠A, ∠B, ∠C and ∠D
- four sides, AB, BC, CD and AD
- two diagonals, AC and BD.

In some shapes:

- some or all of the sides are the same size or may be parallel to each other
- some or all of the angles are the same.

These are called their **geometrical properties**.

Types of triangle

Triangles can be several different shapes.

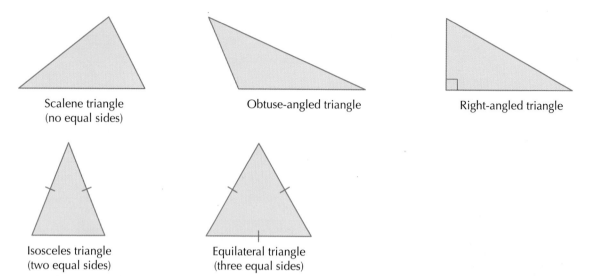

Scalene triangle
(no equal sides)

Obtuse-angled triangle

Right-angled triangle

Isosceles triangle
(two equal sides)

Equilateral triangle
(three equal sides)

Example 12

Describe the geometrical properties of the isosceles triangle ABC.

AB = AC

$\angle ABC = \angle ACB$

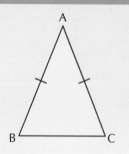

You can use a flow chart like this to identify triangles.

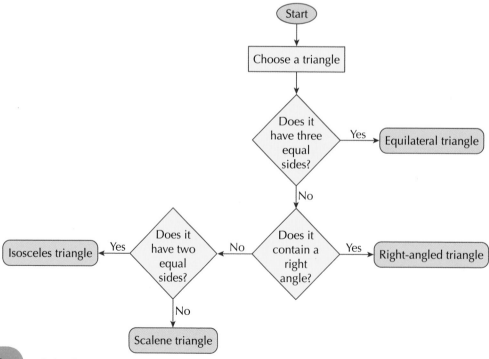

Types of quadrilateral

Quadrilaterals can be several different shapes.

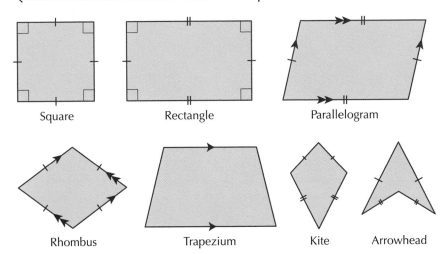

Square   Rectangle   Parallelogram

Rhombus   Trapezium   Kite   Arrowhead

Example 13

Describe the geometrical properties of the parallelogram ABCD.

AB = CD and AD = BC

AB is parallel to CD

AD is parallel to BC

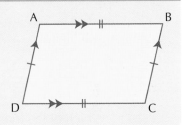

Exercise 9E

1   Sides and diagonals are missing from these shapes.

    i   ii   iii

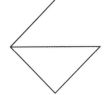   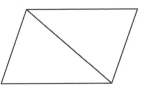   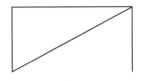

    iv   v   vi

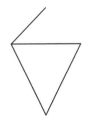   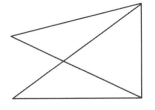   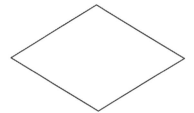

   a   Copy the shapes and draw in any missing lines or diagonals.

   b   What is the name of each shape?

   c   The diagonals of three of the shapes are perpendicular to each other.
       Name the three shapes.

2 Which of the triangles below are isosceles triangles?

a   b   c   d

3 Which of the triangles below are scalene triangles?

a   b   c   d

4 Which of the triangles below are right-angled triangles?

a   b   c   d

5 Which of the triangles below are equilateral triangles?

a   b   c   d

6 Using square dotty grid paper, draw each of these shapes.

a Rectangle   b Isosceles triangle   c Right-angled triangle

· · · ·   · · · ·   · · · ·

· · · ·   · · · ·   · · · ·

· · · ·   · · · ·   · · · ·

· · · ·   · · · ·   · · · ·

d Parallelogram   e Kite   f Trapezium

· · · · ·   · · · · ·   · · · · ·

· · · · ·   · · · · ·   · · · · ·

· · · · ·   · · · · ·   · · · · ·

· · · · ·   · · · · ·   · · · · ·

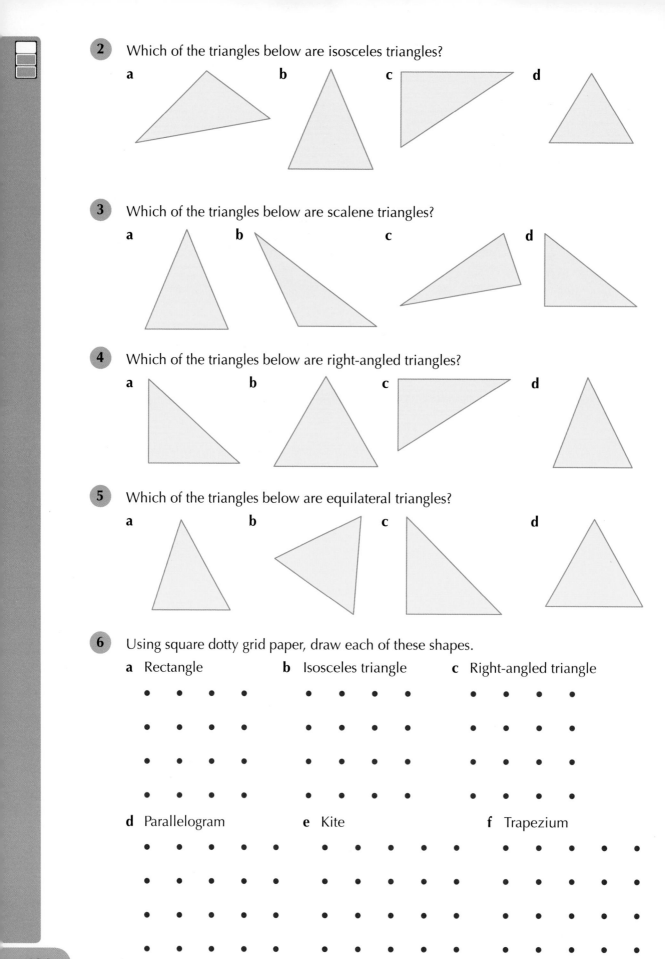

7 Words can be shown by writing them as the shapes they describe. For example:

STRAIGHT LINE   O_BTUSE

Write each of these as word shapes.

PARALLEL LINES   PERPENDICULAR   RIGHT ANGLE

ACUTE   TRIANGLES   RECTANGLES

 8 Write down the geometrical properties for these three shapes.

a Equilateral triangle ABC   **b** Square ABCD   **c** Rhombus ABCD

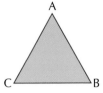   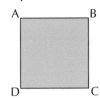   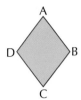

9 Copy this square on a piece of card. Then draw in the two diagonals and cut out the four triangles.

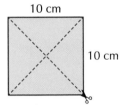

How many different triangles or quadrilaterals can you make with:

a four of the triangles

b three of the triangles

c two of the triangles?

Draw all the different shapes you have made.

Reasoning: Making triangles

Here are six sticks.

| 2 cm | 3 cm | 4 cm |
| 2 cm | 3 cm | 4 cm |

A How many different triangles can you make using any three of these sticks?
Use geosticks to help.

B Draw all the triangles you have made.

Ready to progress?

I can use points of a compass.
I know the names for different types of angles.

I know the names of the different types of triangles and quadrilaterals.

I can draw and measure angles.
I know that angles on a straight line add up to 180°.
I know that angles at a point add up to 360°.
I know the properties of simple 2D shapes.
I can solve simple problems about triangles and quadrilaterals.

Review questions

1   a   Describe how to move from A to B on this grid.

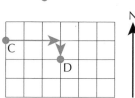

   b   Describe how to move from C to D on this grid.

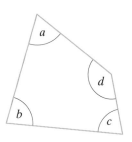

2   Look at this quadrilateral.

   Complete these sentences.

   a   The angle labelled *a* is an ... angle.

   b   The angle labelled *b* is an ... angle.

   c   The angle labelled *c* is an ... angle.

   d   The angle labelled *d* is an ... angle.

 3   Draw three copies of this trapezium.

   a   On one copy draw a line on the trapezium to make
       two triangles.

   b   Now draw one line on another copy of the
       trapezium to make a quadrilateral and a triangle.

   c   Now draw one line on another copy of the trapezium to make two
       quadrilaterals.

   d   Copy this square. Draw two lines on the square to make four
       triangles that are all the same size.

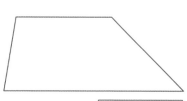

4 Measure each angle.

a

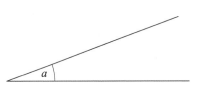

b

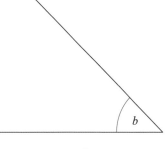

c

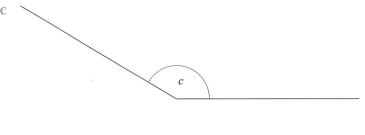

d

5 Draw and label each angle.

   a 50°   b 65°   c 100°   d 145°

6 Calculate the size of each unknown angle.

Give a reason for each answer.

   a   b   c   d

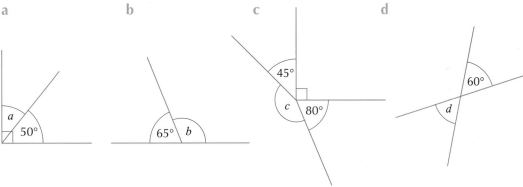

7 Can you put these three sticks together to make a triangle?

Draw a diagram to explain your answer.

2 cm

4 cm

8 cm

Investigation
Snooker tables

You will need centimetre-squared paper for this investigation.

A snooker ball starts at Corner A. It moves along a line at at an angle of 45° to the side of the table. It always bounces at 45° off the sides of the table.

The ball must end up in a corner after a number of bounces.

Example 1

This is a 6 by 2 snooker table.

This ball finally ends up in Corner C after two bounces.

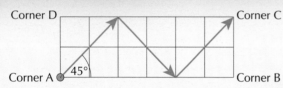

Example 2

This is a 6 by 4 snooker table.

This ball finally ends up in Corner D after three bounces.

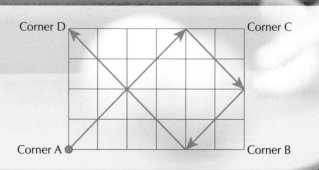

The results for these two examples can be shown in a table.

Example	Size of table	Final corner	No. of bounces
1	6 by 2	C	2
2	6 by 4	D	3

Here are some more examples for you to try.

Example	Size of table	Final corner	No. of bounces
3	2 by 2		
4	2 by 3		
5	2 by 4		
6	2 by 5		
7	2 by 6		
8	3 by 2		
9	3 by 3		
10	4 by 2		

Copy and complete the table.

Write down anything you notice.

10

Coordinates and graphs

This chapter is going to show you:

- how to use coordinates
- how to draw graphs from functions and input/output diagrams
- how to recognise lines of the form $x = a$, $y = b$
- how to recognise the line $y = x$
- how to interpret and draw graphs that show real-life problems.

You should already know:

- how to read a simple map.

About this chapter

Graphs can save lives. If the doctor thinks you have a heart problem, you will be linked up to an electrocardiogram machine that will turn the rhythm of your heartbeat into a graph on a screen. This makes it easy to see instantly if there are any problems. It also helps to monitor very ill people, or those having operations, as any problem with their heartbeat can be seen on the graph. Graphs of all types make it easier to interpret data visually and see what is happening.

10.1 Coordinates

Learning objective

• To understand and use coordinates to locate points

Key words	
axes	coordinate
origin	quadrant
x-axis	x-coordinate
y-axis	y-coordinate

The **coordinate** grid consists of two **axes**, called the **x-axis** and the **y-axis**. The x-axis runs horizontally, while the y-axis runs vertically.

The two axes meet at a point called the **origin**, which is labelled O.

You can use coordinates to locate any point on a grid.

The point A on the grid is 1 unit across and 2 units up.

You can say that the coordinates of A are (1, 2), which you usually write as A(1, 2).

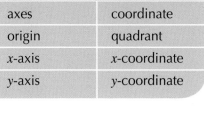

• The first number, 1, is the **x-coordinate** of A.

• The second number, 2, is the **y-coordinate** of A.

The x-coordinate is always written first.

When plotting a point on a grid, you should use a small, neat cross (×), a small cross inside a circle (⊗) or a dot (•).

The coordinates of the origin are (0, 0) and the coordinates of the point B are (3, 4).

Exercise 10A

1 Write down the coordinates of the points A, B, C, D, E and F.

2 **a** Copy the grid in Question 1, but do not mark the lettered points A–F. Then plot the points G(2, 1), H(5, 3) and J(2, 3).

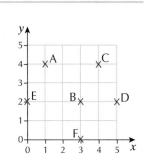

    b The three points are the corners of a rectangle. Plot point K to complete the rectangle.

    c Write down the coordinates of K.

3 The square ABCD is drawn on this grid.

    a Write down the coordinates of A, B, C and D.

    b The point E is halfway between points A and B. Write down the coordinates of E.

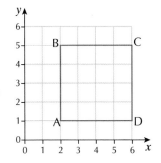

    c The point F is the mid-point of the line AD. Write down the coordinates of F.

    d G is the point at the centre of the square. Write down the coordinates of G.

4 Each of the points plotted on this grid is marked with a letter.

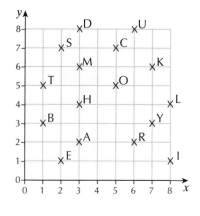

The coordinate code for the word STAR is (2, 7), (1, 5), (3, 2), (6, 2).

a Write down the coordinate code for each of these words.

   i CAKE   **ii** MATHS

   iii MOBILE   **iv** HOLIDAY

b Ben uses this coordinate code to send a message to Tom.

His message reads:

   (2, 7), (2, 1), (2, 1), (7, 3), (5, 5), (6, 8), (3, 2), (1, 5), (1, 3), (6, 2), (2, 1), (3, 2), (7, 6)

What is Ben's message?

c Draw a different grid with points and letters. Make up your own coordinate code messages.

5 From this grid, write down the coordinates of the points A, B, C, D, E, F, G, H, I and J.

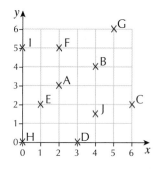

6 Copy the grid from question **5**, but do not mark the lettered points.

On your grid, draw the points with these coordinates.

   P(5, 2), Q(2, 4), R(3, 3), S(4, 0), T(0, 5)

7 Look at this grid.

a Write down the coordinates of A, B and C.

b A, B and C are three corners of a square.

Write down the coordinates of the fourth corner.

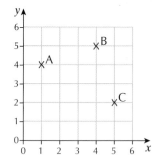

8 Look at this grid.

a Write down the coordinates of L, M and N.

b The points L, M and N are three corners of a parallelogram.

Write down two possible coordinates for the position of the fourth corner.

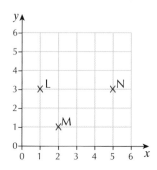

Investigation: More space

Look at the grid.

The point A has coordinates (4, −3).

The point B has coordinates (−4, 4).

The point C has coordinates (−5, −3).

Write down the coordinates of the points D, E, F, G, H, I and J.

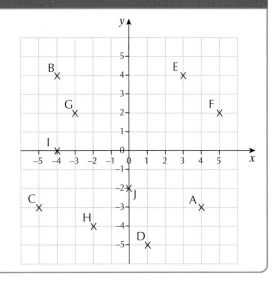

10.2 From mappings to graphs

Learning objectives

- To work out coordinates from a rule
- To draw a graph for a simple rule

Key words	
graph	rule

Think about the **rule**: 'add one'.

You can show this rule in a diagram.

Add one		
Start		**Finish**
1	→	2
2	→	3
3	→	4
4	→	5
5	→	6

Putting the numbers together to form pairs of coordinates gives:

(1, 2), (2, 3), (3, 4), (4, 5), (5, 6)

These are just five starting points. There are many more.

Now you can use these ordered pairs as coordinates, and plot them on a pair of axes.

- You always count the first number along to the right (→) from the origin.
- You always count the second number up (↑) from the origin.

Then you can join up all the points with a straight line, as shown on this **graph**.

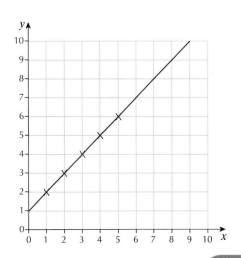

1 Sam throws two six-sided dice. Each dice is numbered from 1 to 6.

One dice is blue. The other dice is red.

Sam's dice show blue 5, red 3.

His total score is 8.

He marks a cross on the grid to show his score for this throw.

When Sam rolls the dice again, the total score is 6.

Copy the grid and put crosses on it to show all the different pairs of numbers that Sam's dice could show.

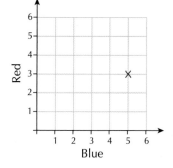

MR **2** Faye joins Sam now to play a game with the dice.

Winning rule: Win a point if the number on the blue dice is the same as the number on the red dice.

Draw a grid like the one in question **1**, but without any points marked.

Put crosses on your grid to show all the different winning throws.

MR **3** The friends play a different game.

This grid shows all the different winning throws.

Complete this sentence to explain the winning rule.

Winning rule: Win a point if the number on the blue dice is ….

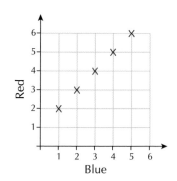

4 Look at each table, below.

i Copy and complete the table for the rule.

ii Complete the coordinates alongside.

iii Plot the coordinates and draw the graph.

You will need to draw a new grid for each graph. Label each axis from 0 to 10.

a Add 2	Coordinates	b Multiply by 2	Coordinates
0 → 2	(0, 2)	0 → 0	(0, 0)
1 → 3	(1, 3)	1 → 2	(1, 2)
2 →	(2,)	2 →	(2,)
3 →	(3,)	3 →	(3,)
4 →	(4,)	4 →	(4,)
5 →	(5,)	5 →	(5,)

c	Divide by 2	Coordinates
	$0 \to 0$	(0, 0)
	$2 \to 1$	(2, 1)
	$4 \to 2$	(4,)
	$6 \to$	(6,)
	$8 \to$	(8,)
	$10 \to$	(10,)

d	Add 4	Coordinates
	$1 \to 5$	(1, 5)
	$2 \to 6$	(2, 6)
	$3 \to$	(3,)
	$4 \to$	(4,)
	$5 \to$	(5,)
	$6 \to$	(6,)

5 This is a special rule. The second number is the same as the first.

a Copy and complete the table to show these coordinates.

The same	Coordinates
$0 \to 0$	(0, 0)
$1 \to$	(1, 1)
$2 \to$	(2,)
$3 \to$	(3,)
$4 \to$	(4,)
$5 \to$	(5,)

b Use the coordinates to draw a graph on a copy of the grid.

This is the line $y = x$ because the x-coordinate is always the same as the y-coordinate.

This is an important line and you should remember it.

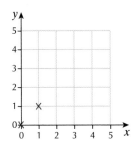

 6 Look at each graph.

i Write down the coordinates of the points marked with crosses.

ii Set up a table like those in questions **4** and **5**.

iii Write down the rule for the table.

a

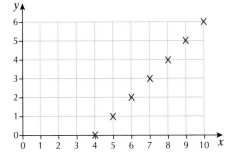

b

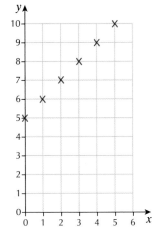

7 Look at each table, below.

   i Copy and complete the input/output diagram.

   ii Draw a grid for the values given.

   Plot the coordinates and draw the graph.

a

Add 3	Coordinates
0 → 3	(0, 3)
1 → 4	(1, 4)
2 →	(2,)
3 →	(3,)
4 →	(4,)
5 →	(5,)

Label the x-axis from 0 to 5 and the y-axis from 0 to 10.

b

Multiply by 3	Coordinates
0 → 0	(0, 0)
1 → 3	(1, 3)
2 →	(2,)
3 →	(3,)
4 →	(4,)
5 →	(5,)

Label the x-axis from 0 to 5 and the y-axis from 0 to 15.

c

Divide by 3	Coordinates
0 → 0	(0, 0)
3 → 1	(3, 1)
6 →	(6,)
9 →	(9,)
12 →	(12,)
15 →	(15,)

Label the x-axis from 0 to 15 and the y-axis from 0 to 5.

d

Subtract 3	Coordinates
3 → 0	(3, 0)
4 → 1	(4, 1)
5 →	(5,)
6 →	(6,)
7 →	(7,)
8 →	(8,)

Label the x-axis from 0 to 8 and the y-axis from 0 to 5.

Challenge: It all adds up

A Write down five pairs of values that are true for each rule.

   a The two numbers add up to 6.   **b** The two numbers add up to 8.

   c The two numbers add up to 5.

B Plot the values on a graph.

C Describe anything you notice.

10.3 Naming graphs

Learning objective

• To recognise and draw line graphs of fixed values

You know that when you use coordinates the first number is the x-coordinate and the second number is the y-coordinate. This means that you can write a general coordinate pair as (x, y).

What do you notice about the set of coordinates (0, 3), (1, 3), (2, 3), (3, 3), (4, 3)?

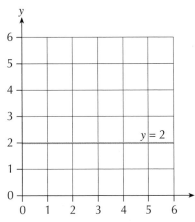

The second number, the y-coordinate, is always 3. In other words, $y = 3$.

Look what happens when you plot the coordinates on a graph.

Although the x-value is changing, the value of y is staying the same. This graph is called $y = 3$.

The graphs of $y = 2$ and $y = 5$ are shown below.

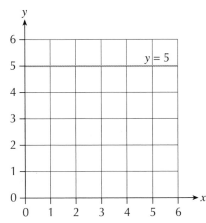

When y has a fixed value, the graph is always a horizontal line.

What happens when x has a fixed value?

For a fixed x-value, such as $x = 2$, the graph is a vertical line, like this.

The name of this graph is $x = 2$.

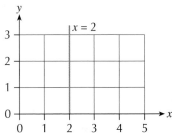

Exercise 10C

1 The diagram shows the line $y = 4$.

Write down the coordinates of six points that are on this line.

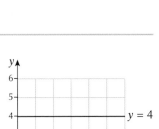

2 The diagram shows the lines $y = 1$ and $x = 3$.

a Write down the coordinates of five points that are on the line $y = 1$.

b Write down the coordinates of five points that are on the line $x = 3$.

c What are the coordinates of the point where the two lines cross?

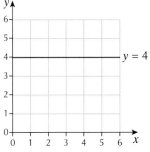

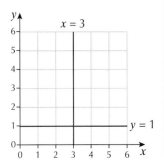

3 Write down the name of the straight line that goes through each pair of points on the diagram.

a A and B

b C and D

c E and F

d G and H

e I and D

f J and B

g K and I

h J and K

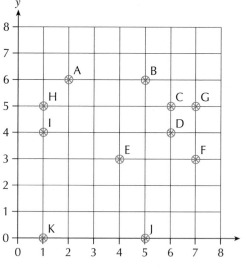

4 Draw a set of axes. Label the *x*-axis from 0 to 7 and the *y*-axis from 0 to 7. On your grid, draw and label each graph.

a $y = 2$

b $y = 3$

c $y = 5$

d $x = 3$

e $x = 5$

f $x = 0$

5 Look at the grid and write down the letters of the points that are on each line.

a $x = 0$

b $y = 0$

c $y = 5$

d $y = 1$

e $x = 2$

f $x = 1$

g $y = 3$

h $x = 4$

i $x = 5$

j $y = 2$

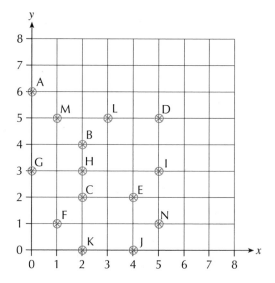

MR **6** These are the coordinates of eight points.

A(2, 3)   B(3, 5)   C(8, 3)   D(2, 5)   E(8, 7)   F(7, 4)   G(3, 4)   H(7, 7)

Here are eight pairs of letters.

a A and C

b B and D

c F and H

d A and D

e E and H

f F and G

g B and G

h C and E

Here are the names of eight lines.

$y = 4$ $x = 2$ $x = 3$ $y = 7$

$y = 5$ $x = 7$ $y = 3$ $x = 8$

Match each line to a pair of coordinates.

Challenge: Rectangles on grids

The lines $x = 2$, $x = 5$, $y = 1$ and $y = 6$ have been drawn on the grid.

They enclose a rectangle with an area of $3 \times 5 = 15$ square units.

Work out the area of the rectangles enclosed by each set of lines.

a $x = 2$, $x = 8$, $y = 3$ and $y = 5$

b $x = 2$, $x = 7$, $y = 3$ and $y = 6$

c $x = 4$, $x = 1$, $y = 1$ and $y = 8$

d $x = 5$, $x = 1$, $y = 2$ and $y = 7$

e $x = 3$, $x = 2$, $y = 8$ and $y = 6$

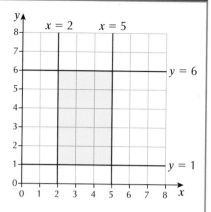

10.4 Graphs from the real world

Learning objectives

- To learn how graphs can be used to represent real-life situations

- To draw and use real-life graphs

Key word

conversion graph

When someone fills their car with petrol, the pump displays the amount of petrol they have taken and the total cost.

One litre of petrol costs about £1.40, although the rate changes from time to time.

The table below shows the costs of different quantities of petrol, as displayed on a petrol pump.

Petrol (litres)	5	10	15	20	25	30
Cost (£)	7	14	21	28	35	42

This information can also be represented by these coordinates.

(5, 7) (10, 14) (15, 21) (20, 28)
(25, 35) (30, 42)

This graph relates the cost of petrol to the quantity bought.

This is an example of a **conversion graph**. You can use it to work out the cost of any quantity of petrol, or to work out how much petrol can be bought for different amounts of money.

Conversion graphs are usually straight-line graphs.

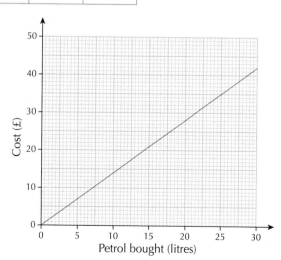

Kg = lb   lb

FS **1** A survey showed these results about the number of mobile phones used in the UK from 1992 to 2002.

Use the graph to find the missing numbers to complete the sentences below.

- In 1992, there were about … million mobile phones.

- Ten years later, there were about … million mobile phones.

- From 1998 to 1999, the number of mobile phones increased by about … million.

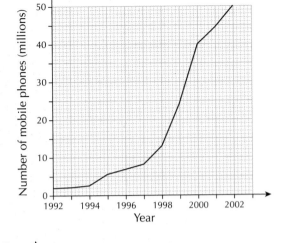

FS **2** Another survey showed these results about the number of mobile phones used in the UK from 1992 to 2013.

a How many mobile phones were used in 2013 in the UK?

b What was the first year that over 70 million mobile phones were used in the UK?

c Use the graph to estimate how many mobile phones might be in use in the UK in the year 2016.

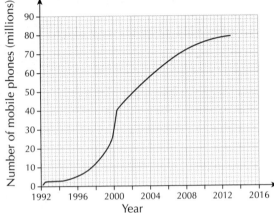

3 The conversion graph shows the link between kilograms and pounds (weight).

Use it to answer the questions.

a Work out the number of pounds weight equivalent to:

   i 5 kg   **ii** 8 kg   **iii** 20 kg.

b Work out the number of kilograms equivalent to:

   i 15 pounds   **ii** 20 pounds

   iii 80 pounds.

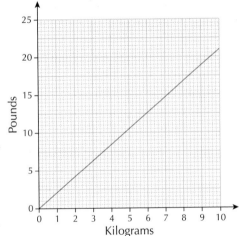

4 The graph opposite shows the distance travelled by a cyclist during an interval of 4 hours.

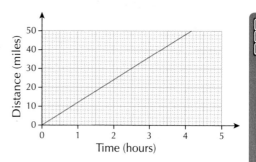

a How far has the cyclist travelled in the first 3 hours?

b Work out the distance travelled during the second hour of the journey.

c Work out the time taken to travel 30 miles.

5 The table shows the approximate comparison of pints and litres.

Pints	0	30	60
Litres	0	17	34

a Use the data from this table to draw a conversion graph between pints and litres.

b Use your graph to work out an approximate conversion to pints for:

  i 10 litres   **ii** 25 litres   **iii** 30 litres.

c Use your graph to work out an approximate conversion to litres for:

  i 10 pints   **ii** 25 pints   **iii** 40 pints.

(PS) d You can buy a 4-pint plastic bottle of milk. How many litres is this equivalent to?

(PS) e You can buy a 2-litre plastic bottle of milk. How many pints is this equivalent to?

Challenge: Taxi!

This graph shows how CityCabs works out how much to charge for a taxi ride.

There is a fixed charge of £1.50 and then a charge of £1 per kilometre.

A a Why is this graph different to all those you used in Exercise 10D?

b How much does a 5 km taxi ride cost with CityCabs?

Another taxi firm, AceCars, has a fixed charge of £1.50 per kilometre.

B a Copy the graph above and draw a line to show how much AceCars charges.

b For what distance do the two firms charge the same amount?

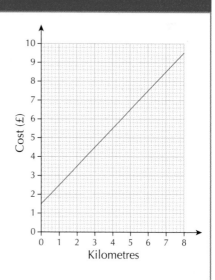

Ready to progress?

I can read coordinates.

I can plot coordinates.

I can work out and plot coordinates from a simple rule.
I can recognise and draw lines such as $x = 3$ and $y = 1$.
I can read values from conversion graphs.

Review questions

1   The rectangle ABCD is drawn on this grid.

   a   Write down the coordinates of the points A, B, C and D.

   b   The point E is halfway between points A and B. Write
       down the coordinates of E.

   c   The point F is the mid-point of the line AD. Write down
       the coordinates of F.

   d   G is the point at the centre of the rectangle. Write down
       the coordinates of G.

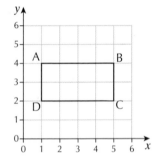

2   Lewis recorded the temperature outside
   his house throughout one day in March.
   Then he drew this graph.

   a   What was the temperature at
       8:00 am?

   b   What was the temperature at
       12 noon?

   c   When did the temperature first
       go above 8 °C?

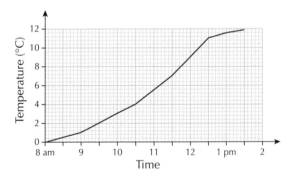

3   Ann throws a blue and a red dice. She scores 6 on the blue
   dice and 2 on the red dice.

   Her total score is 8.

   The cross on the grid shows her throw.

   a   Karl throws the two dice and his total score is 4.

       Copy the grid and put three crosses on it to show all the
       different pairs of numbers that Karl's dice could show.

   b   Ann and Karl play a game. They win a point if the
       number on the blue dice is higher than the number on the red dice.

       Put yellow crosses on the grid to show all the different winning throws.

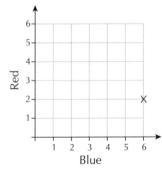

4 **a** The point M is halfway between points A and B.
What are the coordinates of point M?

b Shape ABCD is a rectangle.
What are the coordinates of point D?

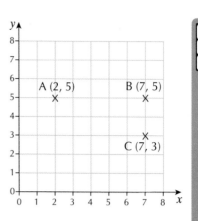

5 The diagram shows the lines $y = 5$ and $x = 4$.

a Write down the coordinates of five points that are on the line $y = 5$.

b Write down the coordinates of five points that are on the line $x = 4$.

c What are the coordinates of the point where the two lines cross?

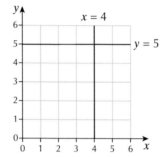

6 The diagram shows a pentagon drawn on a coordinate grid.

The points A, B, C, D and E are at the vertices of the pentagon.

a Match the correct line to each equation. One is done for you.

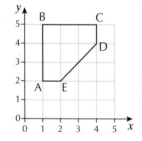

$x = 1$ Line through C and D

$x = 4$ Line through A and E

$y = 2$ Line through A and D

$y = x$ Line through B and D

$y = 5$ Line through B and C

     Line through A and B

     Line through E and D

b By counting squares, work out the area of the pentagon.

7 Ten points are marked on this grid.

Write down the equation of the line that passes through each pair of points.

a A and B   **b** E and G   **c** G and J

d C and D   **e** I and D   **f** C and E

g H and F   **h** I and J   **i** H and D

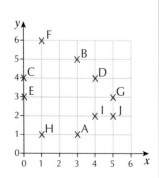

Challenge
Global warming

Our world is getting warmer. Many scientists think that a major cause of this global warming is the amount of carbon dioxide in the atmosphere.

Carbon dioxide is a greenhouse gas. It traps more of the Sun's heat close to the Earth. Higher temperatures have many effects on our world, including the melting of sea ice at the north pole.

The rise of carbon dioxide

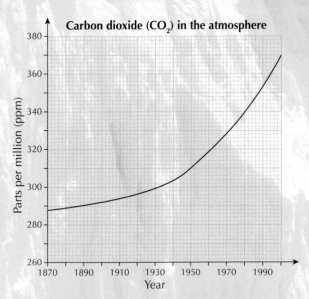

The graph shows the rise in carbon dioxide in the atmosphere from 1870 until 2000. Carbon dioxide is measured in parts per million (ppm).

Use the graph and answer the questions here to work out what might happen to carbon dioxide in the future.

1 Haw many ppm of CO_2 were there in the atmosphere in:

    a 1870   **b** 1900   **c** 1930   **d** 1960   **e** 1990?

2 How much did the number of ppm of CO_2 increase, approximately, in each 30-year period from 1870 until 1930?

    a 1870–1900   **b** 1900–1930

3 How much did the number of ppm of CO_2 increase, approximately, in each 30-year period from 1930 until 1990?

    a 1930–1960   **b** 1960–1990

4 **a** Comment on the increases in the periods from 1870 to 1930 and from 1930 to 1990.

    b What reasons might you give for these changes?

5 Use the graph and your answers to questions 2 and 3 to estimate the ppm levels in 2020.

6 Scientists agree that the dangerous level of CO_2 in the atmosphere is 450 ppm. Between 1990 and 2000 the ppm level of CO_2 increased by 15 to 370.

    If the CO_2 level continues to increase by 15 ppm every 10 years, in approximately what year will the ppm level reach 450?

11

Percentages

This chapter is going to show you:

- how to interpret percentages as fractions
- how to work out a fraction or a percentage of a quantity
- how to write percentages as decimals
- how to work out a percentage of a quantity with or without a calculator
- how to work out the result of a simple percentage increase or decrease.

You should already know:

- what the % sign means
- how to write fractions
- how to write decimals with up to two decimal places
- about units such as centimetres, metres, grams, kilometres and litres.

About this chapter

Few people can resist a good sale. The percentages taken off prices tell you instantly how much they have been reduced and help you judge straight away if you might be getting a good bargain. A reduction of £5 is a good deal when the original price was £10 (50% off), but it's less attractive when the starting price is £500 – a reduction of just 1%! Becoming comfortable working with percentages will help you to become a better bargain hunter. It will enable you to compare lots of other kinds of important data as well such as the interest you will get on bank savings accounts.

11.1 Fractions and percentages

Learning objectives

- To understand what a percentage is
- To know the equivalence between some simple fractions and percentages

Key words

fraction	per cent (%)
percentage	sector

You can use **percentages** to compare quantities or measurements.

Look at this circle. It is divided into four **sectors**.

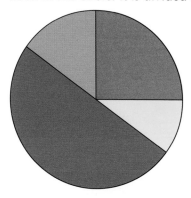

The blue sector is half the circle.

The red sector is a quarter of the circle.

Now imagine that the whole circle is divided into 100 equal sectors.

A half of 100 is 50. 50 out of 100 sectors will be blue.

This means that 50 **per cent** of the circle is blue.

You may see the symbol % written instead of 'per cent'. It means 'out of 100'.

A quarter of 100 is 25. 25 out of 100 sectors are red. 25% of the circle is red.

Example 1

One tenth of the circle is yellow.

What percentage of the circle is yellow?

One tenth of 100 is 10, so 10 parts out of 100 are yellow.

10% of the circle is yellow.

Example 2

What percentage of the circle is green?

The red, blue and yellow sectors make up 25% + 50% + 10% = 85%.

The whole circle is 100% so the green sector must be 100% − 85% = 15%.

1 These three shapes each have 100 small squares.
What percentage of each shape is red?

a   b 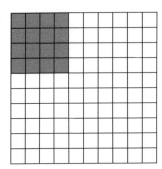 c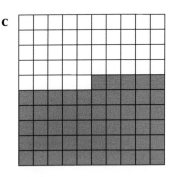

2 Work out the percentage of this shape that is:
     a   blue   b red   c green   d yellow.

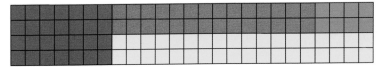

3   a   What percentage of this shape is blue?
     b   What **fraction** of this shape is blue?

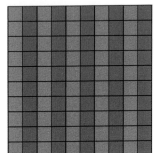

4   a   What percentage of this shape is yellow?
     b   What percentage of this shape is green?
     c   What fraction of this shape is yellow?
     d   What fraction of this shape is green?

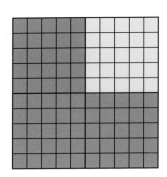

5 Copy and complete this table.

Percentage	25%	50%	75%
Fraction			

6 This rectangle is divided into 100 equal parts.

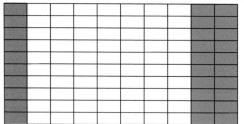

   a How many parts are red?

   b What percentage is red?

   c What fraction is red?

   d How many parts are blue?

   e What percentage is blue?

   f What fraction is blue?

7 Copy and complete this table.

Percentage	10%	20%	30%	40%	50%	60%	70%	80%	90%
Fraction	$\frac{1}{10}$	$\frac{1}{5}$						$\frac{4}{5}$	$\frac{9}{10}$

8 **a** Work out the fraction of the shape that is blue.

   b Work out the percentage of the shape that is blue.

   c Work out the fraction of the shape that is yellow.

   d Work out the percentage of the shape that is yellow.

9 Look at this circle.

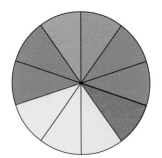

Work out the percentage of the circle that is:

   a red   **b** blue   **c** yellow   **d** green

   e not red   **f** not yellow   **g** red or green.

PS **10** Copy this shape.

   a Colour 20% red and 50% blue.

   b What percentage is not coloured?

11 There are two colours in this shape.

Work out the percentage of each colour.

12 **a** What percentage of this shape is red?

b What percentage is blue? Justify your answer.

Challenge: Eighths as percentages

Look at these numbers.

$\frac{1}{2}$ 50%

Halve both the numbers.

$\frac{1}{4}$ 25%

Half of $\frac{1}{2}$ is $\frac{1}{4}$ and half of 50% is 25%.

A $\frac{1}{8}$ is half of $\frac{1}{4}$.   What percentage is $\frac{1}{8}$?

B $\frac{3}{8}$ is three times $\frac{1}{8}$.   What percentage is $\frac{3}{8}$?

C Work out the percentages that are equal to $\frac{5}{8}$ and $\frac{7}{8}$.

D Draw diagrams to show the percentages you have found in this activity.

11.2 Fractions of a quantity

Learning objective

• To find a fraction of a quantity

You can work out fractions by a mixture of multiplication and division.

Example 3

There are 96 runners in a race.

Two-thirds of them are women. How many is that?

To work out two-thirds of 96, first work out one third.

$\frac{1}{3}$ of 96 is 96 ÷ 3 = 32

$\frac{2}{3}$ is 32 × 2 = 64   There are 64 women.

Exercise 11B ✗

1. Work out:

   a $\frac{1}{3}$ of 15 people **b** $\frac{2}{3}$ of 15 people **c** $\frac{1}{3}$ of £18 **d** $\frac{2}{3}$ of £18.

2. Work out:

   a $\frac{1}{4}$ of 20 kg **b** $\frac{3}{4}$ of 20 kg **c** $\frac{1}{4}$ of 80 m **d** $\frac{3}{4}$ of 80 m.

3. Work out one-fifth of:

   a £10 **b** £40 **c** 60 people **d** 200 cm **e** 125 litres.

4. Work out one-tenth of:

   a 40 people **b** £90 **c** 100 hours **d** 270 km **e** £2.00.

5. Work out these fractions of £30.

   a $\frac{1}{5}$ **b** $\frac{2}{5}$ **c** $\frac{3}{5}$ **d** $\frac{4}{5}$

6. Work out these fractions of 70 km.

   a $\frac{1}{10}$ **b** $\frac{3}{10}$ **c** $\frac{7}{10}$ **d** $\frac{9}{10}$

7. Work out:

   a $\frac{3}{8}$ of 24p **b** $\frac{5}{8}$ of 40 g **c** $\frac{5}{6}$ of 60 seconds **d** $\frac{2}{9}$ of 36 months.

8. The length of this rectangle is 12 cm.
   The width is two thirds of the length.
   Work out the width of the rectangle.

   12 cm
   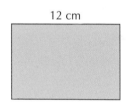

9. Isabel is swimming 120 lengths of a swimming pool.
   She has completed two thirds of them.
   How many lengths is that?

10. 65 people work for a company.
    $\frac{2}{5}$ of them are under 30 years old.

    a How many are under 30?

    b What fraction are not under 30?

    c How many are not under 30?

(PS) 11. A marathon is approximately 26 miles.

   a How far is a half marathon?

   b Alex has run three-quarters of a marathon. How far has he still got to run?

12 There are 2400 people at a festival.

    a Three-quarters of them are teenagers.

       How many is that?

    b Two-thirds stayed overnight in a tent.

       How many is that?

    c Three-eighths arrived by bus.

       How many is that?

    d Nine-tenths of them say they will come next year. How many is that?

13 These are four coloured rods. The yellow rod is 180 mm long.

    a The red rod is $\frac{5}{6}$ of the length of the yellow rod. Work out its length.

    b The blue rod is $\frac{4}{5}$ of the length of the yellow rod. Work out its length.

    c The green rod is $\frac{2}{3}$ of the length of the yellow rod. Work out its length.

     d Another rod is $\frac{3}{4}$ of the length of the yellow rod. Show that it is longer than the green rod but shorter than the blue one.

Challenge: Fractions of a minute

There are 60 seconds in a minute.

Some fractions of a minute are whole numbers of seconds. Here are two examples.

• $\frac{1}{3}$ of one minute is 20 seconds.   • $\frac{3}{5}$ of one minute is 36 seconds.

What other fractions of one minute can you find that are whole numbers of seconds?

11.3 Percentages of a quantity

Learning objective

• To find a percentage of a quantity

You know that $25\% = \frac{1}{4}$ and $75\% = \frac{3}{4}$.

You should remember these from Exercise 11A.

Percentage	10%	20%	30%	40%	50%	60%	70%	80%	90%
Fraction	$\frac{1}{10}$	$\frac{1}{5}$	$\frac{3}{10}$	$\frac{2}{5}$	$\frac{1}{2}$	$\frac{3}{5}$	$\frac{7}{10}$	$\frac{4}{5}$	$\frac{9}{10}$

You have learnt how to find a fraction of a quantity. You can find a percentage of a quantity by first changing the percentage to a fraction.

Example 4

There are 280 people in a meeting. 75% are over 30 years old. How many people is that?

$75\% = \frac{3}{4}$

$\frac{1}{4}$ of 280 = 280 ÷ 4 = 70 $\frac{3}{4}$ of 280 = 70 × 3 = 210

210 people are over 30 years old.

Example 5

Work out 35% of £60.

35% = 25% + 10%

Find 25% of £60 and 10% of £60 and add them together.

25% of £60 = $\frac{1}{4}$ of £60 = £15   10% of £60 = $\frac{1}{10}$ of £60 = £6

So 35% of £60 = £15 + £6 = £21.

With money it is useful to remember that 1% of £1 is 1p.

1% of any number of pounds is equal to the same number of pence.

Example 6

Find 12% of £8.

1% of £8 is 8p

12% of £8 = 12 × 8p = 96p or £0.96

Exercise 11C

1   **a**   Write 10% as a fraction.
  b   Find 10% of:
      i   20 cm   **ii**   50 people   **iii**   130 km   **iv**   300 ml.

2   **a**   Write 80% as a fraction.
  b   Find 80% of:
      i   10 g   **ii**   55 m   **iii**   £20   **iv**   125 ml.

3   Work out these percentages of 80 cm.
  a   50%   **b**   75%   **c**   30%   **d**   80%   **e**   60%

4   Work out:
  a   25% of 32 people   **b**   30% of 5000 people   **c**   40% of 2500 people.

5 There are 480 cars in a car park.

    a 10% are red.

       Work out the number of red cars.

    b 75% are hatchbacks. Work out the number of hatchbacks.

    c 60% have been in the car park for more than one hour. How many cars is that?

    d 90% belong to people who have driven to work.

       How many is that?

6 Copy the lists of percentages and answers.

Draw a line from each percentage to the correct answer.

20% of 1300	225
30% of 800	240
50% of 450	256
80% of 320	260
90% of 300	270

7 **a** Work out: **i** 25% of 180 people   **ii** 10% of 180 people.

    b Use your answers to part **a** to work out:

        i 35% of 180 people   **ii** 15% of 180 people.

8 **a** Work out: **i** 75% of 440 animals   **ii** 20% of 440 animals.

    b Use your answers to part **a** to work out:

        i 95% of 440 animals   **ii** 55% of 440 animals.

9 There are 160 trees in a park.

30% are lime trees.

25% are oak trees.

5% are beech trees.

Work out the number of each type of tree.

(FS) **10** Work out:

    a 1% of £6   **b** 7% of £6   **c** 21% of £6   **d** 54% of £6   **e** 99% of £6.

(FS) **11** Work out:

    a 1% of £23   **b** 3% of £23   **c** 10% of £23   **d** 40% of £23.

(PS) **12** 10% of £123 is £12.30.

Use this fact to work out:

    a 20% of £123   **b** 30% of £123   **c** 5% of £123.

(PS) **13** 30% of £714 is £214.20.

Use this fact to work out:

    a 60% of £714   **b** 90% of £714   **c** 15% of £714.

14 Work out these percentages of 640 kg.

    a 50%   **b** 25%   **c** 35%   **d** 90%   **e** 99%

(PS) 15 38% of £49.00 is £18.62.

    Use this fact to work out 62% of £49.00.

Investigation: Fractions for percentages

Zoe knows how to use simple fractions to work out these percentages.

10% 20% 25% 30% 40% 50% 60% 70% 75% 80% 90%

She can use these to work out other percentages.

For example, Zoe wants to know 65% of 320 m.

She could easily find 25% and 40% and add them together.

Or she could find 75% and 10% and subtract one from the other.

A Show that both Zoe's methods give the same answer.

B Zoe wants to work out 45% of 860 kg.

    a Describe two different ways Zoe can do this.

    b Show that both ways give the same answer.

C a Find different ways to work out 95% of 620 litres.

    b Show that they give the same answer.

D a Find different ways to work out 35% of £26.00.

    b Show that they give the same answer.

11.4 Percentages with a calculator

Learning objectives

- To write a percentage as a decimal
- To use a calculator to find a percentage of a quantity

Key word

decimal

It is easy to write a percentage as a **decimal**.

Look at these numbers.

1% = 0.01   7% = 0.07   20% = 0.2   45% = 0.45   70% = 0.7   95% = 0.95

You can compare percentages and decimals on a number line.

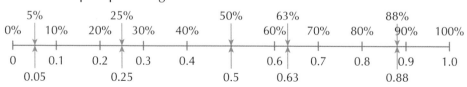

Sometimes you can work out a percentage easily using fractions.

For harder percentages it is more efficient to use a calculator.

Example 7

In an election 850 people vote. 28% vote for Ms White.

How many people vote for Ms White?

Write 28% as a decimal. It is 0.28.

Multiply the decimal by 850. $0.28 \times 850 = 238$

238 people vote for Ms White.

Exercise 11D

1 Write these percentages as decimals.

    a 45%   **b** 13%   **c** 9%

    d 3%   **e** 30%   **f** 70%

2 Write these decimals as percentages.

    a 0.63   **b** 0.24   **c** 0.07

    d 0.2   **e** 0.6   **f** 0.99

3 **a** Write 42% as a decimal.

    b Work out:

        i 42% of 32 kg   **ii** 42% of 12 metres

        iii 42% of 7400 people   **iv** 42% of £29.

4 **a** Write 30% as: **i** a fraction   **ii** a decimal.

    b Use a fraction to work out 30% of 210 children.

    c Use a calculator to work out 30% of 210 children. Check you get the same answer as you did for part **b**.

5 Work out:

    a 17% of £28.00   **b** 69% of 4200 km   **c** 83% of 5800 people

    d 91% of 7200 years   **e** 46% of 6.50 m   **f** 77% of £77.

6 Work out:

    a 80% of £3   **b** 8% of £3   **c** 88% of £36.

7 Work out:

    a 7% of 380   **b** 77% of 380   **c** 70% of 3800.

8 **a** Work out:

        i 17% of £62   **ii** 83% of £62.

    b Show that the two answers in part **a** add up to £62. Explain why.

9 **a** Work out:

        i 7% of 30 kg   **ii** 17% of 30 kg   **iii** 27% of 30 kg   **iv** 37% of 30 kg.

    b The questions and answers in part **a** form a sequence. What is the next term in the sequence?

10 In an election 7100 people voted.

The Reds gained 32% of the votes. The Blues gained 41%. The Yellows gained 16%. How many votes did each party gain?

11 A politician is talking to a meeting of 450 people.

He says: 'I know that 90% of the people in this room agree with me.'

How many people is that?

(FS) **12** A festival charges 3% of the ticket price as a booking fee. Martin buys a ticket for £140. How much is the booking fee?

13 This information was found on a website.

15% of the population of England live in Greater London.
5% of the population of England live in the North East.
The population of England is 53 million.

Work out the population of Greater London and of the North East.

Financial skills: Booking a holiday

When you book a holiday or order something you want to buy, you often have to pay a deposit.

The deposit will not be returned if you change your mind about going on the holiday or buying the item you have ordered.

A Mr White books a holiday for his family. The holiday costs £1400.

He pays a deposit of 25%. Work out the deposit.

B Ms Smith is getting new glasses. The cost is £290. She is asked to pay a deposit of 35%. How much is that?

C Zelda orders a new car.

The car costs £13 250. She adds metallic paint for £485 and alloy wheels for £455.

She is asked to pay a deposit of 15%. How much is that?

D Three friends are going on holiday together. The cost for each person is £692. They must pay a deposit of 15%.

Work out the total deposit for all three.

11.5 Percentage increases and decreases

Learning objective

• To work out the result of a simple percentage change

Key words	
decrease	increase
reduction	

In a sale, prices are often reduced by a percentage.

When the value of something increases or decreases, the change is often described using a percentage.

To find the new value, you calculate the percentage of the original value.

Add it on for an **increase**. Subtract it for a **decrease**.

A decrease is often called a **reduction**.

Example 8

This sign was in a shop window.

The original price of a dress is £120.

In the sale the price is reduced by 25%.

What is the sale price?

SALE
NOW ON
Selected
prices
reduced
by 25%

The reduction is 25% of £120.

25% of £120 = $\frac{1}{4}$ of £120 = £120 ÷ 4 = £30

The reduction is £30.

The sale price is £120 − £30 = £90.

Exercise 11E

(FS) **1** The price of a train ticket was £48.

Then prices increased by 25%.

a Work out 25% of £48.

b Work out the new price of a ticket.

2 On Friday Jan gets 18 emails.

On Saturday she gets 50% more emails than she did on Friday.

a Work out 50% of 18.

b Work out how many emails she gets on Saturday.

3 A tree is 540 cm high. In a year the height increases by 10%.

a Work out 10% of 540 cm.

b Work out the new height.

4 A woman weighs only 40 kg and she is trying to increase her weight.

She successfully increases her weight by 10%.

a Work out 10% of 40 kg.

b Work out her new weight.

5 At 8:00 am there are 80 cars in a car park.

At 9:00 am the number has increased by 60%.

a Work out 60% of 80.

b Work out the number of cars at 9:00 am.

6 A shop has 60 copies of a magazine. They sell 30% of them.

a Work out 30% of 60.

b Work out how many magazines are left.

(FS) 7 The price of a TV is £600.

In a sale the price is reduced by 20%.

   a   Work out 20% of £600.

   b   Work out the new price.

(FS) 8 The price of a car is decreased by 3%.

The original price was £14 800.

   a   Write 3% as a decimal.

   b   Work out 3% of £14 800.

   c   Work out the new price.

9 The population of a village has increased by 45% over the last ten years.

Ten years ago the population of the village was 720 people.

   a   Work out 45% of 720.

   b   Work out the population now.

(FS) 10 The price of a washing machine is £520.

   a   Work out 5% of £520.

   b   Work out the new price of the washing machine if the price is increased by 5%.

   c   Work out the new price of the washing machine if the price is decreased by 5%.

(FS) 11 A woman earns £2800 a month.

   a   Work out 2% of £2800.

   b   If the woman has a pay rise of 2%, how much will she earn each month?

   c   If the woman has a pay cut of 2%, how much will she earn each month?

Financial skills: VAT

VAT is a tax that is added to goods and services.

If you buy something or have work done by someone, VAT is probably included in your bill.

The rate of VAT can vary.

In January 2011 the rate of VAT in the UK increased to 20%.

A The cost of a computer game before adding VAT is £45.

   20% VAT must be added to this.

   a   Work out the VAT, 20% of £45.

   b   Add the VAT onto £45 to find the selling price of the game.

B The cost of a camera before VAT is added is £390.

   a   Work out the VAT, 20% of £390.

   b   Work out the cost of the camera including the VAT.

C Copy and complete this table to show the effect of VAT on prices.

Cost before VAT (£)	10	20	50	100	200	500	1000
20% VAT (£)	2			20			
Cost including VAT (£)	12			120			

Ready to progress?

I can write percentages such as 75% or 20% as fractions.

I can work out a fraction of a quantity.
I can find percentages like 75% or 40% of a quantity by using fractions.
I can write a percentage as a decimal.
I can work out percentages of a quantity by changing the percentage to a decimal and by using a calculator.
I know that to increase, or decrease, a quantity by a percentage you either add it to, or subtract it from, the original value.

Review questions

1 a Write down the percentage of this shape that is:

      i yellow   ii green   iii red   iv blue.

   (MR) b Explain why, looking at the shape, you can see that the four answers to part **a** must add up to 96%.

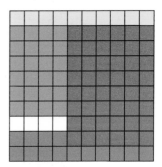

2 a Copy this rectangle. Shade 25% of it in one colour.

   b Shade 10% in a different colour.

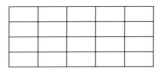

3 The passengers on a train are all men or women. There are no children.

   42% of the passengers are men. Work out the percentage that are women.

4 This table shows the results of a survey of vehicles.

Vehicle	Car	Van	Lorry	Bicycle	Total
Frequency	10	5	1	4	20

   a There are 20 vehicles. What fraction of the vehicles are cars?

   b What percentage of the vehicles are cars?

   c What percentage of the vehicles are vans?

5 Write these percentages as fractions.

   a 75%   b 70%   c 60%   d 30%

6 Work out:

   a $\frac{1}{4}$ of 20   b $\frac{3}{4}$ of 20   c $\frac{1}{5}$ of 20

   d $\frac{4}{5}$ of 20   e $\frac{3}{10}$ of 20.

7 Work out:

  a $\frac{7}{10}$ of 40 cm   b $\frac{7}{10}$ of 150 people   c $\frac{7}{10}$ of 210 kg.

 8 a Write 40% as a fraction.

  b Work out 40% of 30 cm.

  c Work out 40% of 240 kg.

 9 Work out these percentages of 120 m.

  a 75%   b 10%   c 90%   d 80%

 10 Work out:

  a 6% of £5   b 47% of £2   c 3% of £31.

(PS) 11 The diagram shows a square and a rectangle. They are not drawn accurately.

Each side of the square is 5 cm long.

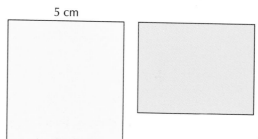
5 cm

  a Work out the perimeter of the square.

  b The perimeter of the rectangle is 80% of the perimeter of the square. Work out the perimeter of the rectangle.

  c Work out the area of the square.

  d The area of the rectangle is 60% of the area of the square. Work out the area of the rectangle.

12 a Write 6% as a decimal.

  b Work out 6% of:

    i 35 g   ii 470 km   iii 5800 people.

(FS) 13 Work out:

  a 19% of £275   b 86% of £72   c 8% of £38.50.

14 Look at this triangle.

Angle C is a right angle.

  a Angle B is 80% of angle C. Work out the size of angle B.

(MR)   b Show that angle A is 20% of angle C.

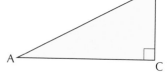

15 The height of a plant is 40 cm.

A month later the height has increased by 30%.

  a Work out 30% of 40 cm.

  b Work out the new height of the plant.

(FS) 16 The price of a pair of shoes is £90.

In a sale the price is reduced by 60%.

  a Work out 60% of £90.

  b Work out the sale price of the shoes.

Financial skills

Income tax

Most people who earn money have to pay income tax.
You can earn a certain amount before you have to pay tax.
This is called your tax allowance.
You pay a percentage of anything over your tax allowance as income tax.
This percentage is called the tax rate.

Peter earns £15 000 in one year. His tax allowance is £10 000. The tax rate is 20%.

1 Copy and complete these sentences.

   a Peter pays tax on £15 000 − £10 000 = £...

   b Peter's tax bill is 20% of ... = £...

2 Copy and complete these sentences.

   a Peter pays tax on £20 000 − £10 000 = £...

   b Peter's tax bill is 20% of ... = £...

3 Copy and complete these sentences.

   a Peter pays tax on £30 000 − £10 000 = £...

   b Peter's tax bill is 20% of ... = £...

4 Copy and complete this table for Peter. Fill in the answers from the first three questions.

Income	£15 000	£20 000	£25 000	£30 000	£35 000
Tax					

5 Look at the pattern of the numbers in the table from question 4. Use this to predict how much tax Peter pays if he earns £40 000. Calculate the tax to test your prediction.

6 Here are three statements. Only one is true.

   • If Peter earns £30 000 he pays twice as much tax as he pays if he earns £15 000.

   • If Peter earns £30 000 he pays more than twice as much tax as he pays if he earns £15 000.

   • If Peter earns £30 000 he pays less than twice as much tax as he pays if he earns £15 000.

   Which of the statements is true? Justify your answer.

7 Use the table from question 4 to draw a graph to show how much tax Peter pays. Draw axes like this. Plot five points and joint them with a straight line that starts at 10 000 on the 'income' axis.

8 Use your graph to find out how much tax Peter will pay if he earns £12 500 in one year.

9 Use your graph to find out how much tax Peter will pay if he earns £27 500 in one year.

10 One year Peter pays £4500 income tax. Use the graph to find out how much he earned.

11 Suppose the tax rate is changed from 20% to 25%.

   a Show that if Peter earns £15 000 he will pay £1250 income tax.

   b Calculate how much income tax Peter will pay if he earns £20 000.

   c Calculate how much income tax Peter will pay if he earns £25 000.

   d Calculate how much income tax Peter will pay if he earns £30 000.

   e Put your values to the previous parts in a table.

   f Use your table to draw a new line on your graph.

12

Probability

This chapter is going to show you:

- how to use words about probability
- how to work with a probability scale
- how to work out theoretical probabilities in different situations
- how to use experimental probability to make predictions.

You should already know:

- some basic ideas about chance and probability
- how to collect data from a simple experiment
- how to record data in a table or chart.

About this chapter

In October 2012 the mayor of New York had a tricky decision to make. Hurricane Sandy, a violent and destructive storm, was heading across the Atlantic towards the east coast of the USA. But where exactly would its main force hit? What effect would it have on New York?

As it approached, scientists calculated and recalculated the probability of it devastating the city. Eventually, with the storm just hours away, the mayor ordered the compulsory evacuation of 375 000 people and so saved many lives.

Assessing the probability of what might happen like this is vital for scientists trying to prevent natural events such as storms and earthquakes from turning into disasters for the people who might be in their way.

12.1 Probability words

Learning objective

• To learn and use the words about probability

Key words	
at random	chance
event	fair
likely	outcome
probability	probability scale
random	

Look at the pictures. Which one has the greatest chance of happening where you live today?

When you do something that may have more than one result, such as roll a dice, this is called an **event**. The **outcomes** of the event are the results that may occur. For example, rolling a dice has six possible outcomes: you may score 1, 2, 3, 4, 5, or 6.

You can use **probability** to decide how **likely** it is that different outcomes will happen. You are talking about the **chance** of something happening.

You will use special words when you are talking about whether something may happen:

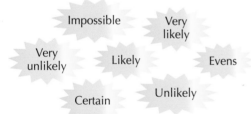

The two complete opposites are 'impossible' and 'certain', with 'an even chance' (evens) in the middle, and so the words you will use can be given in the order:

impossible, very unlikely, unlikely, evens, likely, very likely, certain

You can also show these words on a **probability scale**.

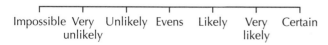

There are lots of other words you can use when describing probability, such as 50–50 chance, probable, uncertain, good chance, poor chance.

When you flip a coin or throw a dice, the outcome is **random**. This means that it cannot be predicted. If you take a coloured ball from a bag without looking, you say you take it **at random**.

Example 1

Show these probabilities on a probability scale.

a A new-born baby will be a girl.

b A person is right-handed.

c It will snow tomorrow.

The probabilities are shown on this scale.

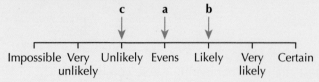

Example 2

Which is a more likely outcome: flipping a tail on a coin or rolling a number less than 5 on a dice?

A coin can only land two ways (heads or tails), so provided the coin is **fair**, there is an even chance of landing on a tail.

On a dice there are four numbers less than 5 and two numbers that are not, so there is more than an even chance of rolling a number less than 5. So, rolling a number less than 5 is more likely than getting tails when a coin is flipped.

Example 3

Match each of these outcomes to a position on a probability scale.

a It will snow in the winter in Birmingham.

b You will come to school in a tractor.

c The next person to walk through the door will be female.

d When an ordinary dice is thrown the score will be 10.

  a It usually snows in the winter but not always, so this event is very likely.

  b Unless you live on a farm this is very unlikely to happen.

  c As the next person to come through the door will be either male or female this is an evens chance.

  d An ordinary dice can only score from 1 to 6 so this is impossible.

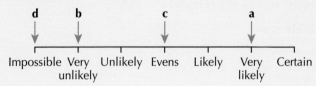

Exercise 12A

1 Here are two grids.

Grid 1   Grid 2

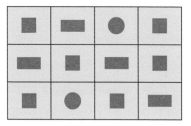

a   **i**   How many triangles are there on grid 1?

     ii   How many triangles are there on grid 2?

b   Complete these sentences.

     i   Picking a triangle from grid … is fifty-fifty

     ii   Picking a triangle from grid … is impossible.

c   **i**   How many rectangles are there on grid 1?

     ii   How many rectangles are there on grid 2?

d   Copy and complete these sentences.

     i   Picking a rectangle from grid … is unlikely

     ii   Picking a rectangle from grid … is very unlikely.

e   **i**   How many squares are there on grid 1?

     ii   How many squares are there on grid 2?

f   Copy and complete these sentences.

     i   Picking a square from grid … is evens.

     ii   Picking a square from grid … is unlikely.

g   Choose a shape to make this sentence true.

     The chance of picking a … from each grid is the same.

h   Choose a probability word to make this sentence true.

     The chance of picking a red shape from grid 1 is ….

i   Choose a probability word to make this sentence true.

     The chance of picking a blue shape from grid 2 is ….

j   Draw your own grid, in which:

     i   picking a triangle is evens

     ii   picking a circle is unlikely

     iii   picking a rectangle is likely

     iv   picking a square is impossible.

2 Tom has a box of coloured squares with shapes on them.

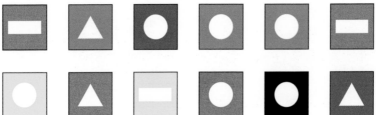

a i How many squares are there altogether?

ii How many squares have a circle on them?

b Choose a probability word to complete this sentence. The chance of picking a square with a circle on it is ....

c i How many red squares are there?

ii Choose a probability word to complete this sentence.

The chance of picking a red square is ....

d i How many squares have a rectangle on them?

ii Choose a probability word to complete this sentence.

The chance of picking a square with a rectangle on it is ....

e Use a phrase from the box to complete each sentence.

equal to	more than	less than

i The chance of picking a blue square is ... the chance of picking a yellow square.

ii The chance of picking a red square is ... the chance of picking a green square.

iii The chance of picking a square with a triangle on it is ... the chance of picking a square with a circle on it.

f Write down the colour to make each sentence true.

i The chance of picking a blue square is more than picking a ... square.

ii The chance of picking a ... square is very unlikely.

iii The most likely colour square to be chosen is ....

g Pick shapes to make this sentences true.

The chance of picking a square with a ... on is equal to the chance of picking a square with a ... on.

3 Pick a word from the box to complete each sentence.

impossible	unlikely	evens	likely	certain

a It is ... that I will meet Queen Victoria.

b It is ... that it will snow in Dronfield during June.

c It is ... that when I toss a coin, I get a tail.

d It is ... that it will be cold in January.

e It is ... that Christmas Day will be on 25 December this year.

4 Emma used Scrabble letters to make the word PROBABILITY.

P_3 R_1 O_1 B_1 A_1 B_1 I_1 L_1 I_1 T_1 Y_4

a How many letters are there altogether in the word?

b Choose a letter to make each statement true.

  i The chance of picking a B is equal to the chance of picking a .....

  ii The chance of picking a P is less than the chance of picking a .....

  iii The chance of picking an A is equal to the chance of picking a .....

c Choose a number to make each statement true.

  i The chance of picking a tile with a value of ... is very likely.

  ii The chance of picking a tile with a value of ... is very unlikely.

d Choose a probability word to complete each sentence.

  i The chance of picking a tile with a vowel is ....

  ii The chance of picking a tile with a letter in the word BILLY is ....

  iii The chance of picking a tile with an even value is ....

  iv The chance of picking a tile with a letter in the word SUM is ....

5 Match the events below to these probability outcomes.

You may need to use some probabilities more than once.

a certain   b impossible   c fifty-fifty chance   d very unlikely

e likely   f very likely   g unlikely

Events

A You are older today than you were last year.

B You will score an even number on an ordinary dice.

C You will live to be 1000 years old.

D Someone in your class will have a pet cat.

E Someone in your class will have a pet spider.

F Someone in your class will have a birthday in January.

G Someone in your class will have a sister.

H You and the person sitting next to you have birthdays in the same month.

I You will flip a coin and it will land on heads.

J The next meal you eat will be a pizza.

K Your family will buy a winning lottery ticket.

6 Rowan has these cards.

He picks a card at random.

Put these outcomes in order of likeliness, with the least likely first.

A The number on the card will be a 1, 2, 3, 4, 6 or 8.

B The number on the card will be even.

C The number on the card will be in the 3 times table.

D The number on the card will be less than 3.

E The number on the card will be more than zero.

F The number on the card will be bigger than 10.

MR 7 Bag A contains 10 red marbles, 5 blue marbles and 5 green marbles. Bag B contains 8 red marbles, 12 blue marbles and no green marbles. A girl wants to pick a marble at random from a bag.

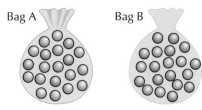

Choose the correct letter to make each sentence true.

a She has a better chance of picking a red marble if she picks a marble from bag ….

b She has a better chance of picking a blue marble if she picks a marble from bag ….

c She has a better chance of picking a green marble if she picks a marble from bag ….

Challenge: Lucky for some

Everyone's lucky number is 7.

Ask at least 30 people what their lucky number is, in the range from 1 to 9.

Do your results back up the claim?

12.2 Probability scales

Learning objectives

- To learn about and use probability scales from 0 to 1
- To work out probabilities based on equally likely outcomes

Key word

probability fraction

You can also measure probability on a scale from 0 to 1. Then you write probabilities as fractions or decimals, and sometimes as percentages. You may see probabilities written like this in the weather forecast.

Then the probability scale looks like this.

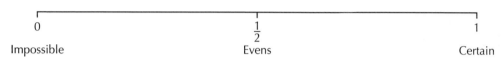

0	$\frac{1}{2}$	1
Impossible	Evens	Certain

Example 4

A bag contains five counters. Two are red and three are blue.

Work out the probability of taking out:

a a red counter   **b** a blue counter   **c** a green counter.

When you take a counter out of the bag without looking, there are five to choose from and each one is equally likely to be taken.

There are five outcomes, all equally likely.

a The probability of choosing a red counter is 2 out of 5.

This is written as:

$$P(\text{red}) = \frac{2}{5}$$

b The probability of choosing a blue counter is 3 out of 5.

This is written as:

$$P(\text{blue}) = \frac{3}{5}$$

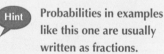

Hint Probabilities in examples like this one are usually written as fractions.

These fractions are called **probability fractions**.

c The probability of choosing a green counter is 0 out of 5.

This is written as:

$$P(\text{green}) = \frac{0}{5} = 0$$

This is because there are no green counters in the bag.

Example 5

What is the chance of scoring a head when tossing a fair coin?

When tossing a fair coin, there are two possible outcomes: head (H) or tail (T).

Each outcome is equally likely to happen because it is a fair coin.

So, the chance of getting a head is the same as the chance of getting a tail, which is $\frac{1}{2}$.

This is written as:

$P(H) = \frac{1}{2}$ and $P(T) = \frac{1}{2}$

You may also say that this is a 1 in 2 chance or a 50–50 chance.

Hint If a coin or a dice is fair, all of the possible outcomes are equally likely.

Example 6

If you throw a dice, what is the probability of scoring: **a** 6 **b** 1 or 2?

When anyone throws a fair dice, there are six equally likely outcomes: 1, 2, 3, 4, 5, 6.

a The chance of scoring 6 is:

$P(6) = \dfrac{1}{6}$

b The chance of scoring 1 or 2.

You can do this in two different ways out of the six that are possible.

This gives the chance of scoring 1 or 2 as:

$P(1 \text{ or } 2) = \dfrac{2}{6} = \dfrac{1}{3}$

Hint Always simplify fractions as much as you can, when writing down your answer.

Exercise 12B

1 Look at this grid of shapes.

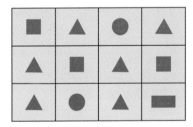

    a **i** How many shapes are there altogether?

       ii How many of the shapes are triangles?

      iii A shape is picked at random. What is the probability it is a triangle?

    b **i** How many of the shapes are rectangles?

       ii A shape is picked at random. What is the probability it is a rectangle?

    c **i** How many of the shapes are squares?

       ii A shape is picked at random. What is the probability it is a square?

d i How many of the shapes are circles?

   ii A shape is picked at random. What is the probability it is a circle?

e What is the probability that a shape chosen at random is red?

2 A bag contains 8 red marbles, 6 blue marbles and 2 green marbles.

  a How many marbles are in the bag altogether?

  b A marble is chosen at random from the bag.
    What is the probability that it is:

    i red   **ii** blue   **iii** green?

3 Cards numbered 1 to 10 are placed in a box.

George takes a card at random from the box. Find the probability that he takes:

a 7

b an odd number

c a number in the 4 times table

d an even number

e 3 or 9

f a number greater than 0

g a number greater than 10

h a 5, 6 or 7

i a number that divides exactly into 12

j a number that can be divided exactly by 3.

4 Arron is using a fair, eight-sided spinner in a game. Find the probability that he scores:

a 4   **b** 1   **c** 2   **d** 3   **e** 0.

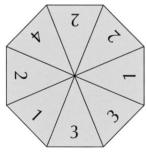

5 In a normal pack of 52 playing cards, there are 2 red suits, Hearts (♥) and Diamonds (♦), and 2 black suits, Clubs (♣) and Spades (♠).
Each suit has 13 cards: Ace, 2, 3, 4, 5, 6, 7, 8, 9, 10, Jack, Queen and King.

The Jack, Queen and King are called the picture cards.

Keira picks a card at random from the pack.

Write down these probabilities.

  a P(red)

  b P(a Club)

  c P(a picture card)

  d P(King of Hearts)

  e P(a 2 or a 3)

  f P(Ace)

6 Fatima rolls a fair dice. Find each of the following probabilities.

    a P(5)   **b** P(even number)   **c** P(1 or 2)

    d P(number less than 6)   **e** P(odd number)   **f** P(4)

    g P(3 or 4)   **h** P(7)   **i** P(1, 2 or 3)

(MR) **7** Mr Ellin has a box of 20 calculators. Five of them do not work very well.

What is the probability that the first calculator he takes out of the box at random does not work very well?

(MR) **8** At the start of a tombola, there are 400 tickets inside the drum. There are 50 winning tickets available.

What is the probability that the first ticket taken out of the drum is a winning ticket?

Activity: Good guess!

Milly and Molly are playing a game with a set of cards numbered 1 to 9.

Milly shuffles the cards and turns one over. Molly then has to guess whether the next card will be higher or lower. If she guesses correctly she guesses whether the next card is higher or lower. If she guesses incorrectly her turn is over.

Milly turns over the first card. It is a 3. Molly then guesses the next three cards correctly.

A What should Molly guess for the next card? Explain your answer.

B The next card is a 4.

    Explain why 'Higher' has a better chance than 'Lower'.

C Now make a set of cards numbered from 1 to 9 and play the game with a partner. Record your results.

    a What is the longest run of cards before either of you gets one wrong?

    b After what numbers can you always guess correctly?

    c What are the worst numbers to get to start with?

    d When a few cards have been turned over, are there any other numbers that you can be sure of a correct guess after?

12.3 Experimental probability

Learning objectives

- To learn about and understand experimental probability
- To understand the difference between theoretical probability and experimental probability

Key words

experimental probability

theoretical probability

trial

You have been calculating probabilities by using equally likely outcomes. The probability worked out this way is called the **theoretical probability**.

Sometimes, you can find a probability by carrying out a series of experiments and recording the results in a frequency table. Then you can estimate the probability of an outcome from these results. A probability found in this way is called an **experimental probability**.

To find an experimental probability, the experiment has to be repeated a number of times. Each separate experiment carried out is known as a **trial**.

$$\text{Experimental probability of an outcome} = \frac{\text{the number of times the outcome occurs}}{\text{the total number of trials}}$$

Example 7

A dice is thrown 50 times. The results of the 50 trials are shown in a frequency table.

Score	1	2	3	4	5	6
Frequency	8	9	8	10	7	8

What is the experimental probability of scoring a 4?

The experimental probability of scoring a 4 is:

$$\frac{\text{the number of times 4 was thrown}}{\text{the total number of throws}} = \frac{10}{50} = \frac{1}{5}$$

It is important to remember that when an experiment is repeated, the experimental probability will be slightly different each time. The experimental probability of an event is an estimate for the theoretical probability.

As the number of trials increases, the value of the experimental probability gets closer to the theoretical probability.

Exercise 12C

1 Work with a partner.

Toss a coin 20 times and record your results in a frequency table like this one.

	Tally	Frequency
Head		
Tail		

a Use your results to find the experimental probability of getting a head.

b What is the experimental probability of getting a tail?

2 Work with a partner.

Throw a dice 24 times and record your results in a frequency table like this one.

Score	Tally	Frequency
1		
2		
3		
4		
5		
6		

a Find the experimental probability of scoring 6.

b Find the experimental probability of scoring an even number.

3 Work with a partner.

Drop a playing card 50 times. Copy and record your results in a frequency table like this one.

Score	Tally	Frequency
Face up		
Face down		

a What is the experimental probability that the card will land face up?

b What is the experimental probability that the card will land face down?

4 **a** Work with a partner.

Take 12 playing cards, three of each suit (♣, ♦, ♥, ♠). Shuffle them. Look at the suit of the top card and record it in a frequency table like this one.

Suit	Tally	Frequency
Clubs ♣		
Diamonds ♦		
Hearts ♥		
Spades ♠		
	Total:	

Shuffle after every turn. Try to complete about 20 shuffles.

b Find your experimental probability that the top card will be a Heart.

c Find your experimental probability that the top card will be a black suit.

d If possible combine your results with the rest of the class.

Now what is the experimental probability of getting:

i a Heart   **ii** a black suit?

5 Joe and Lucy are playing a game of 'Hit the rat'. They each draw a 'rat' on two adjacent squares, on a 4 by 4 grid, without showing each other. Then they take it turns to guess the squares that the other person's rat is in. The first to get both squares is the winner.

This is Joe's board.

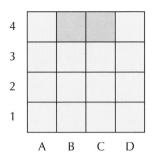

a What is the probability that Lucy guesses one of the correct squares with her first guess?

b Lucy's first guess is B4 and she hits one of Joe's rat squares.

Explain why the probability that Lucy gets the other square on her next go is $\frac{1}{3}$.

 6 Anya wishes to test whether a dice is biased. She rolls the dice 40 times. Her results are shown in the table below.

Score	1	2	3	4	5	6
Frequency	3	16	5	5	7	4

a Do you think the dice is biased? Give a reason for your answer.

b How could Anya improve the experiment?

c From the results, estimate the probability of rolling a 5.

d From the results, estimate the probability of rolling a 2 or a 3.

Activity: Spinners

A Make a six-sided spinner from card and a cocktail stick.

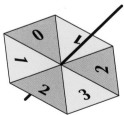

B Spin the spinner 60 times and record the scores in a frequency table.

C Find the experimental probability for each score.

D Repeat the experiment by sticking a small piece of card behind one of the numbers on the card. This will make the spinner unfair or biased. What is the difference in the results?

Ready to progress?

I can use probability words to describe the chance of things happening.

I can use a probability scale in words.
I can use a probability scale marked from 0 to 1.

I can use equally likely outcomes to calculate probabilities.
I can calculate probability from experimental data.
I understand the differences between theoretical and experimental probability.

Review questions

1   Choose the best word from the box to describe the probability for each event.

| impossible   very unlikely   unlikely   evens   likely   very likely   certain |

   a   Chelsea will win every game next season.

   b   A 'lucky dip' ticket will win the National Lottery.

   c   You are reading this question.

   d   When tossing a coin it will land on heads.

   e   This book will turn into a butterfly and fly away.

   f   You will watch TV sometime this week.

   g   New Year's Day will be on 1 January.

2   Anthony put the letters that make up the word:

     LOLLOP

into a bag.

He took a letter out of the bag, at random.

Choose the best word from the box to describe the probability of choosing each letter below.

| impossible   very unlikely   unlikely   evens   likely   very likely   certain |

   a   L   b   P   c   O   d   a consonant

3 a Chris puts 4 white counters and 2 black counters in a bag.

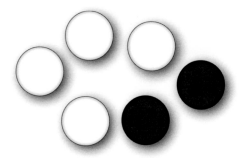

He is going to take out one counter, without looking.

What is the probability that the counter will be black?

b Chris puts the counter back in the bag and then puts more black counters in the bag.

He is going to take one counter without looking.

The probability that the counter will be black is now $\frac{1}{2}$.

How many more black counters did Chris put in the bag?

4 A fair eight-sided spinner has 4 sections coloured yellow, 1 section coloured blue and 3 sections coloured red.

a Mark on the probability scale below the theoretical probability that the spinner lands on:

i red   **ii** blue   **iii** yellow   **iv** green.

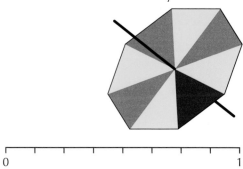

0   1

b a small piece of sticky pad is stuck to one of the sections.

The spinner is now spun 120 times.

The number of times it lands on each colour is

Colour	Red	Blue	Yellow
Frequency	32	46	42

i Which colour of sector do you think the sticky pad was fixed to?

ii Explain your answer.

Highcliffe Comprehensive is having a Christmas Fayre to raise money.

These are three of the games.

Hook a duck

The parents of pupils in Class 8E have donated 20 prizes. They are numbered, in tens, from 10 to 200.

Each duck has a number on its base. The numbers are 1, 2, 3, 4, …. up to 200.

Each player pays 50p to hook a duck.

If the number on the duck ends in 0 then the player wins the prize with that number on it.

Once a duck is hooked it is removed from the pool.

Find the prize bauble

Class 8S have created a large sand tray with 10 whole baubles and 90 half-baubles all half-buried in the sand so that you cannot tell which are whole ones and which are not.

Players pay 50p to pick a bauble.

Once a bauble has been chosen it stays out of the tray.

There are four whole baubles with 50p written on the bottom, three with 75p written on them, 2 with £1 written on them and one with £5 written on it.

Roll a coin

Class 8P are running a game where players roll a 10p coin down a track, If the coin lands exactly on a square the player wins the amount of money shown. Not all squares are winning squares.

Players roll their own coins. They lose if it doesn't land on a winning square.

There are 25 pupils in the class. To work out the chances of winning, each pupil rolled four 10p coins down the board.

These are the results.

	Number of wins
Nothing	90
10p	7
40p	2
50p	1

10p					
					40p
	10p				
			10p		
	40p				
			50p	10p	

Use the information about **Hook a duck** to answer these questions.

1 If 170 people have one go on Hook a duck, how much will that stall make?

2 Barry is the first to have a go. What is the probability of him winning a prize?

3 Mr Buxton tells his daughter that she can have five goes.
   Mrs Kirkland tells her son that he can have three goes.
   Who has the greater chance of winning a prize?

4 Later in the day, 150 ducks have been hooked and 16 prizes have been won.
   Is the chance of winning a prize now greater or smaller than it was at the start of
   the day?
   Explain your answer.

5 Ten minutes before the fayre ends, Hook a duck has taken £90 and the probability of
   winning a prize from the remaining tickets is 0.1.
   How many prizes are left? Show your working.

Use the information about **Find the prize bauble** to answer these questions.

6 If all the baubles are picked how much money will the class make? Show your working.

7 Before the game starts, what is the probability of winning:

   a 50p   **b** 75p   **c** £1   **d** £5?

8 After half the baubles have been chosen there are still two labelled 50p, one labelled
   75p, one labelled £1 and the £5 bauble left as prizes.
   What is the probability now of winning:

   a 50p   **b** 75p   **c** £1   **d** £5?

9 Later in the day the £5 still hasn't been won and the probability of winning it is now $\frac{1}{8}$.

   How many baubles are there still to be chosen? Explain your answer

10 The headteacher buys the very last bauble. She does not know what the last remaining
    prize is. She says:

    'It must be one of four prizes, so the probability that I win the £5 is $\frac{1}{4}$.'

    Is she correct? Explain your answer.

Use the information about **Roll a coin** to answer these questions.

11 What is the experimental probability of winning a prize of:

    a 10p   **b** 40p   **c** 50p?

12 Tom decides to roll five coins. His first four coins win nothing. Is he more likely to win
    or lose with his last coin? Explain your answer.

13 The class expect 500 10p coins to be rolled through the day. Show that they expect to
    make £40.

14 Will the class make exactly £64 if 800 10p coins are rolled?

15 Jess rolled five coins and made a profit of 70p. Work out all the possible scores she
    could have had with the five coins. Explain your answer.

13

Symmetry

This chapter is going to show you:

- how to recognise shapes that have reflective symmetry
- how to use line symmetry
- how to recognise and use rotational symmetry
- how to reflect shapes in a mirror line
- how to tessellate a shape.

You should already know:

- how to recognise symmetrical shapes
- how to plot coordinates
- the mathematical names of triangles and quadrilaterals.

About this chapter

Examples of symmetry are all around. Many animals and plants have symmetrical patterns: think about the wings of a butterfly or the petals on a flower. The peacock uses the symmetry of its tail feathers to attract a partner. Bees recognise flowers by their symmetrical patterns and visit them for nectar, pollinating them at the same time.

In art and architecture, symmetry is an important factor when painting landscapes or designing buildings.

Across all cultures from the ancient Greek to the modern Chinese civilisations, symmetry plays an important part in everyday life.

13.1 Line symmetry

Learning objectives

- To recognise shapes that have reflective symmetry
- To draw lines of symmetry on a shape

Key words	
diagonal	horizontal
line of symmetry	mirror line
reflect	reflective symmetry
vertical	

If you can fold a 2D shape along a line, so that one half fits exactly over the other, the fold line is a **line of symmetry** of the shape.

You can use a mirror or tracing paper to check whether a shape has a line of symmetry.

Some shapes have no lines of symmetry.

A line of symmetry is also called a **mirror line**, because the shapes on each side **reflect** each other. The shape has **reflective symmetry**.

Example 1

Describe the symmetry of this shape.

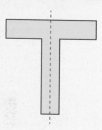

This T-shape has one line of symmetry, as shown.

Put a mirror on the line of symmetry and check that the image in the mirror is exactly half of the T-shape.

Next, trace the T-shape and fold the tracing along the line of symmetry, to check that both halves of the shape fit exactly over each other.

This shape has one **vertical** line of symmetry.

Example 2

Describe the symmetry of this shape.

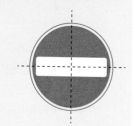

This road sign has two lines of symmetry, as shown.

Check that each line drawn here is a line of symmetry.

Use either a mirror or tracing paper.

This shape has one vertical line of symmetry and one **horizontal** line of symmetry.

Example 3

Describe the symmetry of this shape.

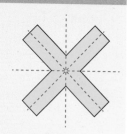

This cross has four lines of symmetry, as shown.

Check that each line drawn here is a line of symmetry.

Use either a mirror or tracing paper.

This shape has one vertical line of symmetry, one horizontal line of symmetry and two **diagonal** lines of symmetry.

Example 4

Describe the symmetry of this shape.

This L-shape has no lines of symmetry.

Use either a mirror or tracing paper to check that there are no lines of symmetry.

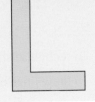

Exercise 13A

For this exercise, you may find it helpful to use tracing paper or a mirror.

1 Each of these 2D shapes has one line of symmetry.

Copy each shape onto centimetre-squared paper and draw on the line of symmetry.

a   b   c   d

2 Each of these 2D shapes has two lines of symmetry.

Copy each shape onto centimetre-squared paper and draw on both lines of symmetry.

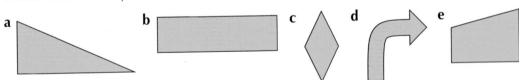

a   b   c   d

3 Only two of these shapes have lines of symmetry.

Which ones are they?

a   b   c   d   e

4 Copy each mathematical shape and draw its lines of symmetry.

Write below each shape the number of lines of symmetry it has.

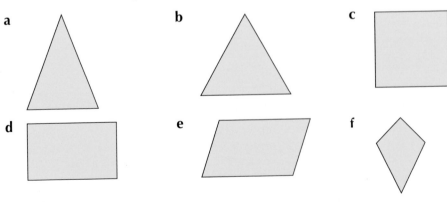

a   b   c

d   e   f

5 Write down the number of lines of symmetry for each shape.

a   b   c   d

6 Write down the number of lines of symmetry for each road sign.

a   b   c   d

7 The flags of many countries are symmetrical.

Use the internet to see how many flags you can find that have:

a 1 line of symmetry   b 2 lines of symmetry   c 4 lines of symmetry.

MR **8** Here is a sequence of symmetrical shapes.

There is one vertical line of symmetry that works for all of these shapes.

a Draw this lie of symmetry on each shape and look carefully at the patterns you make.

b Now draw the next two shapes in the pattern.

c Explain your rule.

Investigation: Paper folding

You will need some sheets of coloured paper and some scissors.

A a Fold a sheet of coloured paper in half.

  b Then cut out some shapes, as shown.

 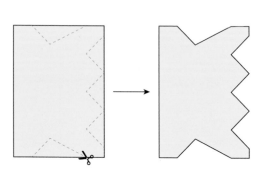

  c Open the paper out to reveal a symmetrical pattern.

B Repeat a few times, using more difficult shapes as cutouts.

C Now try folding the paper twice before you cut it.

Make a display of your paper-folding patterns.

13.2 Rotational symmetry

Learning objectives

- To recognise shapes that have rotational symmetry
- To find the order of rotational symmetry for a shape

Key words

order of rotational symmetry

rotational symmetry

A shape has **rotational symmetry** if you can rotate it so that it looks exactly the same in a new position.

The **order of rotational symmetry** is the number of different positions in which the shape looks the same, as you rotate it through one complete turn (360°).

If you have to rotate a shape through a complete turn before it looks exactly the same, it has no rotational symmetry. You say it has rotational symmetry of order 1.

It is a good idea to use tracing paper to help you find the order of rotational symmetry of a shape.

- First, trace the shape.
- Then rotate the tracing paper until the tracing again fits exactly over the shape.
- Count how many times that the tracing fits exactly over the shape until you return to the starting position.
- The number of times that the tracing fits is the order of rotational symmetry.

Example 5

Describe the symmetry of this shape.

This shape has rotational symmetry of order 3.

Example 6

Describe the symmetry of this shape.

This shape has rotational symmetry of order 4.

Example 7

Describe the symmetry of this shape.

This shape has no rotational symmetry.

Therefore, it has rotational symmetry of order 1.

Exercise 13B

For this exercise, you may find it helpful to use tracing paper.

1 Copy each of these capital letters.
Write the order of rotational symmetry under each letter.

a   b   c

d    e   f

2 Write down the order of rotational symmetry for each shape.

a    b    c

d 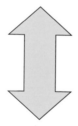   e 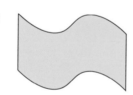   f

3 Write down the order of rotational symmetry for each shape.

a    b 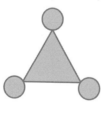   c    d

4 Write down the order of rotational symmetry for each shape.

a   b   c    d

PS **5** These four squares are identical.

Use centimetre-squared paper to make three copies of this grid.

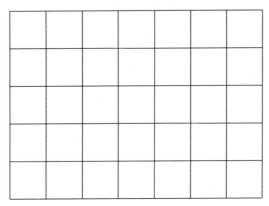

a On the first copy, use the four squares to make a shape that has rotational symmetry of order 1.

b On the second copy, use the four squares to make a shape that has rotational symmetry of order 2.

c On the third copy, use the four squares to make a shape that has rotational symmetry of order 4.

MR **6** Copy the table.

	Name of shape	Number of lines of symmetry	Order of rotational symmetry
a			
b			
c			
d			
e			
f			
g			
h			

Complete the table, to describe each shape.

a  **b** 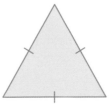 **c** 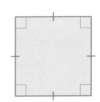 **d**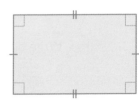

e 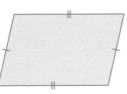 **f**  **g**  **h**

Copy the table.

	Number of sides	Number of lines of symmetry	Order of rotational symmetry
a			
b			
c			
d			
e			

Complete the table, to describe each shape.

a   b   c   d   e

What do you notice?

Activity: Domino-go-round

You will need a set of dominos for this activity.

This domino has rotational symmetry of order 2.

Draw diagrams of any other dominoes that you can find that have rotational symmetry of order 2.

13.3 Reflections

Learning objectives

- To understand how to reflect a shape
- To use a coordinate grid to reflect shapes

Key words

image
object
reflect
reflection

The picture shows an L-shape **reflected** in a mirror.

You can use a mirror line to draw the **reflection**, like this.

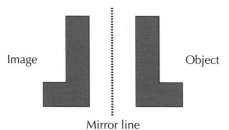

Image   Object

Mirror line

The **object** is reflected in the mirror line to give the **image**.

The mirror line becomes a line of symmetry. So, if the paper is folded along the mirror line, the object will fit exactly over the image.

The image is the same distance from the mirror line as the object is, but is on the other side of the line.

Example 8

Reflect this shape in the mirror line.

Notice that:

- the image is the same size as the object
- the mirror line is a line of symmetry.

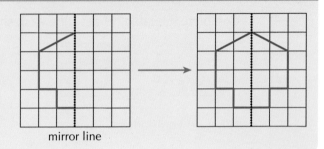

mirror line

Example 9

Describe the reflection in this diagram.

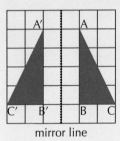

mirror line

Triangle A'B'C' is the reflection of triangle ABC in the given mirror line.

Notice that:

- the point A and the point A' are the same distance from the mirror line
- the line joining A and A' crosses the mirror line at 90°.

This is true for all the points on the object and its image.

Example 10

Describe the reflection in this diagram.

The coordinates of the points X, Y and Z on the grid are X(1, 5), Y(0, 3) and Z(2, 1).

The three points are reflected in the mirror line to give the image points X', Y' and Z'.

The coordinates of the image points are X'(5, 5), Y'(6, 3) and Z'(4, 1).

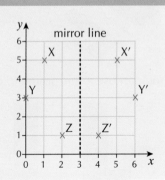

Exercise 13C

For this exercise, you may find it helpful to use tracing paper or a mirror.

1 Copy each diagram onto squared paper.

Draw the reflection of each shape in the given mirror line.

a 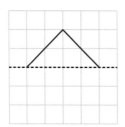 **b**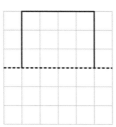

c 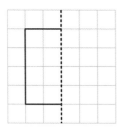 **d**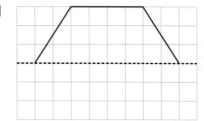

2 Copy each diagram onto squared paper.

Draw the reflection of each shape in the given mirror line.

a 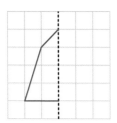 **b**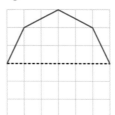

c 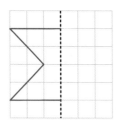 **d**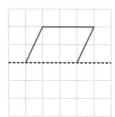

3 Copy each diagram onto squared paper.

Draw the reflection of each shape in the given mirror line.

a 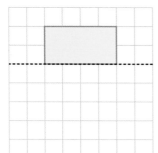 **b**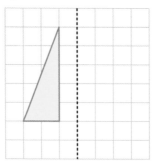

c 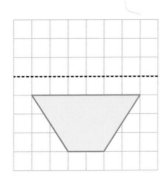   **d**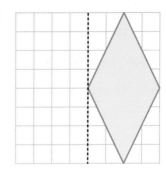

4 The points A(1, 5), B(2, 4), C(3, 1) and D(5, 0) are shown on the grid.

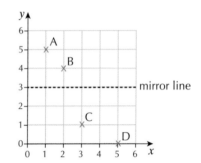

a Copy the grid onto centimetre-squared paper.

Plot the points A, B, C and D.

Draw the mirror line.

b Reflect the points in the mirror line.

Label them A′, B′, C′ and D′.

c Write down the coordinates of the image points.

5 Copy the grid onto centimetre-squared paper.

Draw the shape and the mirror line.

Label the points P, Q, R and S.

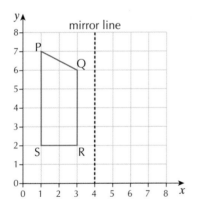

a Reflect the shape in the mirror line.

Label the image points P′, Q′, R′ and S′.

b Copy and complete the table.

Object		Image	
Point	Coordinates	Point	Coordinates
P		P′	
Q		Q′	
R		R′	
S		S′	

6 **a** Copy the diagram onto squared paper.

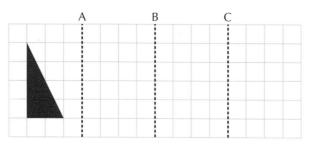

Reflect the triangle in mirror A.

Now reflect this image in mirror B.

Finally, reflect this image in mirror C.

b Use a series of parallel mirror lines to make up your own patterns.

Activity: Ink devils

For this activity you will need a sheet of white A5 paper and some ink or poster paint.

Fold the paper in half and make a firm crease.

Open the paper out and carefully smear some ink or poster paint over one half of the paper.

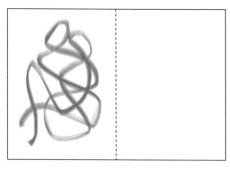

Now quickly fold the paper again, press it down and then open it out.

You should see some interesting symmetrical patterns.

Here are some examples.

13.4 Tessellations

Learning objective

Key word

tessellation

- To understand how to tessellate shapes

A **tessellation** is a pattern made by fitting together copies of the same shape without leaving any gaps.

When you draw a tessellation, use a square or a triangular grid, as in the examples below.

To show a tessellation, you should use about ten repeating shapes.

Example 11

This cross shape makes a tessellation on a square grid.

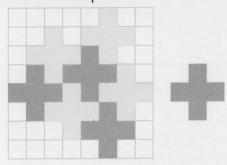

Example 12

This L-shape makes a tessellation on a square grid.

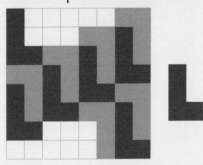

Example 13

This boat-shape makes a tessellation on a triangular grid.

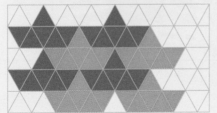

Exercise 13D

1 Make a tessellation from each shape.

Use a square grid.

a   b   c    d

2 Make a tessellation from each shape.

Use a triangular grid.

a   b   c   d

(PS) 3 This tessellation uses curves.

Look at it carefully, then see if you can design a different tessellation that uses curves.

4 This tessellation uses two shapes.

They are squares and equilateral triangles.

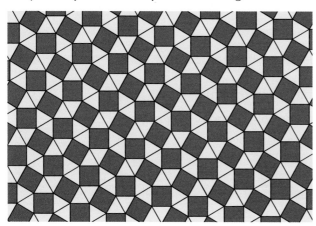

Look at it carefully, then see if you can make a different tessellation that uses two different shapes.

There are lots of different examples on the internet.

Activity: A tessellation poster

Work in pairs or groups.

Design a tessellation of your own.

Make an attractive poster to show all of your different tessellations.

Ready to progress?

I can draw lines of symmetry on 2D shapes.

I can reflect 2D shapes in a mirror line.

I can find the order of rotational symmetry of a 2D shape.
I know how to make a tessellation from 2D shapes.

Review questions

1   Look at these shapes. Which ones have no lines of symmetry?

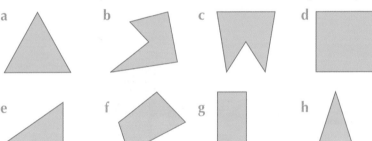

a   b   c   d

e   f   g   h

2   These are examples of symmetry from nature.

Write down the number of lines of symmetry for each one.

a   butterfly   b   four-leaf clover   c   starfish   d   snowflake

         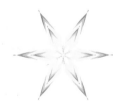

(PS)   3   Copy this diagram. Use squared paper.

a   b   c

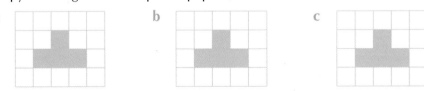

Shade in an extra square so that the shape has:

a   no lines of symmetry   b   one line of symmetry

c   four lines of symmetry.

4 Copy each shape onto squared paper. Draw its reflection in the given mirror line.

a 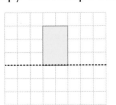   b 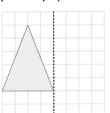   c 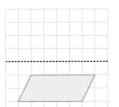   d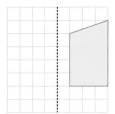

5 Copy the grid onto centimetre-squared paper.

Draw the triangle and the mirror line.
Label the points A, B and C.

a   Write down the coordinates of A, B and C.

b   Reflect the triangle in the mirror line and label
    the image points A', B' and C'.

c   Write down the coordinates of A', B' and C'.

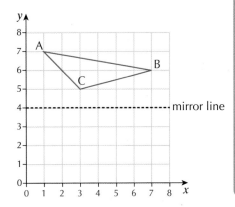

6 Write down the order of rotational symmetry for
   each design.

a    b 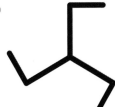   c    d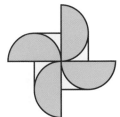

(MR) 7 This is a tessellating mosaic tiling pattern, similar to some found in Roman villas.

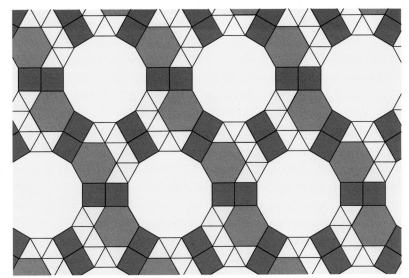

a   How many different shapes can you find?

b   Write down the number of sides each shape has.

Activity
Landmark spotting

Look at the symmetry of these famous landmarks.

1 Describe any symmetry in the five landmarks.

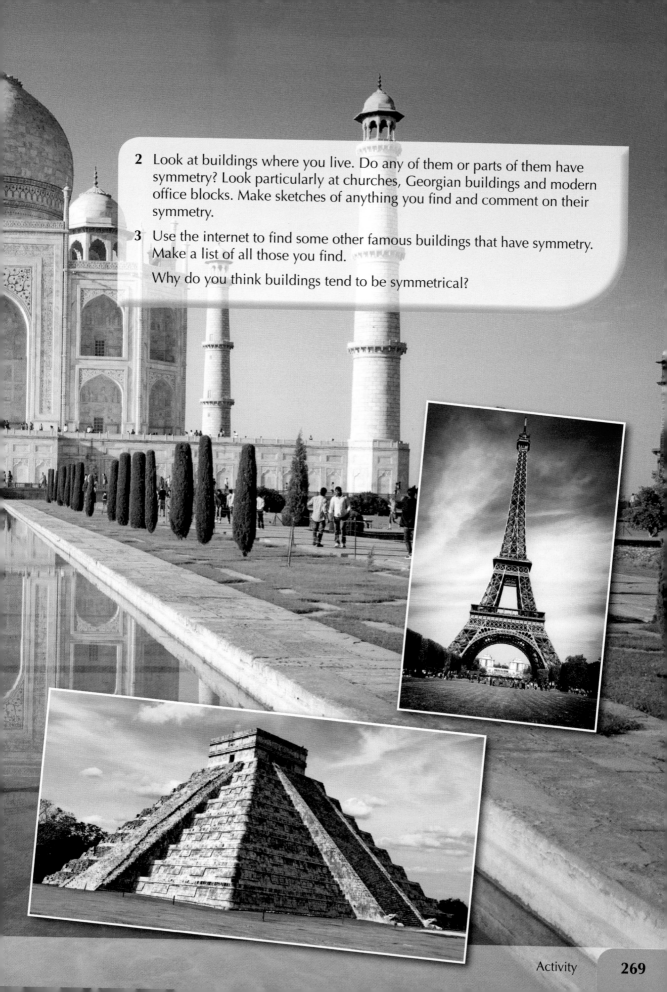

2 Look at buildings where you live. Do any of them or parts of them have symmetry? Look particularly at churches, Georgian buildings and modern office blocks. Make sketches of anything you find and comment on their symmetry.

3 Use the internet to find some other famous buildings that have symmetry. Make a list of all those you find.

Why do you think buildings tend to be symmetrical?

14

Equations

This chapter is going to show you:

- how to solve simple equations
- how to set up equations to solve simple problems.

You should already know:

- how to write and use simple expressions, using letters for numbers
- how to substitute numbers into expressions to work out their value
- how to use words and symbols to write and use simple formulae.

About this chapter

Algebra is the branch of mathematics where we use letters to stand for numbers. When you wrote formulae in Chapter 7 you were using algebra. You also used algebra in Chapter 10, when you learnt about graphs.

An understanding of algebra helps you in studying mathematics and many other subjects that use mathematics.

Algebra started developing when the ancient Babylonians first worked out rules for doing calculations.

In the third century AD, a Greek mathematician called Diophantus wrote a book about solving equations, which is what you will be doing in this chapter.

Modern algebra started with the work of the Arabic mathematician Al-Khwarizmi (780–850 AD). He called his method *al-jabr*, which is Arabic for 'restoration' or 'completion'. From *al-jabr* we get the English word 'algebra'.

14.1 Finding unknown numbers

Learning objective

- To find missing numbers in simple calculations

Key words

| algebra | unknown number |

In Chapter 7 you learnt how to use **algebra** to write expressions. You used letters to represent **unknown numbers**. You are going to use those skills again in this chapter.

This is Nat.

He is thinking of a number.

He doubles it and then adds 1.

Suppose Nat's number is n.

If he doubles n he gets $2n$.

If he then adds 1 he gets $2n + 1$.

Now Nat says that the answer is 13.

Can you guess the value of n that makes $2n + 1$ equal to 13?

You should be able to see that it is $n = 6$ because $2 \times 6 + 1 = 13$.

Example 1

a Work out the value of the letter a if $a + 5 = 12$.

b Work out the value of the letter c if $c - 10 = 4$.

c Work out the value of the letter d if $3d = 21$.

a $a + 5 = 12$	What number do you add to 5 to make 12? The answer is 7.
$a = 7$	
b $c - 10 = 4$	You need to start with a number and subtract 10 to leave 4.
$c = 14$	Check that $14 - 10 = 4$.
c $3d = 21$	$3 \times$ a number $= 21$
$d = 7$	Check that $3 \times 7 = 21$.

Example 2

In this number wall, the number in each brick is the sum of the numbers in the two bricks below it.

For example, in this wall, $11 + 9 = 20$.

Work out the values of x and y.

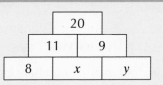

11 is above 8 and x.

$8 + x = 11$ What must you add to 8 to make 11?

$\quad x = 3$

In the same way:

$9 = x + y$

So $9 = 3 + y$.   What must you add to 3 to make 9?

$\quad y = 6$

Example 3

Molly thinks of a number.

She multiplies it by 3.

The answer is 24.

Work out Molly's number.

If you write M for Molly's number, then $3M = 24$.

What number $\times$ 3 makes 24?

The answer is $M = 8$.

Molly's number is 8.

Exercise 14A

1 Work out the number that each letter represents.

    a $a + 5 = 8$
    b $b + 10 = 14$
    c $c + 3 = 11$
    d $d + 19 = 24$

    e $e + 2 = 9$
    f $f + 3 = 16$
    g $g + 5 = 9$
    h $h + 7 = 16$

2 Work out the number that each letter represents.

    a $2k = 8$
    b $2m = 12$
    c $2n = 16$
    d $2p = 22$

    e $3q = 6$
    f $3r = 21$
    g $3s = 30$
    h $4t = 20$

3 Work out the number that each letter represents.

    a $a - 1 = 7$
    b $t - 1 = 12$
    c $x - 2 = 5$
    d $y - 2 = 8$

    e $a - 3 = 3$
    f $k - 5 = 3$
    g $w - 6 = 5$
    h $x - 10 = 4$

4 Work out the number that each letter represents.

    a $5 + a = 11$
    b $b + 5 = 11$
    c $c - 6 = 7$
    d $d - 8 = 3$

    e $12 = x + 4$
    f $11 = 7 + y$
    g $15 = z - 4$
    h $4 = w - 3$

5 Work out the number that each letter represents.

    a $2t = 12$ **b** $3t = 12$ **c** $4t = 12$ **d** $6t = 12$

6 In these number walls, the number in each brick is the sum of the two numbers below it.

Work out the number that each letter represents.

7 Here are some more number walls.

Work out the number that each letter represents.

PS 8 Jake says:

My mother is three times my age.

Jake's mother is 36. Work out Jake's age.

PS 9 Lisa says:

In nine years' time I shall be 21.

How old is Lisa?

PS FS 10 Harry counts the money in his pocket.

If I had another £3.25 I could buy that t-shirt.

The t-shirt costs £12.50. How much money does Harry have?

Challenge: Number triangles

Here is a number triangle.

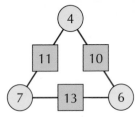

The number in each square is the sum of the numbers in the circles either side of it.

In this example:

$11 = 7 + 4$ $10 = 4 + 6$ $13 = 7 + 6$

A Work out the number that each letter represents in these number triangles.

a
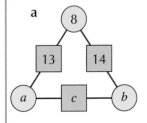

b
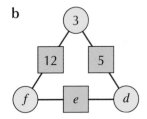

c
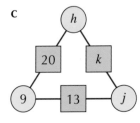

d
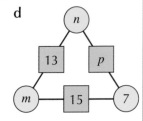

B This one is more difficult.

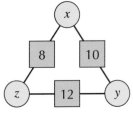

Work out the number that each letter represents.

14.2 Solving equations

Learning objectives

- To understand what an equation is
- To solve equations involving one operation

Key words

equation   solve

At the start of Section 14.1, Nat was thinking of a number, n.

After multiplying by 2 and adding 1 he got the expression $2n + 1$.

Nat's answer was 13.

From this, you can write:

$2n + 1 = 13$

This is an **equation**.

There is only one value of n that makes $2n + 1$ equal to 13. It is $n = 6$.

Finding the value of n is called **solving** the equation.

Example 4

Solve these equations.

a $x + 10 = 25$ **b** $y - 11 = 6$ **c** $3t = 39$

  a $x + 10 = 25$ This means 'a number + 10 = 25'.

                           You could try to guess the answer, but it is easier do it by subtraction.

        $x = 25 - 10$ The number is $25 - 10$.

        $x = 15$

  b $y - 11 = 6$ This means 'a number $- 11 = 6$'.

        $y = 6 + 11$ Add 11 on to 6 to get the answer.

        $y = 17$ Check that $17 - 11 = 6$.

  c $3t = 39$ This means '$3 \times$ a number $= 39$'.

        $t = 39 \div 3$ The number is $39 \div 3$.

        $t = 13$

Example 5

The perimeter of this triangle is 17 cm.

a Write down an equation to show this.

b Solve the equation to find the value of x.

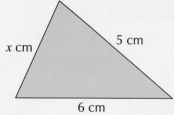

  a The perimeter is $x + 5 + 6 = x + 11$.

     So the equation is $x + 11 = 17$.

  b $x + 11 = 17$ Solve this by subtracting 11 from 17.

        $x = 17 - 11$

        $x = 6$

Example 6

The area of this rectangle is 32 cm².

a Write down an equation to show this.

b Solve the equation to find the value of y.

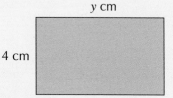

  a The area is the length $\times$ the width.

     The equation is $4y = 32$.

  b $y = 32 \div 4$ Divide by 4 to find the value of y.

        $y = 8$

1 Solve these equations by doing a subtraction.
The first one has been done for you.

   a $t + 7 = 19$ **b** $r + 4 = 15$ **c** $t + 3 = 27$ **d** $x + 2 = 14$
       $t = 19 - 7$
       $t = 12$

   e $a + 10 = 13$ **f** $b + 15 = 21$ **g** $5 + c = 13$ **h** $3 + w = 20$

2 Solve these equations by doing an addition.
The first one has been done for you.

   a $a - 2 = 9$ **b** $a - 3 = 10$ **c** $t - 5 = 12$ **d** $t - 6 = 4$
       $a = 9 + 2$
       $a = 11$

   e $x - 10 = 11$ **f** $b - 20 = 5$ **g** $m - 8 = 28$ **h** $r - 40 = 10$

3 Solve these equations.
   a $2x = 6$ **b** $2x = 18$ **c** $2y = 24$ **d** $3y = 9$
   e $3w = 15$ **f** $3t = 21$ **g** $4z = 12$ **h** $4p = 20$

4 For each triangle:
   i write down an equation   **ii** solve it to find the length of the lettered side.
   The first one has been done for you.

a 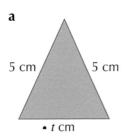   **b** 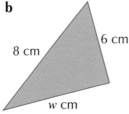   **c**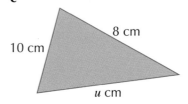

Perimeter = 17 cm   Perimeter = 23 cm   Perimeter = 30 cm

   i $t + 10 = 17$
   ii $t = 17 - 10$
          $t = 7$

d 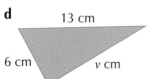   **e** 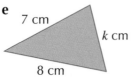   **f**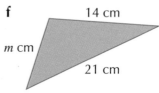

Perimeter = 33 cm   Perimeter = 22 cm   Perimeter = 50 cm

5 For each rectangle:

i write down an equation   **ii** solve it to find the length of the lettered side.

The first one has been done for you.

a
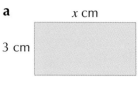
x cm

3 cm

Area = 24 cm²

b
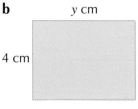
y cm

4 cm

Area = 36 cm²

c
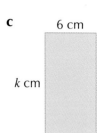
6 cm

k cm

Area = 72 cm²

i $3x = 24$

ii $x = 24 \div 3$

$x = 8$

d
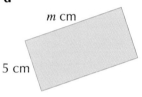
m cm

5 cm

Area = 60 cm²

e
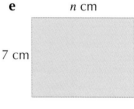
n cm

7 cm

Area = 49 cm²

f
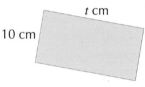
t cm

10 cm

Area = 200 cm²

6 The angles on a straight line add up to 180°.

For each diagram:

i use this fact to write down an equation

ii solve the equation to find the lettered angle.

The first one has been done for you.

a

m° / 55°

b

y° / 78°

c
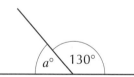
a° 130°

i $m + 55 = 180$

ii $m = 180 - 55$

$m = 125$

d
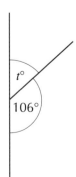
t°

106°

e
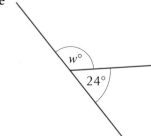
w°

24°

f
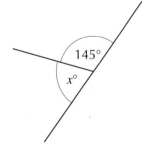
145°

x°

7 The angles at a point add up to 360°.

For each diagram:

  i use this fact to write down an equation

  ii solve the equation to find the lettered angle.

The first one has been done for you.

a

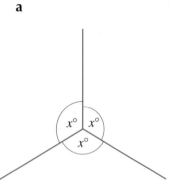

b

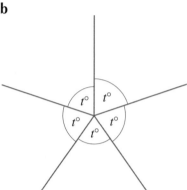

c

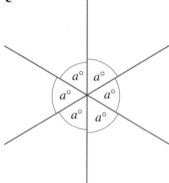

  i $3x = 360$

  ii $x = 360 \div 3$

       $x = 120$

d

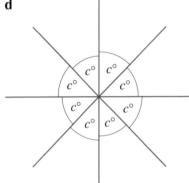

e

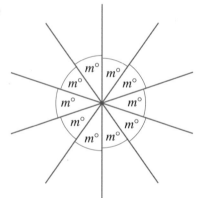

8 In each diagram, the numbers in the squares add up to the number in the circle.

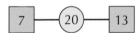

$7 + 13 = 20$

For each diagram:

i write down an equation

ii solve the equation to find the missing number.

a 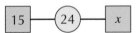   **b**    **c**

9 In each diagram, the numbers in the squares are multiplied together to give the number in the triangle.

$7 \times 4 = 28$

For each diagram:

   i write down an equation

   ii solve the equation to find the missing number.

a    **b**    **c**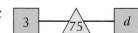

Challenge: Making equations

A Suppose $x = 4$.

Complete each equation.

   a $2x = \ldots$ **b** $x + 1 = \ldots$ **c** $2x + 1 = \ldots$ **d** $2(x + 1) = \ldots$

B Repeat question **A** for $x = 5$.

C Repeat question **A** for $x = 10$.

14.3 Solving more complex equations

Learning objective

- To solve equations involving two operations

Key words

| inverse | operation |

Each of the equations you solved in Section 14.2 had an **operation**, such as addition, subtraction or multiplication.

You have seen the equation $2n + 1 = 13$ before.

It involves two operations, first multiplication and then addition.

Example 7

Solve this equation.

$2a + 3 = 17$

$$2a + 3 = 17$$

$\quad 2a = 17 - 3$ First subtract 3 from both sides.

$\quad 2a = 14$ $17 - 3 = 14$

$\quad\quad a = 14 \div 2$ Now divide both sides by 2.

$\quad\quad a = 7$

You can see that to 'undo' add 3 you subtract 3.

To 'undo' multiply by 2 you divide by 2. These are **inverse** operations.

Example 8

Solve these equations.

a $2a - 3 = 17$ **b** $4c + 7 = 39$

a $2a - 3 = 17$

$\quad\quad 2a = 17 + 3$ First add 3 to both sides.

$\quad\quad 2a = 20$ Now divide by 2.

b $4c + 7 = 39$

$\quad\quad 4c = 32$ First subtract 7 from both sides. $39 - 7 = 32$

$\quad\quad c = 8$ Then divide both sides by 4. $32 \div 4 = 8$

The inverse of 'multiply by 4' is 'divide by 4'.

Example 9

Solve these equations.

a $2(x + 5) = 18$ **b** $2(x - 5) = 18$

a $2(x + 5) = 18$ The brackets mean the last operation is 'multiply by 2'.

$\quad\quad x + 5 = 9$ First divide both sides by 2. $18 \div 2 = 9$

$\quad\quad x = 4$ Now subtract 5. $9 - 5 = 4$

b $2(x - 5) = 18$ Again, the last operation is 'multiply by 2'.

$\quad\quad x - 5 = 9$ First divide both sides by 2. $18 \div 2 = 9$

$\quad\quad x = 14$ Now add 5 to both sides. $9 + 5 = 14$

Example 10

a Write an expression for the perimeter of this rectangle.

b The perimeter of the rectangle is 30 cm.
  Write an equation to show this.

c Solve your equation to find the value of t.

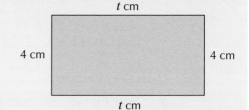

a The perimeter is $t + 4 + t + 4$.

  This simplifies to $2t + 8$. $t + t = 2t$ and $4 + 4 = 8$

b If the perimeter is 30 cm, then $2t + 8 = 30$.

c $2t + 8 = 30$

$\quad\quad 2t = 22$ Subtract 8 from both sides. $30 - 8 = 22$

$\quad\quad t = 11$ Divide both sides by 2. $22 \div 2 = 11$

An alternative equation for the perimeter is $2(t + 4)$.

In that case the equation is $2(t + 4) = 30$.

This equation has the same solution.

Exercise 14C

1 Solve each equation. Start by subtracting 3, each time.

    a $2a + 3 = 11$ **b** $2a + 3 = 19$ **c** $2a + 3 = 31$

2 Solve each equation. Start by adding 3 each time.

    a $2a - 3 = 7$ **b** $2a - 3 = 15$ **c** $2a - 3 = 29$

3 Solve each equation. Think about what you will add or subtract, each time.

    a $3a + 1 = 13$ **b** $3a + 2 = 20$ **c** $3a + 4 = 25$

    d $3a - 1 = 11$ **e** $3a - 2 = 19$ **f** $3a - 4 = 32$

4 Solve each equation. Start by dividing by 2, each time.

    a $2(a + 1) = 10$ **b** $2(a + 3) = 20$ **c** $2(a + 2) = 28$

    d $2(a - 1) = 6$ **e** $2(a - 4) = 10$ **f** $2(a - 3) = 30$

5 Look at this rectangle.

    a Show that an expression for the perimeter is $2a + 10$ cm.

    b The perimeter is 26 cm so $2a + 10 = 26$.

        Solve this equation.

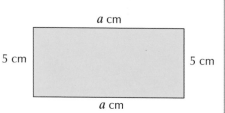

6 Look at this rectangle.

    a Show that an expression for the perimeter is $2t + 24$ cm.

    b The perimeter is 40 cm so $2t + 24 = 40$.

        Solve this equation.

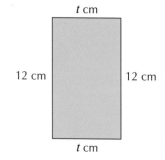

7 Look at this rectangle.

    a Show that an expression for the perimeter is $2(m + 4)$ cm.

    b The perimeter is 22 cm so $2(m + 4) = 22$.

        Solve this equation.

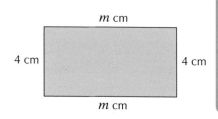

8 Look at this rectangle.

    a Work out an expression for the perimeter, in centimetres.

    b The perimeter is 52 cm.

        Write an equation to show this.

    c Solve your equation to find the value of x.

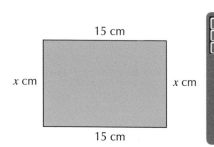

9 Three sides of this trapezium are t cm long.

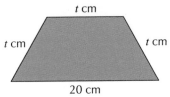

t cm

t cm   t cm

20 cm

   a Show that an expression for the perimeter, in centimetres, is $3t + 20$.

   b The perimeter is 62 cm. Write an equation to show this.

   c Solve your equation to find the value of t.

10 Three sides of this trapezium are a cm long.

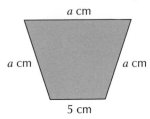

a cm

a cm   a cm

5 cm

   a Work out an expression for the perimeter, in centimetres, of the shape.

   b The perimeter is 38 cm. Write an equation to show this.

   c Solve your equation to find the value of a.

11 Four sides of this shape are x cm long.

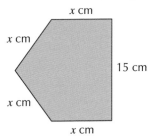

x cm

x cm

15 cm

x cm

x cm

   a Work out an expression for the perimeter, in centimetres, of the shape.

   b The perimeter is 51 cm. Write an equation to show this.

   c Solve your equation to find the value of x.

Challenge: Using tables to solve equations

A If $x = 4$, work out the value of $2x + 1$.

B Copy and complete this table to show values of $2x + 1$ for different values of x.

x	4	6	8	10	12	14	16	18
$2x + 1$	9		17			29		37

C Use the table to solve these equations.

   a $2x + 1 = 17$ **b** $2x + 1 = 29$ **c** $2x + 1 = 37$

D Use the values in your table to help you solve these equations.

   a $2x + 1 = 11$ **b** $2x + 1 = 23$ **c** $2x + 1 = 35$

14.4 Setting up and solving equations

Learning objective

• To use algebra to set up and solve equations

You can solve many real-life mathematical problems by first setting up an equation.

Example 11

Tickets for a concert cost £24 each.

There is also a £5 booking fee.

a Work out the total cost of three tickets.

b Write a formula for the total cost of n tickets, including the booking fee.

c Sam buys some tickets. They cost him £197.

  i Write an equation to show this.

  ii Solve the equation to work out how many tickets Sam buys.

  a The cost, in pounds, is $24 \times 3 + 5 = 72 + 5 = 77$.

    The booking fee is £5, however many tickets you buy.

  b The formula is $24n + 5$. Multiply 24 by the number of tickets, then add 5.

  c $24n + 5 = 197$ The total cost for Sam is £197. Do not put £ signs in the equation.

      $24n = 197 - 5$ First subtract 5 from both sides.

      $24n = 192$

        $n = 192 \div 24$ Now divide by 24.

        $n = 8$

  Sam bought 8 tickets.

Example 12

Kate thinks of a number.

First she subtracts 3, then she multiplies by 2.

a Suppose the number Kate thinks of is k.

  Write an equation to show that the answer is 72.

b Solve the equation to find the number Kate thought of.

My answer is 72.

  a After subtracting 3 Kate has $k - 3$.

    Then she multiplies by 2 to get $2(k - 3)$.

    Kate's answer is 72 so the equation is $2(k - 3) = 72$.

  b $2(k - 3) = 72$

      $k - 3 = 36$ First divide both sides by 2. $72 \div 2 = 36$

          $k = 39$ Then add 3 to both sides. $36 + 3 = 39$

  Kate's starting number is 39.

Exercise 14D

(FS) 1 Tickets for a football match cost £17 each.

When you buy them online there is a £4 booking fee.

   a Max buys t tickets online. Write an expression for the total cost, in pounds.

   b The total cost for Max's tickets is £106.

      Write an equation to show this.

 Hint Use your expression from part a.

   c Solve the equation to find the number of tickets Max buys.

(FS) 2 Theatre tickets cost £22 each. There is a booking fee of £3.

   a Jen buys j tickets. Write an expression for the cost, in pounds.

   b The tickets cost Jen £179. Write an equation to show this.

   c Solve the equation to find how many tickets Jen buys.

(FS) 3 Concert tickets cost £34 each and there is an £8 booking fee.

   a Yasmine buys y tickets and the total cost is £314. Write an equation to show this.

   b Solve the equation to find the number of tickets Yasmine bought.

4 Dave thinks of a number, d.

He doubles it and adds 3.

   a Write down an expression for Dave's answer.

   b Write down an equation to show Dave's answer.

   c Solve your equation to find Dave's initial number.

My answer is 59.

5 Cathy thinks of a number, c.

She adds 1 and then doubles the result.

   a Write an expression to show what she did.

   b Cathy's answer is 24. Write an equation to show this.

   c Solve your equation to find Cathy's starting number.

6 Mark thinks of a number, n.

He doubles it and adds 7 to the result. The answer is 41.

   a Write an equation to show this.

   b Solve your equation to find the value of n.

7 George thinks of a number, g.

He subtracts 5, then multiplies the result by 3. The answer is 36.

   a Write an equation to show this.

   b Solve your equation to find the value of g.

8 Look at this rectangle.

   a The perimeter is 28 cm. Write an equation to show this.

   b Solve your equation to find the value of a.

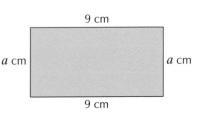

9 cm

a cm a cm

9 cm

9 Look at this rectangle.

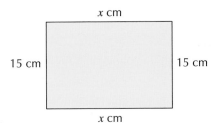

x cm

15 cm   15 cm

x cm

    a The perimeter is 72 cm. Write an equation to show this.

    b Solve your equation to find the value of x.

  10 This shape is a pentagon.

Four sides are the same length, c cm.

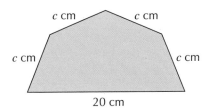

c cm   c cm

c cm   c cm

20 cm

    a The perimeter of the pentagon is 76 cm.

       Write an equation to show this.

    b Solve your equation to find the value of c.

Challenge: Changing temperatures

In Europe, temperatures are measured in degrees Celsius (°C).

In the USA, temperatures are measured in degrees Fahrenheit (°F).

This is a formula for degrees Fahrenheit in terms of degrees Celsius.

$$F = 1.8C + 32$$

A a Change 40 °C to degrees Fahrenheit by putting C equal to 40 in the formula.

   b Change 60 °C to degrees Fahrenheit.

B Copy and complete this table.

°C	0	20	40	60	80	100
°F		104				

C To change 86 °F to degrees Celsius you need to solve this equation.

$$1.8C + 32 = 86$$

Solve the equation.

D To change 122 °F to degrees Celsius you need to solve this equation.

$$1.8C + 32 = 122$$

Solve the equation.

E Change 194 °F to degrees Celsius.

Ready to progress?

I can solve simple equations that involve one operation.

I can solve simple equations that involve two operations.
I can set up and solve an equation for a simple real-life problem.

Review questions

1 Solve these equations.

   a $x + 5 = 13$ b $y - 5 = 13$ c $t - 13 = 5$
   d $6 + a = 20$ e $b - 15 = 2$ f $14 = c + 3$

2 Solve these equations.

   a $2x = 6$ b $2y = 26$ c $3t = 90$
   d $5a = 35$ e $10b = 150$ f $36 = 9c$

3 a Show that an expression for the volume of this cuboid is $8x$ cm³.

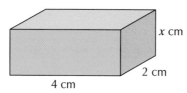

   x cm
   2 cm
   4 cm

   Suppose the volume of the cuboid is 24 cm³.

   b Write down an equation involving x.
   c Solve the equation.

4 a Write an expression for the perimeter of this triangle, in terms of x.

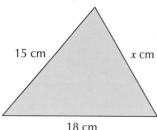

   15 cm x cm

   18 cm

   b The perimeter of the triangle is 55 cm.
      Write an equation for x.
   c Solve the equation to find the value of x.

5 Solve these equations.

   a $2t + 7 = 17$ **b** $2r - 7 = 17$ **c** $3z - 2 = 40$

6 Solve these equations.

   a $2(m + 1) = 24$ **b** $2(p - 3) = 28$ **c** $3(z - 2) = 27$

 7 A pattern is made from matchsticks.

   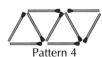

Pattern 1   Pattern 2   Pattern 3   Pattern 4

An expression for the number of matches in pattern p is $2p + 1$.

   a Show that this expression has the correct value if p is 1.

   b Show that this expression has the correct value if p is 2.

   c Show that this expression has the correct value if p is 4.

   d Use the expression to work out how many matches there are in pattern 7.

   e A particular pattern has 33 matches.

      i Write down an equation involving p to express this.

      ii Solve the equation to work out the value of p.

 8 The cost, £c, of hiring a car for d days is given by the formula $c = 25 + 13d$.

   a Work out the cost of hiring the car for four days.

   b Gemma hires the car for d days and pays £207.

     Write an equation to show this.

   c Solve your equation to find how long Gemma had the car.

   d Harry hired the car and paid £142.

     Work out how long Harry had the car.

9 Tom thinks of a number, t.

He doubles it and adds four.

The answer is 80.

   a Write an equation to show this.

   b Solve your equation to find the value of t.

 10 Laura thought of a number, L.

She did two things to it.

Her final answer was 42.

She wrote down this equation to show what she did.

    $3(L - 4) = 42$

   a Work out the two things Laura did, and the order in which she did them.

   b Work out the number Laura started with.

Challenge
Number puzzles

Here is a common type of number puzzle.

Each letter stands for a different number.

The row and column totals are given.

The task is to find the value of each letter.

A	B	C	A	22
B	C	D	A	23
C	C	C	C	20
D	B	A	D	26
23	16	25	27	

Using equations can help you do this.

Start by looking for a row or column with just one letter.

Row 3 has just C. The total is 20 so you can write:

$4C = 20$
$\rightarrow C = 20 \div 4 = 5$

A	B	5	A	22
B	5	D	A	23
5	5	5	5	20
D	B	A	D	26
23	16	25	27	

Now look for a row or column with just one other letter.

Column 2 has just B.

$2B + 10 = 16$
$\rightarrow 2B = 16 - 10 = 6$
$\rightarrow B = 6 \div 2 = 3$

Now you know B and C.

Row 1 has just one letter.

$2A + 8 = 22$
$\rightarrow 2A = 22 - 8 = 14$
$\rightarrow A = 14 \div 2 = 7$

Column 1 gives:
$D + 15 = 23$
$\rightarrow D = 23 - 15 = 8$

You should check that all the row and column totals are correct.

A	3	5	A	22
3	5	D	A	23
5	5	5	5	20
D	3	A	D	26
23	16	25	27	

7	3	5	7	22
3	5	D	7	23
5	5	5	5	20
D	3	7	D	26
23	16	25	27	

Solve these number squares. Use equations to help you.

1

A	A	12
B	C	16
13	15	

2

A	B	19
C	B	17
14	22	

3

A	B	20
C	C	30
18	32	

4

A	A	B	23
C	C	B	43
C	A	B	33
35	25	39	

5

A	B	C	32
A	C	A	31
A	B	B	38
36	33	32	

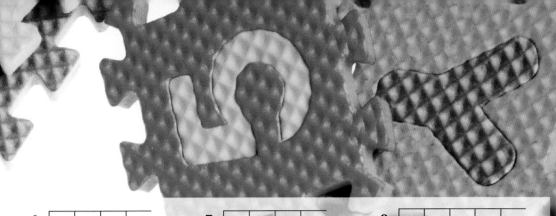

6

A	A	C	17
B	B	B	9
C	A	B	15
15	13	13	

7

A	C	B	17
B	C	A	17
C	C	B	20
17	21	16	

8

A	A	A	B	22
B	C	A	A	31
C	B	A	C	40
D	D	A	D	29
38	38	8	38	

9

A	B	C	D	35
C	A	C	C	42
D	D	C	B	29
D	B	C	A	35
34	32	40	35	

10

A	B	C	D	51
D	D	D	D	56
A	D	A	C	52
D	B	B	A	45
50	48	51	55	

11

A	B	C	D	22
C	B	A	D	22
D	B	A	D	25
C	C	C	D	17
23	11	26	26	

12 Now make your own puzzle.
Make sure it is possible to solve it.
Give it to someone else to solve.

15 Interpreting data

This chapter is going to show you:
- how to read data from a pie chart
- how to use the median and range to compare sets of data
- how to carry out and interpret a statistical survey.

You should already know:
- how to work out the median and range of a set of data
- how to draw tally charts.

About this chapter

You often see pie charts used to represent information – on television, in newspapers and, of course, in textbooks! This chapter will show you how to interpret and compare information presented in this way. It also shows you how you can compare sets of data by using the medians or ranges.

Whether it is better to use the median or range depends on what you want to know. This chapter will help you decide which is more suitable for solving different types of problems. Finally it shows you how to gather and collate your own data for interpretation, by carrying out statistical surveys.

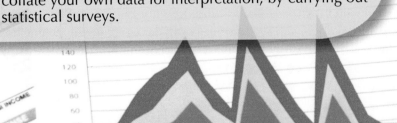

15.1 Pie charts

Learning objective

- To read data from pie charts, where the data is given in simple sectors

Key words

| pie chart | sector |

You will often see **pie charts** that are divided into ten **sectors**. The information may be about 100 people, so each section represents 10 people, as in the next example.

Example 1

The pie chart shows the favourite drinks of 100 Year 7 pupils.

What does it tell you?

The pie chart is divided into ten sectors, so each sector represents 10 pupils.

'Tea' takes up 1 sector, so 10 pupils chose tea as their favourite.

'Milk' takes up 3 sectors, so 30 pupils chose milk as their favourite.

'Cola' takes up 4 sectors, so 40 pupils chose cola as their favourite.

'Coffee' takes up 2 sectors, so 20 pupils chose coffee as their favourite.

Favourite drinks

Sometimes the information may be about a different number of people, as in the next examples.

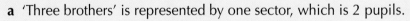

Example 2

Twenty Year 7 pupils were asked how many brothers they had.

The pie chart shows the results.

a How many pupils had three brothers?

b How many pupils had two brothers?

c How many pupils had one brother?

d How many pupils had no brothers?

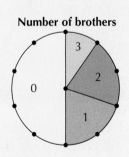
Number of brothers

The pie chart represents 20 pupils.

There are ten sectors in the pie chart.

Each sector of the pie chart represents 20 ÷ 10 = 2 pupils.

a 'Three brothers' is represented by one sector, which is 2 pupils.

b 'Two brothers' is represented by two sectors, which is 2 × 2 = 4 pupils.

c 'One brother' is represented by two sectors, which is 2 × 2 = 4 pupils.

d 'No brothers' is represented by five sectors, which is 2 × 5 = 10 pupils.

Example 3

The pie chart shows the favourite teacher of all 60 girls in Year 7.

a How many girls chose Mr Evans?

b How many girls chose Mrs Wyn?

c How many girls chose Miss Take?

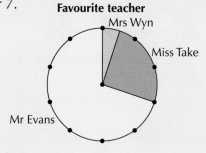

Favourite teacher

The pie chart represents 60 pupils.

There are ten sectors in the pie chart.

Each sector of the pie chart represents $60 \div 10 = 6$ pupils.

a Mr Evans is represented by seven sectors, which is $6 \times 7 = 42$ girls.

b Mrs Wyn is represented by half a sector, which is $6 \div 2 = 3$ girls.

c Miss Take is represented by two and a half sectors.

This is $6 \times 2\frac{1}{2} = 15$ girls.

Exercise 15A

1 This pie chart shows the colours of 100 cars in the school car park.

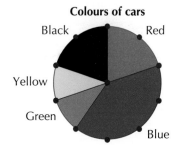

Colours of cars

How many of the cars were:

a red   **b** blue   **c** green   **d** yellow   **e** black?

2 This pie chart shows the favourite pets out of a school year of 100 pupils.

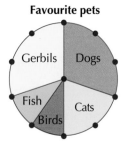

Favourite pets

How many of the pupils chose:

a dogs   **b** cats   **c** birds   **d** fish   **e** gerbils?

3 This pie chart shows the school subjects that 100 pupils chose as their favourite.

Favourite school subjects

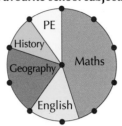

How many of the pupils said their favourite subject was:

a Maths   **b** English   **c** Geography   **d** History   **e** PE?

4 This pie chart shows the soap operas chosen by the 40 teachers in the school.

Favourite TV soap operas

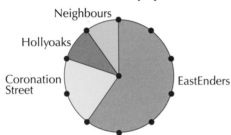

How many of the teachers said their favourite soap opera was:

a Neighbours   **b** Hollyoaks   **c** Coronation Street   **d** EastEnders?

5 This pie chart shows the numbers of people in various age groups, in a community of 60 people.

Ages in the community

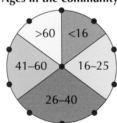

How many of the people in the community are aged:

a under 16   **b** 16–25   **c** 26–40   **d** 41–60   **e** over 60?

6 A social club has 80 members. The pie chart shows the numbers of people in various age groups who regularly use the social club.

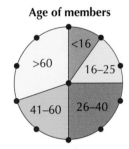

Age of members

How many of the people who go to the social club are aged:

a under 16   **b** 16–25   **c** 26–40   **d** 41–60   **e** over 60?

7 This pie chart shows the school subjects that 120 Year 7 pupils chose as their favourite.

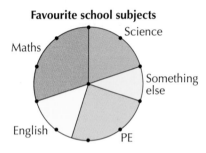

Favourite school subjects

How many pupils chose:

a Maths   **b** English   **c** PE   **d** Science   **e** something else?

8 The pie chart below shows what the 140 boys in a year group chose as their favourite sport.

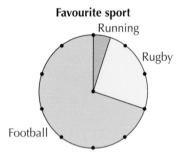

Favourite sport

How many of the boys chose:

a football   **b** running   **c** rugby?

9 This pie chart was pinned to a supermarket staff noticeboard.

It shows that they sold 200 pumpkins one week.

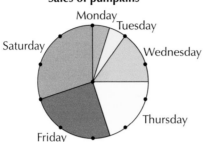

Sales of pumpkins

Karen, one of the staff, looked at the chart and worked out how many pumpkins were sold on each day.

How many pumpkins were sold on:

a   Monday
b   Tuesday
c   Wednesday
d   Thursday
e   Friday
f   Saturday?

Problem solving: Journeys to school

The pie charts show the ways in which two different groups of 40 pupils travel to school most days.

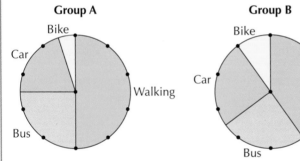

Here are some facts about group A and group B.

In each case, decide whether the statement is:

* true for group A
* true for group B
* true for both
* true for neither.

A Most of the pupils walk to school.

B More travel by car than by bus to school.

C Only six of the pupils come to school on their bikes.

D Ten pupils in the group come to school by car.

15.2 Comparing data by median and range

Learning objectives

- To use the median and range to compare data
- To make sensible decisions by comparing the median and range of two sets of data

Key words	
data	median
range	

When you compare the **median** of two sets of **data**, you are comparing an average.

For example, in a group of pupils:

- median height of the boys = 1.83 m
- median height of the girls = 1.75 m.

From this data you could say that boys are taller than girls.

When you compare the **range** of two sets of data, you are comparing how far the data is spread out, or which data is more consistent.

In the example above:

- range of the height of boys = 0.3 m
- range of the height of girls = 0.5 m.

For this data you can say that the boys' heights are more consistent. This is because the height difference between the shortest and tallest boys is 0.3 m, compared to a height difference of 0.5 m between the shortest and tallest girls.

Example 4

You are organising a ten-pin bowling match.

You have one team place to fill.

These are the last five scores for Neil and Helen.

Neil	122	131	114	162	146
Helen	210	91	135	99	151

Who would you pick to be in the team?

Explain why.

The median for Neil is the middle value of the data, in order:

114, 122, 131, 146, 162

which is 131.

The range is the difference between the highest and lowest values.

162 − 114 = 48

The median for Helen is the middle value of the data, in order:

91, 99, 135, 151, 210

which is 135.

The range is the difference between the highest and lowest values.

210 − 91 = 119

You could pick Helen, as she has the greater median score, so her scores are higher on average.

You could pick Neil, as his range of scores is smaller, so he is more consistent. This means that he has higher scores most of the time.

Example 5

A teacher thinks that the girls in her class are absent more often than the boys are.

There are 10 boys in the class.

These are the numbers of days they were absent, over last term.

　5　0　3　4　6　3　0　8　6　5

There are 12 girls in the class.

These are the numbers of days they were absent, over last term.

　2　1　0　0　15　3　1　2　13　16　2　3

Is the teacher correct? Give reasons for your answer.

The median for the boys is the middle value of the data, in order:

　0, 0, 3, 3, 4, 5, 5, 6, 6, 8

but there are two numbers in the middle.

The two values are 4 and 5, so the median is 'in the middle' of those numbers.

This is $4\frac{1}{2}$.

The range is $8 - 0 = 8$.

The median for the girls is the middle value of the data, in order:

　0, 0, 1, 1, 2, 2, 2, 3, 3, 13, 15, 16

which is 2.

The range is $16 - 0 = 16$.

Using these results, the teacher is wrong because, on looking at the median, the girls are absent less than the boys.

However, if you look at the range, then the teacher could argue she is correct as the girls have three of the worst attendances.

Exercise 15B

1 Alan has to choose someone to play darts for his team. He asked Murray and Ali to throw, nine times each. These are their scores.

Murray	52	16	25	85	12	24	63	121	31
Ali	43	56	40	31	37	49	49	30	31

a Work out the median for Murray.

b Work out the range for Murray.

c Work out the median for Ali.

d Work out the range for Ali.

e Who would you choose? Give a reason for your answer.

2 You have to catch a bus regularly. You can catch bus A or bus B. On the last seven times you caught these buses, you noted down, in minutes, how late they were.

Bus A	1	2	4	12	1	3	5
Bus B	6	5	5	6	2	4	4

a Work out the median value for bus A.

b Work out the range for bus A.

c Work out the median value for bus B.

d Work out the range for bus B.

e Which bus should you catch? Give a reason for your answer.

3 Each day I buy a bag of biscuits from a school canteen. I can buy them from canteen A or canteen B. I made a note of how many biscuits were in each bag I bought from each canteen.

Canteen A	12	11	14	10	13	12	9	12	15
Canteen B	5	18	13	15	7	15	17	8	13

a Work out the median for canteen A.

b Work out the range for canteen A.

c Work out the median for canteen B.

d Work out the range for canteen B.

e Which canteen should I use? Give a reason for your answer.

 4 You have to choose someone for a quiz team.

These are the last ten quiz scores (out of 20) for Lily and Josh.

Lily	1	19	2	12	20	13	2	6	5	10
Josh	8	7	9	12	13	8	7	11	7	8

Who would you choose for the quiz team? Give a reason for your answer.

 5 Andrew and Oliver take the same five tests.

The table gives information about their scores.

	Median	Range
Andrew	17	7
Oliver	14	10

a The teacher wants to give Andrew and Oliver some feedback.

Use the information to compare their scores.

b Can you work out their scores on each test?

Andrew and Oliver retake the tests one week later.

This table shows their new scores.

	Maths	English	Science	History	RE
Andrew	25	20	23	16	15
Oliver	16	15	13	14	12

c Andrew says that he has improved.

Give a reason to support this.

d Oliver says that he has improved.

Give a reason to support this.

Activity: How long are your fingers?

Work in pairs.

A a Measure the length of the fingers on each hand with a ruler as accurately as you can.

b Repeat this for both of you.

c Calculate the median and the range of the lengths of the fingers, for each of you.

d Comment on your results.

B a Try to compare your results with others in your class.

b Compare the results for boys and for girls. What do you notice?

15.3 Statistical surveys

Learning objective

• To use charts and diagrams to interpret data

Key words

experiment	frequency
questionnaire	statistical survey
tally	

You can use **statistical surveys** to collect data.

To obtain data, you could carry out:

• a survey

• an **experiment**.

You can record data on:

• a **questionnaire**

• a data-collection form or sheet.

As you saw in chapter 6 you can use a **tally** chart and a **frequency** table to record the data. There are several ways to present the data to make it easier to interpret. You could use bar charts, pie charts and line graphs.

Exercise 15C

1 In a survey, 30 pupils were asked:

'Approximately how many hours do you spend on homework in a week?'

The results of the survey are shown in this table.

Time (hours)	Tally	Frequency
Less than 2 hours	ЖТ ЖТ ||	
2 hours or more but less than 4 hours	ЖТ ||||	
4 hours or more but less than 8 hours	ЖТ	
More than 8 hours	||||	

a Copy and complete the table.

b Draw a bar chart for the collected data.

2 A sample of 30 girls were asked:

'Which sports do you enjoy watching?'

The results of the survey are shown in this table.

Sport	Tally	Frequency
Football	ЖТ ||||	
Cricket	||	
Tennis	||||	
Badminton	ЖТ ЖТ |	
Something else	|||	

a Copy and complete the table.

b Draw a suitable chart to illustrate the data.

3 A sample of 60 pupils were asked:

'Whose tracks have you downloaded recently?'

The results of the survey are shown in this table.

	Tally	Frequency
Will i Am	ЖТ ЖТ ||	
Pink	ЖТ ЖТ ЖТ	
Little Mix	ЖТ |||	
Bruno Mars	ЖТ ЖТ ЖТ ЖТ ||	
None of them	|||	

a Copy and complete the table.

b Draw a suitable chart for the collected data.

MR **4** These two questions were given to 40 teachers.

    i   Have you ever used a caravan for your holiday?   Yes / No

    ii   Are you intending to go abroad on holiday this year?   Yes / No

The results are shown in this two-way table.

	Going abroad this year	Not going abroad this year
Have used a caravan	16	8
Have never used a caravan	12	2

    a Draw a suitable chart to illustrate these results.

    b From the results, is it true to say: 'More people are using caravans this year'?

5 In a survey of pupils who walked to school, 100 pupils from each of two local schools were asked:

'How long does it take you to walk to school?'

The results are shown in this table.

Time	Highcliffe School	Low Edges School
10 minutes or less	60	75
Between 10 and 15 minutes	30	20
More than 15 minutes	10	5

    a Draw two pie charts, each with ten sectors, to illustrate this data.

    b Which of the schools looks as if its pupils who walk to school live closer?

Activity

A Choose a suitable sample of 20 or more people and investigate this statement.

B Write a report on your findings.

    Remember to:

    • use a data-collection sheet

    • use statistical diagrams in your report

    • write a conclusion.

Smaller people have smaller feet.

Ready to progress?

I can read data from tally charts and create bar charts.
I can use the median and range to compare data.

I can read data from pie charts marked into ten sectors.
I can use charts and diagrams to interpret data.

Review questions

1   20 teachers were asked to name their favourite drink.

One half chose tea.

Eight chose coffee.

The rest chose water.

Use a pie chart like this to show the information.

Remember to give your chart a title.

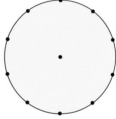

2   In a survey, a shop asked 50 customers about the
quality of customer service over the last year.

The pie chart shows the results.

a   How many said that customer service had
improved?

b   How many customers said there had been no
change?

Quality of customer service

3   Rachel and Joe played nine holes of crazy golf.

These are their scores on each hole.

Rachel	3	5	4	4	4	6	4	3	4
Joe	4	5	4	5	4	5	5	3	3

a   What is the modal score for each player?

b   What is the range of scores for each player?

c   What is the median score for each player?

d   Which player is more consistent? Why?

e   Who is the better player? Why?

4   Make a data-collection sheet to compare how long boys and girls usually spend
watching TV each week.

5 There are 30 pupils in a class.

12 of them are girls.

Pupils in class

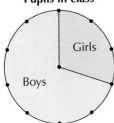

a Is this pie chart drawn correctly, to show the information?

b If not, redraw the pie chart accurately.

(FS) 6 The pie chart shows how Lindsey spent her money one week.

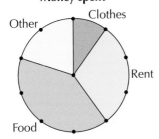

a She spent £30 on clothes that week.

How much did she spend on food?

b The table shows how Chas spent his money in the same week.

Clothes	£20
Rent	£120
Food	£50
Other	£10

Draw a ten-sector pie chart to illustrate this data.

c Who spent a larger proportion of their money on food that week?

7 This pie chart represents the people in a club.

There were ten people aged under 12.

Ages of people in a club

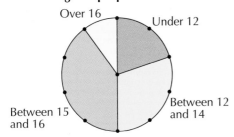

a How many were over 16?

b How many were between 12 and 14?

Challenge
Dancing competition

Five couples take part in a dancing competition.

Each week the couples are given scores by three judges.

Each judge gives a score out of 10. These scores are added up to give the overall scores. These are the scores for weeks 1–4.

Couple	Week 1	Week 2	Week 3	Week 4	Week 5
David and Hanna	16	17	19	21	
James and Helena	10	13	15	16	
Joy and Chris	15	18	19	20	
Tom and Eve	8	9	12	15	
Bain and Kathy	18	19	21	22	

These are the judges' scores for week 5.

Couple	Judge X	Judge Y	Judge Z
David and Hanna	7	8	8
James and Helena	6	6	5
Joy and Chris	7	8	7
Tom and Eve	5	6	5
Bain and Kathy	8	8	7

Questions

1 Copy the table for the couples' scores. Include the totals for week 5.

2 What was the median weekly total for each couple?

3 Comment on the range of scores for each judge in week 5.

4 Draw a graph or chart to illustrate the data for all five weeks.

5 Who would you say has improved the most over the weeks? Give reasons for your choice.

6 The final week of the competition is week 6. Who do you expect to win the competition? Give reasons for your answer.

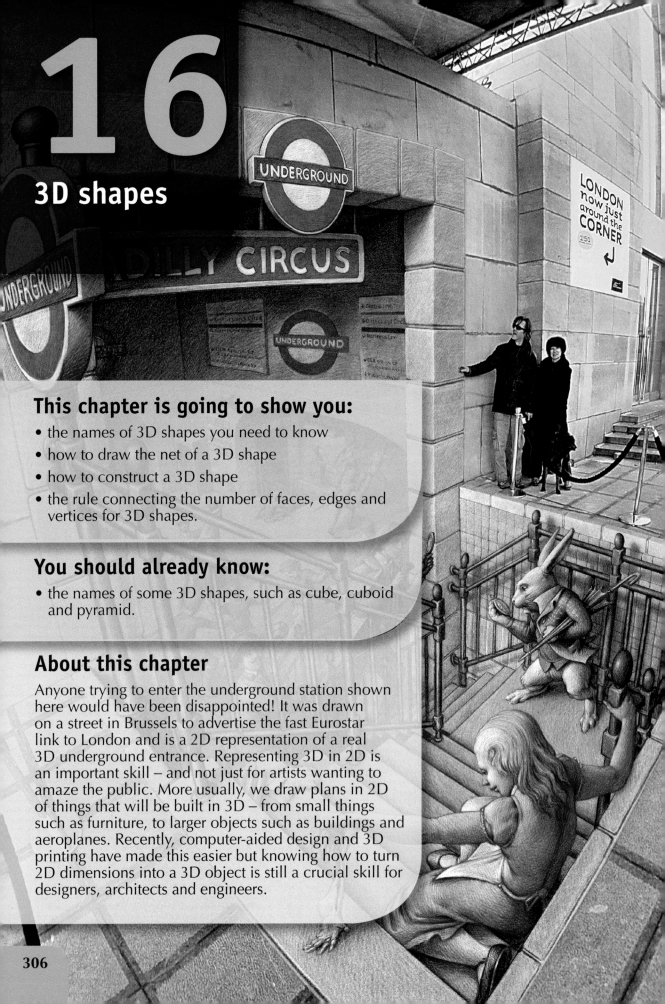

16

3D shapes

This chapter is going to show you:
- the names of 3D shapes you need to know
- how to draw the net of a 3D shape
- how to construct a 3D shape
- the rule connecting the number of faces, edges and vertices for 3D shapes.

You should already know:
- the names of some 3D shapes, such as cube, cuboid and pyramid.

About this chapter

Anyone trying to enter the underground station shown here would have been disappointed! It was drawn on a street in Brussels to advertise the fast Eurostar link to London and is a 2D representation of a real 3D underground entrance. Representing 3D in 2D is an important skill – and not just for artists wanting to amaze the public. More usually, we draw plans in 2D of things that will be built in 3D – from small things such as furniture, to larger objects such as buildings and aeroplanes. Recently, computer-aided design and 3D printing have made this easier but knowing how to turn 2D dimensions into a 3D object is still a crucial skill for designers, architects and engineers.

16.1 3D shapes and nets

Learning objectives

- To know how to count the faces, vertices and edges on a 3D shape
- To draw nets for 3D shapes

Key words

3D	edge
face	net
square-based pyramid	tetrahedron
triangular prism	

Each of these shapes has three dimensions: length, width and height.

 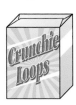  

They are called three-dimensional shapes (**3D**).

You should be able to recognise and name these 3D shapes.

| Cube | Cuboid | **Square-based pyramid** | **Tetrahedron** | **Triangular prism** |

Example 1

What can you say about these 3D shapes?

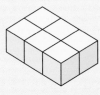 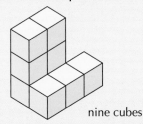

six cubes   nine cubes

Both of these 3D shapes can be made from cubes.

Example 2

What is a **net**?

A net is a 2D shape that is used to make a 3D shape.

This net can be folded to make an open cube.

The shaded square of the net is at the bottom of the open cube.

 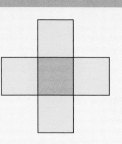

Example 3

Describe a cuboid.

A cuboid has 6 **faces**, 8 vertices and 12 **edges**.

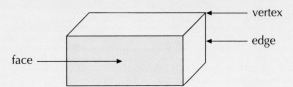

Exercise 16A

① Write down the number of cubes in each 3D shape.

a 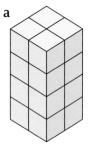 b 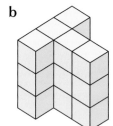 c 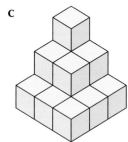 d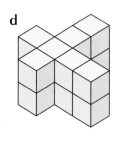

② Each of these 3D shapes has been made from six cubes. There are three pairs of identical shapes. Write down the letters of each pair that are identical.

a   b 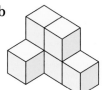 c

d 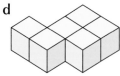 e 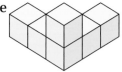 f

③ How many faces, vertices and edges does each 3D shape have?

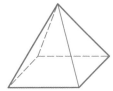 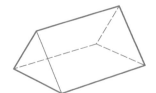 

Square-based pyramid   Triangular prism   Tetrahedron

Copy and complete the table to show your answers.

3D shape	Number of faces	Number of vertices	Number of edges
Cuboid	6	8	12
Square-based pyramid			
Triangular prism			
Tetrahedron			

4 How many faces, vertices and edges does this 3D shape have?

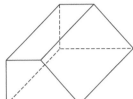

(MR) 5 Decide whether each statement is true or false.

a   A cuboid has 12 vertices.

b   A cube is a cuboid.

c   A tetrahedron has 4 triangular faces.

d   A cube has 8 identical faces.

e   A square-based pyramid has 5 triangular faces.

f   A triangular prism has 3 rectangular faces.

(PS) 6 Use centimetre-squared paper for this question.

Draw as many different nets as you can, to make an open cube.

You may need to cut them out to see if they fold up correctly.

One has been drawn for you.

On each net, shade the square that is at the bottom of the open cube.

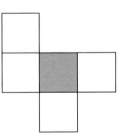

7 Draw a sketch of a net for each 3D shape.

a   A square-based pyramid   b   A triangular prism

c   A tetrahedron

Challenge: Nets for a cube

Work in pairs.

There are 11 different nets for a cube.

A Try to draw them all on centimetre-squared paper.

   If you need help, they can be found on the internet.

B Cut them out and check they are all correct.

16.2 Using nets to construct 3D shapes

Learning objective

- To construct 3D shapes from nets

Key word

construct

A net is a 2D shape that can be cut out and folded up to make a 3D shape.

So you can **construct** a 3D shape from its net.

To construct the 3D shapes in this section, you will need:

- sheets of thin card
- a ruler
- a pair of scissors
- a sharp pencil
- a protractor
- a glue-stick or sticky tape.

Always score the card along the fold lines. This makes the card much easier to fold properly.

 Hint You will need scissors and a ruler to do this.

You can glue the edges together, using the tabs, or you can just use sticky tape. If you decide to use glue, then always keep one face of the shape free of tabs and glue down this face last.

Example 4

Construct a square-based pyramid.

Step 1 Carefully cut out the net. Use scissors.

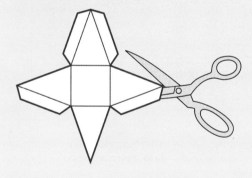

Step 2 Score along each fold line. Use a ruler and scissors.

Step 3 Fold along each fold line.
Stick the shape together by gluing each tab.

Step 4 The last face to stick down is the one without any tabs.

For questions 1 to 4, draw each net accurately on card.
Cut out the nets and construct the 3D shapes.

1   A cube

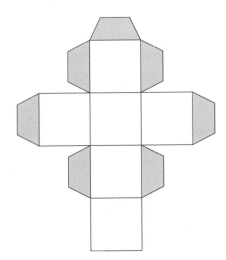

Each square has 4 cm sides.

4 cm

4 cm

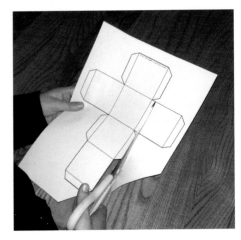

2   A cuboid

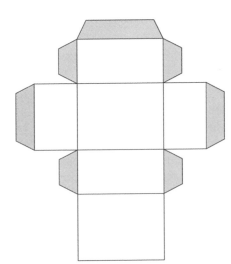

The rectangles have
these measurements.

8 cm

6 cm

8 cm

4 cm

4 cm

6 cm

3 A tetrahedron

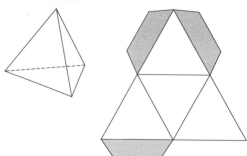

Each equilateral triangle has these measurements.

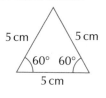

4 A triangular prism

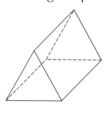

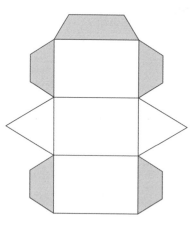

Each rectangle has these measurements.

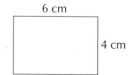

Each equilateral triangle has these measurements.

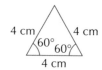

(PS) **5** The diagram shows a different net for a cuboid.

Copy the net. Show where the tabs could go.

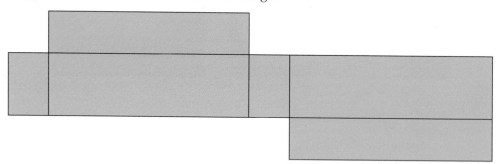

Activity: Making an octahedron

An octahedron is a 3D shape with eight faces.

This is the net for an octahedron.

Choose suitable measurements for the equilateral triangles and draw the net on card.

The tabs have not been included. You will need to decide where to add them.

Fold up your net to make the 3D shape.

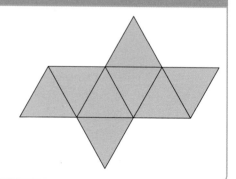

16.3 3D investigations

Learning objectives

- To work out the rule connecting faces, edges and vertices of 3D shapes
- To solve problems involving 3D shapes

Key words	
Euler	hexagonal prism
octahedron	pentagonal-based pyramid

Leonard **Euler** was a famous eighteenth-century Swiss mathematician. He discovered a rule connecting the number of faces, edges and vertices of 3D shapes.

Work through this exercise, to find out more.

Exercise 16C

  1 Here are eight 3D shapes.

Cube   Cuboid   Square-based   Tetrahedron   Triangular prism
                              pyramid

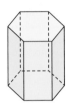 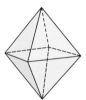

Hexagonal prism   **Octahedron**   **Pentagonal-based pyramid**

a   Copy and complete the table.

3D shape	Number of faces	Number of edges	Number of vertices
Cube	6	12	8
Cuboid			
Square-based pyramid	5	8	5
Tetrahedron			
Triangular prism	5	9	6
Hexagonal prism			
Octahedron			
Pentagonal-based pyramid			

b   Can you spot the rule connecting the number of faces, the number of edges and the number of vertices?

 Hint Add the number of faces to the number of vertices and compare with the number of edges.

2   You will need 12 cubes for this investigation.

Arrange all 12 cubes to make a cuboid.

How many different cuboids can you make?

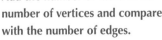

Ready to progress?

I can make 3D shapes using cubes.
I know the mathematical words for various 3D shapes.

I can count the faces, vertices and edges on a 3D shape.

I can draw nets for 3D shapes.
I can use nets to construct 3D shapes.

Review questions

1   Each of these 3D shapes is made with six cubes.
    Which drawings are different views of the same shape?

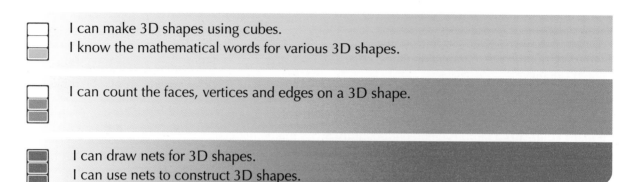

2   a   One of these 3D shapes has one square face and four triangular faces. Write the letter of this shape.

    b   Two of the shapes have six faces. Write the letters of these shapes.

    c   One of the shapes has no vertices. Write the letter of this shape.

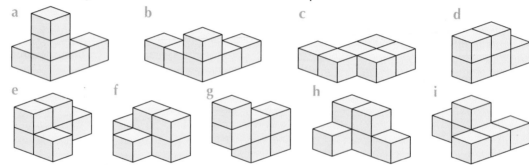

3   The diagram shows a 3D shape. It is called a pentagonal prism.

    How many faces, vertices and edges does this shape have?

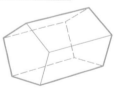

 (MR) 4   Which of these 2D shapes could be a net for a square-based pyramid?

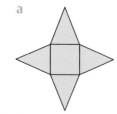 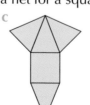 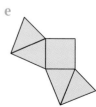

5   Peta uses cubes to make a sequence of towers.

      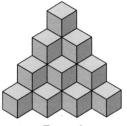

Tower 1   Tower 2   Tower 3   Tower 4

a   How many cubes are there in each tower?

b   Copy and complete this sequence.

Number of cubes
in each tower   …   …   …   …

c   Describe the sequence made by the numbers that are added on each time.

d   Use your rule to work out the number of cubes in Tower 5.

6   The diagram shows the measurements of an open box.

a   Draw an accurate net for the open box.
    Use centimetre-squared paper.

  An open box is a
box with no top.

b   What is the area of the net?

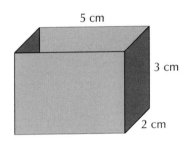

 7   Copy this net for a triangular prism.

Think about when the net is folded up and
glued, to make the prism.

a   Which edge is tab 1 glued to? On your
    copy, label this edge A.

b   Which edge is tab 2 glued to? Label this
    edge B.

c   Which edge is tab 3 glued to? Label this
    edge C.

d   Which edge is tab 4 glued to? Label this
    edge D.

e   Which edge is tab 5 glued to? Label this
    edge E.

f   The corner marked • meets two other
    corners. Label these other two corners •.

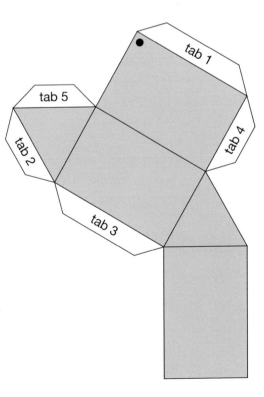

Problem solving
Delivering packages

Hamza is a delivery driver.

He delivers packages from a warehouse to stores in different towns.

He has to drive from the warehouse to the stores and back to the warehouse each day.

He delivers to all the stores in the five towns shown on the map.

He wants to visit all the five towns by driving to each town only once.

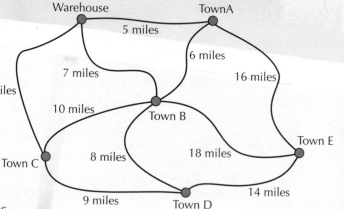

Here is an example of a route he could take.

Warehouse → A → E → B → D → C → Warehouse

The total distance travelled for this route is 5 + 16 + 18 + 8 + 9 + 12 = 68 miles.

(This would be the same route if he did it in reverse.)

1 How far does he travel if he takes this route?

Warehouse → B → A → E → D → C → Warehouse

2 Copy and complete the table to show all the different routes he could take.

Route	Miles travelled	Total mileage
W → A → E → B → D → C → W	5 + 16 + 18 + 8 + 9 + 12	68
W → B → A → E → D → C → W		

3 a What is his shortest route?

  b How far does he travel on this route?

4 On one day he does not have to visit Town C.

  a What is his shortest route?

  b How far does he travel on this route?

5 On another day he only visits four of the five towns.
He travels 40 miles, using the shortest route.
Work out his route.
Write down the towns he visited, in the correct order.

6 On average, Hamza's van uses one gallon of petrol for every 25 miles travelled. In a five-day period, he visits all the five towns each day, using the shortest route. How many gallons of petrol does he use?

17

Ratio

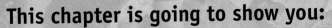

This chapter is going to show you:

- how to use ratio notation
- how to use ratios to compare quantities
- how to simplify ratios
- how to use ratios to find missing quantities
- the connection between ratios and fractions.

You should already know:

- how to simplify fractions
- how to find a fraction of a quantity
- how to interpret bar charts and pie charts.

About this chapter

Why do bicycles have gears?

Many bicycles have cogs on the pedals and on the rear wheel. Different cogs give you different gears.

If you want to cycle uphill it helps if you have a low gear.

If you want to cycle very fast you need a high gear.

We use ratios to describe gears – that is what you will learn about in this chapter.

17.1 Introduction to ratios

Learning objectives

• To introduce ratio notation

• To use ratios to compare quantities

Key words

| quantity | ratio |

Ratios are used to compare **quantities**.

Look at the beads on this bracelet.

There are two red beads for every blue bead.

You can say that the ratio of red beads to blue beads is 2 to 1.

You will see that the colon symbol (:) is used to show ratios. Read it as 'to'.

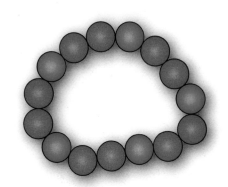

> The ratio of red beads to blue beads is 2 : 1.
>
> You can also say that the ratio of blue beads to red beads is 1 : 2.

Example 1

The mass of a lion is 150 kg.

The mass of a domestic dog is 10 kg.

a Complete this sentence: The lion is ... times heavier than the dog.

b What is the ratio of the mass of the lion to the mass of the dog?

> **a** Divide the mass of the lion by the mass of the dog.
>
> $150 \div 10 = 15$ The lion is 15 times heavier than the dog.
>
> **b** The ratio of the lion's mass to the dog's mass is 15 : 1.

Exercise 17A

1 Look at this bracelet.

Write down the ratio of white beads to red beads.

PS 2 Draw a bracelet with black beads and white beads.

Make the ratio of black beads to white beads 3 : 1.

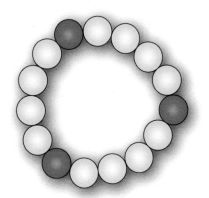

3 Jamie made this bracelet.

   a How many red beads are there for each blue bead?

   b Write down the ratio of red beads to blue beads.

4 Lee is making a bracelet from beads.
He uses 12 green beads and 4 yellow beads.
Work out the missing number in this sentence.
The ratio of green beads to yellow beads is … : 1.

5 Ali makes a necklace from beads.
She uses 20 red beads and 2 blue beads.
Work out the ratio of red beads to blue beads.

6 Alice has saved £12 and Ben has saved £4.

   a What is the missing number in this sentence?
      Alice has saved … times as much as Ben.

   b Copy and complete this sentence.
      The ratio of Alice's savings to Ben's savings is … to 1.

7 Gary buys 1000 g of rice and 250 g of pasta.

   a Work out the missing number in this sentence.
      The mass of rice is … times the mass of pasta.

   b Write down the ratio of rice to pasta.

8 Here are some of the ingredients to make 16 cheese scones.

Flour	400 g
Butter	50 g
Cheese	200 g

   a Work out the missing number in this sentence.
      The mass of flour is … times the mass of butter.

   b Write down the ratio of flour to butter.

   c Work out the ratio of flour to cheese.

9 A website gives these ingredients for making concrete.

6 buckets of gravel

5 buckets of sand

2 buckets of cement

1 bucket of water

    a Write down the ratio of sand to water.

    b Write down the ratio of gravel to water.

    c Work out the missing number.

       The number of buckets of gravel is … times the number of buckets of cement.

    d Work out the ratio of gravel to cement.

10 Katy is 8 years old. Her mother is 32 years old. Her father is 40 years old.

Work out:

    a the ratio of her mother's age to Katy's age

    b the ratio of her father's age to Katy's age.

11 **a** How many squares in this picture are:

       i red   **ii** blue?

    b Find a number to complete this sentence.

       For every red square there are … blue squares.

    c Work out the ratio of red squares to blue squares.

In this picture more red squares have been added.

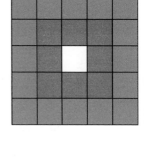

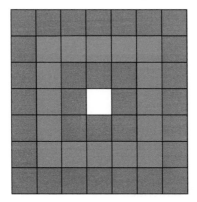

    d Work out the ratio of red squares to blue squares now.

12 A science book has 240 pages. An English book has 80 pages. A maths book has 60 pages.

Work out these ratios:

    a the number of pages in the science book to the number of pages in the English book

    b the number of pages in the science book to the number of pages in the maths book.

13 The size of the engine in a car is given in litres.

Here are the sizes of some car engines.

Car	Engine size (litres)
Peugeot 205	1.3
Ford Fiesta	1.6
Mazda RX7	2.6
BMW M3	3.2
TVR 390	3.9
Lexus LFA	4.8
Audi R8	5.2

a Which car has an engine twice the size of a Peugeot 205?

b Write your answer to part **a** as a ratio.

c Which car has an engine three times the size of a Ford Fiesta?

d Write your answer to part **c** as a ratio.

e Work out the ratios of the sizes of these car engines.

   i TVR 390 to Peugeot 205

   ii Audi R8 to Peugeot 205

14 Here are the populations of some countries.

Country	Population (millions)
USA	300
Brazil	180
Japan	120
UK	60

a Work out the ratio of the population of each country below to the population of the UK.

   i Japan   **ii** Brazil   **iii** USA

b The ratio of the population of the UK to the population of Australia is 3 : 1.

Work out the population of Australia.

Investigation: It's in the bag

When cash is paid into a bank, the coins are put in bags.

Each bag is used for just one type of coin.

This is the label on a bag.

The number of coins must make up a certain value.

For example, a bag of 20p coins must be worth £10.

A a What is the value of a bag of £2 coins?

  b What is the value of a bag of 20p coins?

  c Work out the ratio of the value of a bag of £2 coins to the value of a bag of 20p coins.

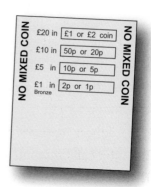

(continued)

B a What is the value of a bag of 50p coins?

  b What is the value of a bag of 2p coins?

  c Work out the ratio of the value of a bag of 50p coins to the value of a bag of 2p coins.

C Find two bags where the ratio of their values is 4 : 1.

D Find two bags where the ratio of their values is 20 : 1.

E a How many coins are there in a bag of 1p coins?

  b How many coins are there in a bag of 10p coins?

  c Work out the ratio of the number of coins in a 1p bag to the number of coins in a 10p bag.

  d Work out the ratio of the number of coins in a £1 bag to the number of coins in a £2 bag.

F a Choose two different bags. Work out the ratio of the number of coins in the two bags.

  b Is the ratio of the value of two bags the same as the ratio of the number of coins in the bags? Justify your answer.

17.2 Simplifying ratios

Learning objective

- To write a ratio as simply as possible

Key word

simplify

You have looked at some simple ratios such as 2 : 1 or 10 : 1.

In this section you will look at more complicated ratios. You will find out how to simplify a ratio. This means to write it as simply as possible.

Look at this bracelet.

There are three blue beads to every two white beads.

You can say the ratio of blue beads to white beads is 3 : 2.

You can also write this the other way round.

  The ratio of white beads to blue beads is 2 : 3.

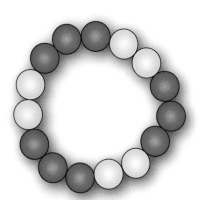

Example 2

A necklace has 10 green beads and four orange beads.

Work out the ratio of green beads to orange beads.

Write the ratio as simply as possible.

  The ratio is 10 : 4.

  Both of these numbers can be divided by 2.

  The ratio can be simplified to 5 : 2, because 10 ÷ 2 = 5 and 4 ÷ 2 = 2.

  This means there are five green beads for every two orange beads.

Example 3

Bottled water comes in two sizes, 500 millilitres (ml) and 750 ml.
What is the ratio of the two sizes?

Imagine each bottle divided into 250 ml sections.

There are three sections in the larger bottle and two sections in the smaller one. You can say:

- the ratio of the amount in the larger bottle to the amount in the smaller one is 3 : 2, or

- the ratio of the smaller to the larger is 2 : 3.

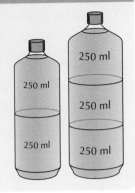

Exercise 17B

Write your ratio answers for this exercise as simply as possible.

1 Look at this bracelet.

a Work out the ratio of blue beads to red beads.

b Write down the ratio of red beads to blue beads.

2 Look at this pattern.

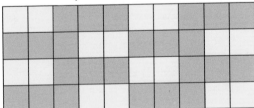

a Work out the ratio of yellow squares to blue squares.

Give the answer as simply as possible.

b Write down the ratio of blue squares to yellow squares.

3 Look at this pattern.

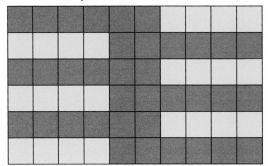

    a Work out the ratio of red squares to yellow squares.
       Give the answer as simply as possible.

    b Write down the ratio of yellow squares to red squares.

4 Look at these beads.

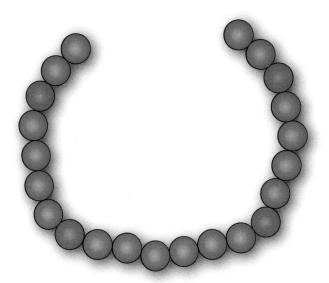

    a How many blue beads are there?

    b Work out the ratio of blue beads to red beads.
       Give your answer as simply as possible.

    c Write down the ratio of red beads to blue beads.

5 In a hedge there are six holly trees and nine beech trees.

    a Work out a number to complete this sentence.
       For every two holly trees there are … beech trees.

    b Work out the ratio of holly trees to beech trees as simply as possible.

    c Write down the ratio of beech trees to holly trees.

6 Look at this picture.

    a Work out the ratio of people wearing glasses to people not wearing glasses.
       Write the answer as simply as possible.

    b Work out the ratio of men to women.
       Write your answer as simply as possible.

7 A drink is made from 50 ml of squash and 125 ml of water.
Work out the ratio of squash to water.
Write your answer in the form 2 : ….

8 A gardener plants these bulbs.
Work out the ratio of the number of:

10 daffodils
15 crocuses
25 snowdrops

    a daffodils to crocuses in the form 2 : …
    b crocuses to daffodils
    c daffodils to snowdrops
    d snowdrops to daffodils.

9 Here are some coins Max has in his pocket.
Work out the ratio of:

2p coins	6
5p coins	4
10p coins	12

    a 2p coins to 5p coins   **b** 5p coins to 10p coins
    c 10p coins to 2p coins.

10 A recipe uses 100 g of flour and 40 g of raisins.
Work out the ratio of:

    a flour to raisins   **b** raisins to flour.

11 **a** This is the label on a shirt.
       Work out the ratio of cotton to acrylic.
       Give your answer as simply as possible.

20% cotton
80% acrylic

    b This is the label on another shirt.
       Work out the ratio of cotton to acrylic.
       Give your answer as simply as possible.

40% cotton
60% acrylic

12 This bar chart shows the numbers of medals won by different countries in the 2012 Olympics.

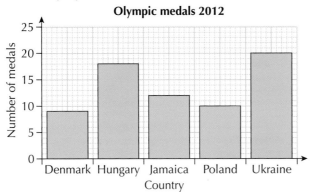

Work out the ratio of:

a the number of medals won by Hungary to the number won by Jamaica

b the number of medals won by Ukraine to the number won by Poland.

13 This bracelet is made from red, white and blue beads.

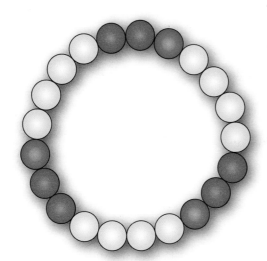

Work out these ratios. Write them as simply as possible.

a blue to red **b** white to blue **c** blue to white **d** red to white.

 14 Here are two rectangles.

Work out the ratio of the areas of the rectangles.

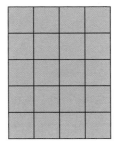 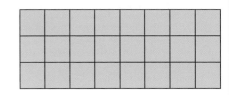

15 This is another red, white and blue necklace.

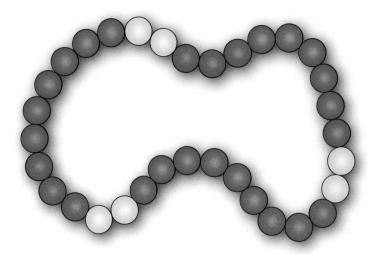

Write these ratios, as simply as possible.

    a blue to white   **b** white to blue   **c** blue to red   **d** red to blue

 16 Peta is five years old and her mother is 25.

   a Work out the ratio of Peta's age to her mother's age.

   b Work out their ages in five years' time.

   c Work out the ratio of their ages in five years' time.

Investigation: Red and green

Here are three patterns in a sequence.

 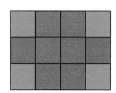 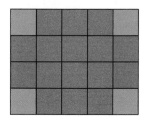

A For each pattern, work out the ratio of red squares to green squares.

   Write the ratios as simply as possible.

B Draw the next two patterns in the sequence.

C Work out the ratio of red squares to green squares in your new patterns.

17.3 Ratios and sharing

Learning objective

● To use ratios to find missing quantities

Up to now you have used ratios to compare two different quantities.

You also use ratios for sharing out a given quantity into different amounts.

Example 4

Tom and Jane share £200 in the ratio 1 : 4. How much does each person get?

Imagine the £200 divided into five equal parts. $1 + 4 = 5$

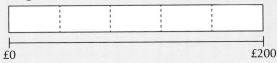

£0   £200

Each share is £200 ÷ 5.

Tom gets one share.   £200 ÷ 5 = £40

Jane gets four shares.   4 × £40 = £160

Check that £40 + £160 = £200.

In Example 4 you knew the total amount.

If you know one of the shares, you can use this to work out the total amount.

Example 5

You are making a drink from lemonade and juice in the ratio 5 : 2.

You have 100 ml of juice that you can use to make the drink.

How much lemonade do you need?

5 parts are lemonade and 2 parts are juice.

The 2 parts of juice make up 100 ml.

1 part is 100 ÷ 2 = 50 ml.

5 parts are lemonade = 5 × 50 = 250 ml.

Exercise 17C

1 In a class of children, the ratio of swimmers to non-swimmers is 1 : 2.
   There are 30 in the class.

   a Work out the number of swimmers.

   b Work out the number of non-swimmers.

2 A farmer harvests oranges and lemons.

The ratio of oranges to lemons is 4 : 1.

There are 1000 fruit all together.

Work out the number of:

a lemons   b oranges.

3 Jake and Marty share £24 in the ratio 1 : 3.

a Work out how much Jake receives.

b Work out how much Marty receives.

4 A necklace is made from 50 pearls altogether.

Some pearls are large and some are small.

The ratio of large pearls to small pearls is 3 : 2.

a How many large pearls are in the necklace?

b How many small pearls are in the necklace?

5 A shop is visited by male and female customers in the ratio 9 : 1.

One day 400 customers use the shop.

Work out the number of:

a male customers   b female customers.

MR **6** In a room, the number of men to women is in the ratio 3 : 2.

There are 20 people altogether. How many women are in the room?

7 A bracelet is made from red and green beads in the ratio 1 : 2.

There are 12 red beads. Work out the number of green beads.

8 The ratio of cars to bicycles using a road is 5 to 1.

There are six bicycles. Work out the number of cars.

9 The ratio of horses to cows in a field is 1 to 6.

There are four horses.

Work out the number of cows.

10 The ratio of sugar to flour in a recipe is 2 : 3.

The recipe uses 50 g of sugar.

Work out the amount of flour.

11 The ratio of men to women in a crowd is 3 : 2.

There are 600 men.

Work out the number of women.

12 There are drawings and painting in an art show.

The ratio of drawings to paintings is 2 : 5.

a Copy and complete this sentence.

For every … drawings there are … paintings.

b There are 14 drawings in the show. Work out the number of paintings.

13 In a fishing contest the numbers of trout and carp caught are in the ratio 1 : 2. The total number of trout and carp is 30. How many carp were caught?

Challenge: All that glitters...

Gold is used to make jewellery.

Gold is a soft metal and it will gradually wear away in everyday use.

To make it harder, it is mixed with other metals.

The other metals used include copper, silver, nickel, palladium and zinc.

Gold is very expensive, so mixing it with other metals makes the jewellery less expensive.

The purity of gold is described in carats.

Pure gold is 24 carats.

21 carat gold has gold and other metals in the ratio 7 : 1.

18 carat gold has gold and other metals in the ratio 3 : 1.

9 carat gold has gold and other metals in the ratio 3 : 5.

A A gold chain is made from 12 g of gold and 4 g of other metals.

  a Work out the ratio of gold to other metals.

  b Is this made from 21 carat gold, 18 carat gold or 9 carat gold?

B A gold brooch is made from 30 g of gold and 50 g of other metals.

  a Work out the ratio of gold to other metals.

  b Is this made from 21 carat gold, 18 carat gold or 9 carat gold?

C a An 18 carat gold ring has a mass of 8 g.

    Work out the mass of gold in the ring.

  b A 9 carat gold ring has a mass of 8 g.

    Work out the mass of gold in the ring.

  c Look at your answers to parts **a** and **b**.

    Compare the amount of gold in an 18 carat ring and a 9 carat ring of the same mass.

D This circle diagram shows the amount of pure gold in 21 carat gold.

  a Draw a circle diagram to show the amount of pure gold in 18 carat gold.

  b Draw a circle diagram to show the amount of pure gold in 9 carat gold.

21 carat gold

Other metals

Gold

17.4 Ratios and fractions

Learning objective

• To understand the connection between fractions and ratios

There is a connection between ratios and fractions.

You have seen this bracelet before.

The ratio of red beads to blue beads is 2 : 1.

Out of every three beads, two are red and one is blue.

$\frac{2}{3}$ of the beads are red.

$\frac{1}{3}$ of the beads are blue.

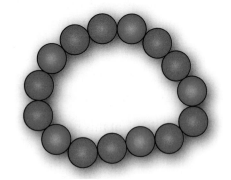

There are 15 beads.

$\frac{2}{3}$ of 15 = 10 red beads.

$\frac{1}{3}$ of 15 = 5 blue beads.

Example 6

Look at this necklace.

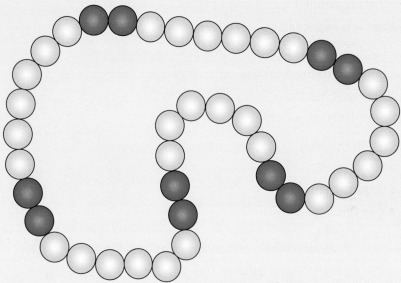

a Work out the ratio of white beads to blue beads.

b Find the fraction of beads that are white.

    a The ratio of white to blue is 6 : 2 and this simplifies to 3 : 1.

    b Three out of every four beads are white.

       The fraction that are white is $\frac{3}{4}$.

Exercise 17D

1 Look at this pattern.

a Write down the ratio of yellow squares to blue squares.

b What fraction of the squares are yellow?

c What fraction of the squares are blue?

2 In a necklace, the ratio of gold beads to silver beads is 1 : 5.

a Write down the fraction of the beads that are gold.

b Write down the fraction of the beads that are silver.

3 Look at this pattern.

a Write down the ratio of blue squares to red squares, as simply as possible.

b What fraction of the squares are red?

4 At a business conference, the ratio of women to men is 3 : 2.

a Copy and complete this sentence.

Out of every five people there are … women and … men.

b Write down the fraction of people at the conference who are women.

c Write down the fraction of people at the conference who are men.

5 Freda has downloaded some music tracks.

The ratio of dance tracks to other music is 4 : 1.

Work out the fraction of dance music tracks.

6 On a bus there are 15 adults and 10 children.

a Write down the ratio of adults to children, as simply as possible.

b What fraction of the passengers are adults?

c What fraction of the passengers are children?

7 On a school trip there are 48 pupils and six teachers.

a Work out the ratio of pupils to teachers as simply as possible.

b What fraction of all the people on the trip are teachers?

PS **8** There are five green bottles and 10 brown bottles on a wall.

    a Work out the ratio of green bottles to brown bottles, as simply as possible.

    b What fraction of the bottles are:

        i green   **ii** brown?

   Two green bottles and one brown bottle accidentally fall off the wall.

    c What is the new ratio of green bottles to brown bottles?

    d What fraction of the bottles now are:

        i green   **ii** brown?

9 Look at this circle.

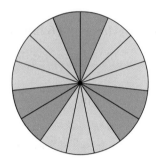

    a Write down the ratio of blue to red in the circle.

    b What fraction of the circle is blue?

    c What fraction of the circle is red?

10 A farmer has sheep and cows.

   One third of his animals are sheep.

    a What fraction are cows?

    b Work out the ratio of sheep to cows.

11 Peter has some £1 coins and £2 coins.

   Three-quarters of his coins are £1 coins.

    a What fraction are £2 coins?

    b Work out the ratio of £1 coins to £2 coins.

PS **12** A hedge has beech trees and holly trees.

   One fifth of the trees are holly trees.

   Work out the ratio of beech trees to holly trees.

13 A fruit cocktail is made from pineapple juice and apple juice in the ratio 3 : 1.

    a What fraction of the drink is pineapple juice?

    b What fraction of the drink is apple juice?

14 Jenny kept a record of the weather each day in June.

Here is part of the tally chart she used for her results.

	Tally	Frequency
Dry day	ЦН ЦН ЦН |||	
Wet day	ЦН ЦН ||	

  a Write down the missing frequencies.

  b Work out the ratio of dry days to wet days.

  c Work out the fraction of the days in June that were:

   i dry days   **ii** wet days.

15 On 21 June, in Aberdeen, there were 18 hours of daylight and 6 hours of night-time.

  a Work out the ratio of the number of hours of daylight to night-time.

  b Work out the fraction of the day when there was daylight.

On the same day in Jersey, there were 16 hours of daylight.

  c Work out the ratio of the number of hours of daylight to night-time in Jersey.

  d Work out the fraction of the day when there was daylight in Jersey.

Challenge: Coloured patterns

Look at this pattern.

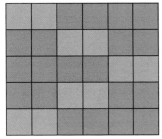

A Copy and complete these sentences.

  a The ratio of blue square to red squares is 1 : ….

  b The fraction of blue squares is ….

  c The fraction of red squares is ….

B a Choose two colours and draw your own pattern to illustrate a simple ratio.

  b Write down the fraction of each colour in your pattern.

Ready to progress?

I can use ratio notation.

I know how to use ratios to compare quantities.
I know how to write a ratio as simply as possible.
I know how to share a quantity in a given ratio.
I know how to write a fraction if I am given a ratio.

Review questions

1   Baby James has a mass of 3 kg. His sister Rachel has a mass of 15 kg.

   a   Copy and complete this sentence.
      Rachel is … times heavier than baby James.

   b   Write down the ratio of Rachel's mass to baby James's mass.

2   These are the ingredients in a recipe.

   a   Work out the ratio of butter to flour.

   b   Work out the ratio of butter to sugar.

> 100 g of flour
> 200 g of butter
> 50 g of sugar

3   Look at this bar chart.

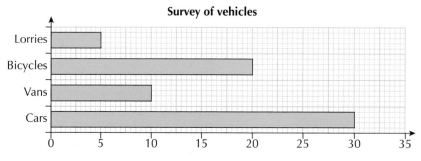

Survey of vehicles

   a   Write down the number of bicycles in the survey.

   b   Work out the ratio of vans to lorries.

   c   Work out the ratio of bicycles to vans.

   d   Work out the ratio of cars to vans.

   e   Work out the ratio of cars to lorries.

4   Some families are visiting a zoo. 25% of them are adults and the rest are children.

   a   What percentage are children?

   b   Complete this sentence.
      There are … children for every adult.

   c   Write down the ratio of children to adults.

5   Look at the triangle.

Work out the ratio of:

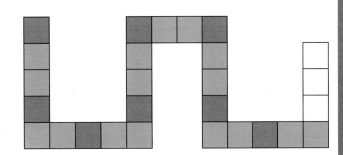

a   the size of angle B to the size of angle A

b   the size of angle C to the size of angle A

c   the size of angle C to the size of angle B.

6   Look at this pattern.

a   What colour should the three white squares be?

b   Write down the ratio of red squares to blue squares.

c   What fraction of the coloured squares are red?

d   What fraction of the coloured squares are blue?

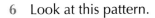

7   A cube has 12 edges.

a   How many faces does it have?

b   Work out the ratio of the number of edges to the number of faces.

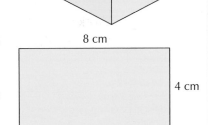

8   a   Work out the ratio of the length to the width of this rectangle.

b   Show that the perimeter of the shape is 24 cm.

c   Work out the ratio of the perimeter to the length of the rectangle.

d   Work out the ratio of the perimeter to the width of the rectangle.

8 cm

4 cm

 9   Sam measures two lines.

a   Draw the two lines.

b   Is Sam correct? Give a reason for your answer.

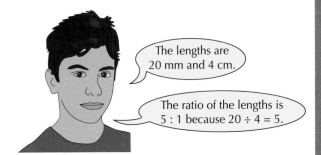

The lengths are 20 mm and 4 cm.

The ratio of the lengths is 5 : 1 because 20 ÷ 4 = 5.

10 On a bicycle the gear ratio is the ratio of the number of teeth on the pedals to the number of teeth on the rear wheel.

a   A high gear for riding fast has 48 teeth on the pedals and 12 on the rear wheel. Work out the gear ratio.

b   A low gear for riding uphill has 32 teeth on the pedals and 16 on the rear wheel. Work out the gear ratio.

Problem solving
Smoothie bar

Recipes are for medium smoothies.

To make a small smoothie:
Use half the ingredients of a medium smoothie.

To make a large smoothie:
Use three times the ingredients of a small smoothie.

Buy any two smoothies and get the cheaper one for half price!

Small	300 ml	£2.00
Medium	400 ml	£3.00
Large	600 ml	£4.00

1 Ingredients

  a List the ingredients of a small Fruity Surprise.

  b List the ingredients of a large Fruity Surprise.

  c List the ingredients of a small Breakfast Boost.

  d List the ingredients of a large Breakfast Boost.

2 Cost and size

  a Find the ratio of the sizes of a medium smoothie and a small smoothie.

  b Find the ratio of the costs of a medium smoothie and a small smoothie.

  c Find ratios to compare the sizes and costs of a large smoothie and a small smoothie.

  d The ratios of the sizes and the ratios of the costs of a medium smoothie and a small smoothie are not the same. Are medium sizes better value than small sizes? Give a reason for your answer.

Breakfast Boost

100 g strawberries
200 g banana
100 g yogurt

Tropical Fruit

250 g tropical fruit
100 ml yoghurt
100 g raspberries

Fruity Surprise

100 g mango
50 g strawberries
100 g bananas
250 ml orange juice

3 Ratios of ingredients

Look at the ingredients of a medium Fruity Surprise.

a Find the ratio of mango to strawberry.

b Find the ratio of banana to mango.

c Are the ratios in a and b the same for a small Fruity Surprise? Justify your answer.

d Are the ratios in a and b the same for a large Fruity Surprise? Justify your answer.

4 Breakfast Boost

Look at the ingredients of a medium Breakfast Boost.

a Work out the total mass of fruit in a medium Breakfast Boost.

b Work out the ratio of the mass of fruit to the mass of yogurt.

c What fraction of the mass of a Breakfast Boost is yogurt?

d What fraction of the mass of a Breakfast Boost is fruit?

5 Selling smoothies

These are the sales of two of the smoothies on one day.

Smoothie	Number sold
Fruity Surprise	20
Tropical Fruit	30
Breakfast Boost	60

Use ratios to compare the quantities of different pairs of smoothies.

Glossary

12-hour clock   A method of measuring the time, based on two groups of twelve hours.

24-hour clock   A method of measuring the time, based on the full twenty-four hours of the day, rather than two groups of twelve hours.

3D   Having three dimensions: length, width and height.

acute angle   An angle between 0° and 90°.

addition   A basic operation of arithmetic, combining two or more numbers or values to find their total value.

algebra   The use of letters to represent variables and unknown numbers and to state general rules or properties; for example: $2(x + y) = 2x + 2y$ describes a relationship that is true for any numbers x and y.

analogue   Continuous; an analogue clock has hands that sweep continuously around the face, so any time can be shown.

anticlockwise   The direction that is opposite to the direction in which the hands of an analogue clock move.

approximation   A value that is close but not exactly equal to another value, and can be used to give an idea of the size of the value; for example, a journey taking 58 minutes may be described as 'taking approximately an hour'; the sign ≈ means 'is approximately equal to'.

area   The amount of flat space a 2D shape occupies; usually measured in square units such as square centimetres (cm^2) or square metres (m^2).

at random   Chosen by chance, without looking; every item has an equal chance of being chosen.

average   A central or typical value of a set of data, that can be used to represent the whole data set; median and mode are both types of average.

axis, plural axes   Fixed lines on a graph, usually perpendicular, numbered and used to identify the position of any point on the graph.

BIDMAS   An agreed order of carrying out operations Brackets, Indices (or powers), Division and Multiplication, Addition and Subtraction.

brackets   Symbols used to show expressions that must be treated as one term or number. Under the rules of BIDMAS, operations within brackets must be done first; for example: $2 \times (3 + 5) = 2 \times 8 = 16$ whereas $2 \times 3 + 5 = 6 + 5 = 11$.

calculate   Work out, with or without a calculator.

calendar   A chart showing the dates in the year and the days on which they occur.

cent- or centi-   A prefix referring to 100; in the metric system, centi- means one hundredth; for example, a centimetre is one hundredth of a metre.

centimetre   A metric unit of length, one-hundredth of a metre; 100 cm = 1 m.

chance   The likelihood, or probability, of an event occurring.

chart   A diagram or table showing information.

class   A small range of values within a large set of data, treated as one group of values.

clockwise   The direction in which the hands of an analogue clock move.

column method   A method for multiplying large numbers, in which you multiply the units, tens and hundreds separately, then add the products together.

compass   An instrument used in navigation, that shows the direction of north.

construct   Draw angles, lines or shapes accurately, using compasses, a protractor and a ruler.

conversion   Expression of a unit or measurement in terms of another unit or scale of measurement.

conversion graph   A graph that can be used to convert from one unit to another, constructed by drawing a line through two or more points where the equivalence is known; sometimes, but not always, a conversion graph passes through the origin.

convert   **1** Express a unit or measurement in terms of another unit or scale of measurement; for example, you can convert inches to centimetres by multiplying by 2.54.

2 To change a number from one form to another, for example, from a fraction to a decimal.

coordinates   Pairs of numbers that show the exact position of a point on a graph, by giving the distance of the point from each axis; on an *x–y* coordinate graph, in the set of coordinates (3, 4), 3 is the *x*-coordinate, and is the horizontal distance of the point from the *y*-axis, and 4 is the *y*-coordinate, and is the vertical distance of the point from the *x*-axis.

data   A collection of facts, such as numbers, measurements, opinions or other information.

data-collection form   A form or table used for recording data collected during a survey.

decimal   A number or number system that is based on 10; a decimal number usually means a number made up of a whole number and fractions, expressed as tenths, hundreds, thousandths, written after a decimal point.

decimal point   A symbol, usually a small dot, written between the whole-number part and the fractional part in a decimal number.

decrease   **1** Reduce or make smaller.

2 The amount by which something is made smaller.

degree   A measure of angle equal to $\frac{1}{360}$ of a complete turn.

denominator   The number below the line in a fraction, which says how many parts there are in the whole; for example, a denominator of 3 tells you that you are dealing with thirds.

diagonal   **1** A straight line joining any two non-adjacent vertices of a polygon.

2 Sloping, not horizontal or vertical.

digital   Data that has fixed values; a digital clock moved in seconds, or minutes, showing no values between.

double function machine   A function machine that includes two operations.

difference   The result of subtracting one number from another; in sequences, the number that is added or subtracted to produce the next term.

edge   The line where two faces or surfaces of a 3D shape meet.

equation   A number sentence stating that two expressions or quantities are of equal value, for example, $x + 2y = 9$; an equation always contains an equals sign (=).

equivalent   The same, equal in value.

equivalent fraction   Fractions that can be cancelled to the same value, such as $\frac{10}{20} = \frac{5}{10} = \frac{1}{2}$.

estimate   **1** State or guess a value, based on experience or what you already know.

2 A rough or approximate answer.

Euler   Leonhard Euler (1707–83), a Swiss mathematician.

event   Something that happens, such as the toss of a coin, the throw of a dice or a football match.

experiment   A test or investigation made to find evidence for or against a hypothesis.

experimental probability   The probability found by trial or experiment; an estimate of the true probability.

expression   Collection of numbers, letters, symbols and operators representing a number or amount; for example, $x^2 - 3x + 4$.

face   One of the flat surfaces of a solid shape; for example, a cube has six faces.

fair   The probability of each outcome is similar to the theoretical probability.

first term   The first number in a sequence.

formula   A mathematical rule, using numbers and letters, that shows how to work out an unknown variable; for example, the conversion formula from temperatures in Fahrenheit to temperatures in Celsius is: $C = \frac{5}{9}(F - 32)$.

formulae   The plural form of formula.

fraction   A part of a whole that has been divided into equal parts, a fraction describes how many parts you are talking about.

fraction wall   A diagram that allows you to compare fractions and see which ones are equivalent.

frequency   The number of times a particular item appears in a set of data.

function machine   A diagram to illustrate functions and their inputs and outputs.

geometrical properties   The properties of a 2D or 3D shape that describe it completely.

graph   A diagram showing the relation between certain sets of numbers or quantities by means of a series of values or points plotted on a set of axes.

grid or box method   A method for multiplying numbers larger than 10, where each number is split into its parts: for example, to calculate 158×67:

158 is 100, 50 and 8

67 is 60 and 7.

These numbers are arranged in a rectangle and each part is multiplied by the others.

grouped frequency table   A table showing data grouped into classes.

hexagonal prism A prism with a hexagonal cross-section and six rectangular faces; it has 8 faces, 12 vertices and 18 edges.

horizontal Parallel to the horizon.

image The result of a reflection or other transformation of an object.

improper fraction A fraction in which the numerator is greater than the denominator. The fraction could be rewritten as a mixed number for example, $\frac{7}{2} = 3\frac{1}{2}$.

increase 1 Enlarge or make bigger.
2 The amount by which something is made bigger.

input The number put into a function machine.

integer Whole number, may be positive or negative, or zero.

intersect To have a common point for example, two non-parallel lines cross or intersect at a point.

inverse Reverse or opposite; inverse operations cancel each other out or reverse the effect of each other.

inverse operation An operation that reverses the effect of another operation; for example, addition is the inverse of subtraction, division is the inverse of multiplication.

length The distance from one end of a line to the other.

like terms Terms in which the variables are identical, but have different coefficients; for example, $2ax$ and $5ax$ are like terms but $5xy$ and $7y$ are not. Like terms can be combined by adding their numerical coefficients so $2ax + 5ax = 7ax$.

likely Having a good chance of happening.

line of symmetry A line that divides a symmetrical shape into two identical parts, one being the mirror image of the other.

long division A method of division showing all the workings, used when dividing large numbers.

long multiplication A method of multiplication showing all the workings, used when multiplying large numbers.

median The middle value of a set of data that is arranged in order; for example, write the data set 4, 2, 6, 2, 2, 3, 7 in order as 2, 2, 2, 3, 4, 6, 7, then the median is the middle value, which is 3. If there is an even number of values the median is the mean of the two middle values; for example, 2, 3, 6, 8, 8, 9 has a median of 7.

metric An internationally agreed decimal system of measurement in which the basic units of mass, length and capacity are grams, metres and litres. Sub-units are obtained from main units by multiplying or dividing by 10, 100, 1000, …. For example, for mass, 1 kilogram = 1000 grams; for length, 1 kilometre = 1000 metres, 1 metre = 100 centimetres, 1 centimetre = 10 millimetres; for capacity, 1 litre = 1000 millilitres.

metric units Units of measurement used in the metric system; for example, metres and centimetres (length), grams and kilograms (mass), litres (capacity).

mill- or milli- A prefix used in the metric system of measurement to indicate a thousandth part, for example, a millimetre is one thousandth of a metre.

millimetre A metric unit of length, one-thousandth of a metre; 1000 mm = 1 m.

mirror line Another name for a line of symmetry.

mixed number A number written as a whole number and a fraction; for example, the mixed number $2\frac{1}{2}$ can be written as the improper fraction $\frac{5}{2}$.

modal The value that occurs most frequently in a given set of data.

modal class In grouped data, the class with the highest frequency.

mode The value that occurs most frequently in a given set of data.

negative number A number that is less than zero.

net A 2D shape that can be folded up to make a 3D shape.

numerator The number above the line in a fraction: it tells you how many of the equal parts of the whole you have; for example, $\frac{3}{5}$ of a whole is made up of three of the five equal parts. The number of equal parts is the denominator.

object The original or starting shape, line or point before it is transformed to give an image.

obtuse angle An angle that is greater than 90° but less than 180°.

octahedron A 3D shape with eight faces.

operation An action carried out on or between one or more numbers; it could be addition, subtraction, multiplication, division or squaring.

opposite angles   The angles on the opposite side of the point of intersection when two straight lines cross, forming four angles. The opposite angles are equal.

order   Arrange numbers or quantities according to a rule, such as size or value.

order of operations   The order in which mathematical operations should be done.

order of rotational symmetry   The number of times a 2D shape looks the same as it did originally when it is rotated through 360°. If a shape has no rotational symmetry, its order of rotational symmetry is 1, because every shape looks the same at the end of a 360° rotation as it did originally.

origin   The point (0, 0) on Cartesian coordinate axes.

outcome   The result of an event or trial in a probability experiment, such as the score from a throw of a dice.

outlier   In a data set, a value that is widely separated from the main cluster of values.

output   The number produced by a function machine.

parallel   Lines that are always the same distance apart, however far they are extended.

pentagonal-based pyramid   A pyramid with a pentagonal base and five triangular faces that meet in a vertex.

per cent (%)   Parts per hundred.

percentage   A number written as a fraction with 100 parts, but instead of writing it as a fraction out of 100, you write the symbol % at the end, so $\frac{50}{100}$ is written as 50%.

perimeter   The total distance around a 2D shape; the perimeter of a circle is called the circumference.

pie chart   A circular graph divided into sectors that are proportional to the size of the quantities represented.

place value   The value of a digit depending on where it is written in a number; for example, in the number 123.4, the place value of 4 is tenths, so it is worth 0.4 and the place value of 2 is tens, so it is worth 20.

positive number   A number that is greater than zero.

power   How many times you use a number or expression in a calculation; it is written as a small, raised number; for example, 2^2 is 2 multiplied by itself, $2^2 = 2 \times 2$ and 4^3 is $4 \times 4 \times 4$.

probability   The measure of how likely an outcome of an event is to occur. All probabilities have values in the range from 0 to 1.

probability fraction   A probability that is not 0 or 1, given as a fraction.

probability scale   A scale or number line, from 0 to 1, sometimes labelled with impossible, unlikely, even chance, etc., to show the likelihood of an outcome of an event occurring. Possible outcomes may be marked along the scale as fractions or decimals.

protractor   A transparent circular or semicircular instrument for measuring or drawing angles, graduated in degrees.

pyramid   A 3D shape with a flat base and triangular sides that meet in a vertex.

quadrant   One of the four regions into which a plane is divided by the coordinate axes in the Cartesian system.

quantity   A measurable amount of something that can be written as a number, or a number with appropriate units; for example, the capacity of a milk carton.

questionnaire   A list of questions for people to answer, so that statistical information can be collected.

random   Chosen by chance, without looking; every item has an equal chance of being chosen.

range   The difference between the greatest value and the smallest value in a set of numerical data. A measure of spread in statistics.

ratio   A way of comparing the sizes of two or more numbers or quantities; for example, if there are five boys and ten girls in a group, the ratio of boys to girls is 5 : 10 or 1 : 2, the ratio of girls to boys is 2 : 1. The two numbers are separated by a colon (:).

rectangle   A quadrilateral in which all four interior angles are 90° and two pairs of opposite sides are equal and parallel; it has two lines of symmetry and rotational symmetry of order 2. The diagonals of a rectangle bisect each other.

reduction   *See* decrease.

reflect   Draw an image of a 2D shape as if it is viewed in a mirror placed along a given (mirror) line.

reflection   The image formed when a 2D shape is reflected in a mirror line or line of symmetry; the process of reflecting an object.

reflective symmetry   A type of symmetry in which a 2D shape is divided into two equal parts by a mirror line.

repeated subtraction   A type of division involving the process of repeatedly subtracting the same number or amount; for example, $35 - 5 - 5 - 5 - 5 - 5 - 5 - 5 = 0$ so $35 \div 5 = 7$, remainder 0.

right angle   One quarter of a complete turn. An angle of 90°.

rotational symmetry   A type of symmetry in which a 2D shape may be turned through 360° so that it looks the same as it did originally in two or more positions.

round   In the context of a number, to express to a required degree of accuracy; for example, 653 rounded to the nearest 10 is 650.

round down   To change a number to a lower and more convenient value; for example, 451 rounded down to the nearest ten is 450.

round up   To change a number to a higher and more convenient value; for example, 459 rounded up to the nearest ten is 460.

rule   The way a mathematical function is carried out. In patterns and sequences a rule, expressed in words or algebraically, shows how the pattern or sequence grows or develops.

sample   A selection taken from a larger data set, which can be researched to provide information about the whole data set.

sector   A region of a circle, like a slice of a pie, bounded by an arc and two radii.

sequence   A pattern of numbers that are related by a rule.

short division   The division of one number by another, usually an integer, that can be worked out mentally rather than on paper.

simplest form   **1** A fraction that has been cancelled as much as possible.
2 An algebraic expression in which like terms have been collected, so that it cannot be simplified any further.

simplify   To make an equation or expression easier to work with or understand by combining like terms or cancelling; for example, $4a - 2a + 5b + 2b = 2a + 7b$, $\frac{12}{18} = \frac{2}{3}$, $5 : 10 = 1 : 2$.

solve   To find the value or values of a variable (x) that satisfy the given equation.

square   A quadrilateral in which all four interior angles are 90° and all four sides are equal; opposite sides are parallel, the diagonals bisect each at right angles; it has four lines of symmetry and rotational symmetry of order 4.

square-based pyramid   A 3D shape with a square base and four isosceles triangular faces.

square centimetre   The area of a square of side 1 centimetre.

square metre   The area of a square of side 1 metre.

square number   A number that results from multiplying an integer by itself; for example, $36 = 6 \times 6$ and so 36 is a square number. A square number can be represented as a square array of dots.

square root   For a given number, a, the square root is the number b, where $a = b^2$; for example, a square root of 25 is 5 since $5^2 = 25$. The square root of 25 is recorded as $\sqrt{25} = 5$. Note that a positive number has a negative square root, as well as a positive square root; for example, $(-5)^2 = 25$ so it is also true that $\sqrt{25} = -5$.

squaring   Multiplying a number or expression by itself; raising a number or expression to the second power; for example, $3^2 = 9$.

statistical survey   The collection of statistical information.

substitute   Replace a variable in an expression with a number and evaluate it; For example, if we substitute 4 for t in $3t + 5$ the answer is 17 because $3 \times 4 + 5 = 17$.

subtraction   Taking one number or quantity away from another, to find the difference.

tally   A mark made to record a data value; every fifth tally is drawn through the previous four.

tally chart   A chart with marks made to record each object or event in a certain category or class. The marks are usually grouped in fives to make counting the total easier.

term   **1** A part of an expression, equation or formula. Terms are separated by + and − signs.
2 A number in a sequence or pattern.

term-to-term rule   The rule that shows what to do to one term in a sequence, to work out the next term.

tessellation   A pattern made of one or more repeating shapes that fit together without leaving any gaps between them.

tetrahedron   A 3D shape with four triangular faces; in a regular tetrahedron, the faces are equilateral triangles. A tetrahedron has 4 faces, 4 verticals and 6 edges.

theoretical probability   Probability that is calculated, based on formulae rather that trials.

trial   An experiment to discover an approximation for the probability of an outcome of an event; it will consist of many trials where the event takes place and the outcome is recorded.

triangle   A 2D shape with three straight sides; the interior angles add up to 180°. Triangles may be classified as:

- scalene – no sides are equal, no angles are equal
- isosceles – two of the sides are equal, two of the angles are equal
- equilateral – all the sides are equal, all the angles are equal
- right-angled – one interior angle is equal to 90°.

triangular number   A number in the sequence $1, 1 + 2, 1 + 2 + 3, 1 + 2 + 3 + 4, \ldots$ 55 is a triangular number since $55 = 1 + 2 + 3 + 4 + 5 + 6 + 7 + 8 + 9 + 10$. A triangular number can be represented by a triangular array of dots, in which the number of dots increases by 1 in each row.

triangular prism   A prism with a triangular cross-section and three rectangular faces; it has 5 faces, 6 vertices and 9 edges.

unknown number   A number that is represented by a letter; it can be treated as a number, following the rules of arithmetic (BIDMAS).

variable   A quantity that may take many values.

vertex   The point at which two lines meet, in a 2D or 3D shape.

vertical   Perpendicular to the horizontal; straight up.

vertices   The plural of vertex.

width   The distance from one side of a 2D shape to the other, usually taken to be shorter than the length.

x-axis   The horizontal axis of a two-dimensional x–y Cartesian coordinate graph, along which the x-coordinates are measured.

x-coordinate   The horizontal distance of the point from the y-axis; the position of a point along the x-axis.

y-axis   The vertical axis of a two-dimensional x–y Cartesian coordinate graph, along which the y-coordinates are measured.

y-coordinate   The vertical distance of the point from the x-axis; the position of a point up the y-axis.

Index

W

X

William Collins's dream of knowledge for all began with the publication of his first book in 1819. A self-educated mill worker, he not only enriched millions of lives, but also founded a flourishing publishing house. Today, staying true to this spirit, Collins books are packed with inspiration, innovation and practical expertise. They place you at the centre of a world of possibility and give you exactly what you need to explore it.

Collins. Freedom to teach.

Published by Collins
An imprint of HarperCollins*Publishers*
77–85 Fulham Palace Road
Hammersmith
London
W6 8JB

Browse the complete Collins catalogue at
www.collins.co.uk

© HarperCollins*Publishers* Limited 2014

10 9 8 7 6 5 4 3 2 1

ISBN-13 978-0-00-753771-6

The authors Kevin Evans, Keith Gordon, Trevor Senior, Brian Speed and Chris Pearce assert their moral rights to be identified as the authors of this work.

All rights reserved. No part of this publication may be reproduced, stored in a retrieval system, or transmitted in any form or by any means, electronic, mechanical, photocopying, recording or otherwise, without the prior written permission of the publisher or a licence permitting restricted copying in the United Kingdom issued by the Copyright Licensing Agency Ltd., 90 Tottenham Court Road, London, W1T 4LP.

British Library Cataloguing in Publication Data
A catalogue record for this publication is available from the British Library.

Commissioned by Katie Sergeant
Project managed by Elektra Media Ltd
Development and copy-edited by Joan Miller
Edited by Helen Marsden
Proofread by Amanda Dickson
Illustrations by Ann Paganuzzi, Nigel Jordan and Tony Wilkins
Typeset by Jouve India Private Limited
Cover design by Angela English

Printed and bound by L.E.G.O. S.p.A. Italy

Acknowledgements
The publishers wish to thank the following for permission to reproduce photographs. Every effort has been made to trace copyright holders and to obtain their permission for the use of copyright materials. The publishers will gladly receive any information enabling them to rectify any error or omission at the first opportunity.

(t = top, c = centre, b = bottom, r = right, l = left)

Cover Nikonaft/Shutterstock, p 6 eska2005/Shutterstock, p 7 Ann Paganuzzi, p 8 Ann Paganuzzi, p 18 godrick/Shutterstock, p 26–27 Cedric Weber/Shutterstock, p 28 Bletchley Park Trust/Getty Images, p 46–47 Alexander Tihonov/Shutterstock, p 48 dea picture library/De Agostini/Getty Images, p 62 Val Thoermer/Shutterstock, p 62–63 Vladimir Badaev/Shutterstock, p 64 Alexey Rezaykin/Shutterstock, p 82–83 oliveromg/Shutterstock, p 84 bbbrrn/iStock, p 104–105 Reinhard Tiburzy/Shutterstock, p 106 Anton Gvozdikov/Shutterstock, p 126–127 Diana Valujeva/Shutterstock, p 128 Hadrian/Shutterstock, p 146–147 Samot/Shutterstock, p 148 Diego Barbieri/Shutterstock, p 168–169 Svetlana Lukienko/Shutterstock, p 170 Babek Tafreshi/SSPL/Getty Images, p 198–199 almonfoto/Shutterstock, p 200 sfam_photo/Shutterstock, p 214–215 Bernhard Staehli/Shutterstock, p 216 Makushin Alexey/Shutterstock, p 221 EDHAR/Shutterstock, p 224t Nikola Bilic/Shutterstock, p 224b skyfish/Shutterstock, p 232–233 Rtimages/Shutterstock, p 234 Lightroom Photos/Alamy, p 250–251 Chantal de Bruijne/Shutterstock, p 252 Melissa Brandes/Shutterstock, p 268–269 RuthChoi/Shutterstock, p 268t Ratikova/Shutterstock, p 268b Alastair Wallace/Shutterstock, p 269t WDG Photo/Shutterstock, p 269b f9photos/Shutterstock, p 270 Jane Sweeney/Getty Images, p 271 ollyy/Shutterstock, p 288–289 zhu difeng/Shutterstock, p 290 ineskoleva/iStock, p 304–305 alysta/Shutterstock, p 306 Barcroft Media/Getty Images, p 311 Ann Paganuzzi, p 316–317 Dmitry Kalinovsky/Shutterstock, p 318 Radu Razvan/Shutterstock, p 326 ollyy/Shutterstock, p 333 baranq/Shutterstock, p 338–339 Africa Studio/Shutterstock.